newreasonstobelieve

To the Creator of everything, God of gods
With heartfelt respect.
With all my love and apologies to the software/hardware team
of the human made virtual reality.

Welcome to the Virtual World

I AM READY LET IT BEGIN

My destiny is in my hand
I hit the roads
May God look at me
And I at Him
We continue hand in hand
On the virtual roads of my God
Let's stop for a while
And announce where we are

Aydın TÜRKGÜCÜ

Stepping Out Of Darkness Into the Light, The Last Step Will Come From Us

New Reasons To Believe

Second Apple Publishing Ltd.

ISBN 978-975-6861-04-2

Cover Design: Aydın Türkgücü, Saadettin Yaşar, Tekajans

Translation : Murat Kırhan, Bonnie Pura

Printing History, March 2009, Exit/Cikis Publishing

© **Aydın Türkgücü 2009 , All Rights Reserved**

www.aydinturkgucu.net

CONTENTS

Thank You

....

9

Foreword

....

10

In Reading

....

11

New Reasons to Believe

....

13

A New Prayer Box

....

32

Visible State / Invisible State

....

35

The Mental Stroke of Thought

....

41

Theory of Everything = Everyone's Theory

....

54

What Good is Space?

....

56

Space is Gods' Recording Apparatus/Archive Cabinet

....

57

Space is not Endless

62

Is the Universe/Space Expanding? Going away?

66

Is the World Round?

70

Blockage of Information Dependent on Perception

73

Intervention in the Simple Perception -Communication System of the Brain

79

There is no Gravity, Blame, Penalty, or Cost

93

in Dreams

93

The Sorrowful end of the Sociological God

105

The Sociological God says "Read"

108

The Technological God says "Read, Understand and Apply"

108

Hollywood and the Need for a Technological God
....
109

Usually racers in a race like this, make the following choices:
....
118

1. Justice applied at birth:
....
122

Application For Earth
....
125

2. Justice during life (fate on the life course):
....
133

The Virtual Does not Realize It Is Virtual
....
136

3. Justice applied after death
....
139

The Heaven of the Sociological God
....
144

The Third Choice in the Afterworld
....
147

Virtual Prophet
....
165

The Fearless Virtual God's Fear of Being Understood!
....
177

1. Fun And Games
....
184

2. Comfort and Healing
....
189

3. Human Resources (Choosing Personnel)
....
196

4. Indivudual Punishment System
....
208

International Space Station = Noah's Ark
....
267

Resources
....
277

Previous Publications
....
279

Reviews
....
282

Back Cover
....
287

Thank You

They asked a dervish, "What is the wisdom of a dervish?"
The Dervish answered, "To be patient when he has nothing,
To give thanks when he has something."
You spoke well brother dervish, but the important thing is this:
"To be patient when you have nothing,
And to be able to share when you have something."

There are two types of writers, the active writer and the passive writer. Those who write books are active writers, those who have a part in writing the book, knowingly or not, are the passive writers.

First and foremost to my family and to those who have shared their knowledge and experience, to all I have had the opportunity to know and to those I haven't met, and to those who have contributed to this book intentionally or unknowingly, I extend my heartfelt gratitude.

Aydın TÜRKGÜCÜ

Special Thanks to:

Prof. Salih Akdemir, Ph.D.   Ankara U. Faculty of Divinity

Prof. Beyza Bilgin, Ph.D.   Ankara U. Faculty of Divinity

Prof. Ahmet İnam, Ph.D.   Professor, Chair
The philosophy department at METU

Prof. Hamdullah Aydın, Ph.D.

Y. Selim Sarıibrahimoğlu, Ph.D.

Sinan Canan, Ph.D.   Başkent U. Faculty of medicine

Robert Abudara   Vice President
The Jewish Community of Turkey

Yusuf Altıntaş   Secretary General of the Chief Rabbi
The Jewish Community of Turkey

Geoffrey B. Evans   St. Nicolas' Church,
British Embassy, Ankara-Turkey

Foreword

'Will a virtual reality destroy belief or renew it?'

If technological issues are not reflected in the Holy Books, the books would remain entangled in everyday sociological issues and lose their status of being the Theory of Everything and the books of all times. If indeed, the technological issues are addressed, it opens a passage from a Sociological God to a Technological God and to the renewal of belief through science.

Since the very beginning, mankind who observed the universe with its exceptional grandeur and diversity made assumptions relating to religious and scientific scenarios of creation. The assumptions that "it is not possible that man, or a group of men, created the universe" and "everything I touch, see or in short, perceive is real" are valid even today.

A period in which mankind believes that he did not create the universe, whose existence he does not doubt, is a period of some-what calm. The opposite turns the old and deep consciousness into doubt, resulting in real chaos.

Those who, inspired by the physical space man takes up on earth, or the space earth takes up in space say: *"We are a mere drop in the ocean,"* similarly say to those who want to reach the information concerning that divine puzzle that is the beginning of the universe: "what we know does not even constitute a dot compared to what we should know. It is virtually zero." **In a situation where we do not know what it is that we should know, how can we make any assumptions concerning the ratio of what we do know to what we do not know (x/? = 0).**

There are two types of people on earth; those who have come to earth to decipher the system, and those who have come to earth to be deciphered by the system. If you are content with the belief in the God you are familiar with, the earth is still large enough for you and you are not yet weary of it, you are in the group that has already deciphered the system or has come here to be deciphered. You do not need to ascend to the skies in order to solve the divine puzzle.

Please, don't even bother!

In Reading

From the beginning of time through the present, man has been so preoccupied with debating the source of the Holy Books or those who transmitted them, that he has not studied their contents. Yet it is what's written inside a book that makes it sacred.

Religions also suffer from the illness of inward withdrawal. In religion this illness can be seen as remaining chained to the past and holding on to the old. Man's closing in on himself is an act of holding on to his past and to the information he has accumulated. As a result, instead of giving persuasive, credible new answers to questions posed by today's people, the responses are based on past hearsay, and depend on legends and stories. Rote defense of the thoughts of those who came before us, therefore copying the conservatism of the past, (fixation on imitation) has, historically, never been accepted.

Questioning with our clogged intelligence, relying on historical hearsay, legends and stories, and trying to stop the evolution of knowledge and time does not amount to questioning, but to conservatism. Is it not the command of the Creator that we produce new thoughts through the books for all times until the day of reckoning?

The extreme reaction (forbidden by the Creator) shown by conservative people who regard any thinking that is outside the system as a threat, is the result of the conservative person meeting the other. **The ability to re-express the existing knowledge or the practices of the past (the traditions) without changing its core or by keeping its essence, is to be able to see what's new and to evolve.**

Fear of questioning that stems from a lack of self-confidence, is fear of losing. This book, like all new points of view, is the product of years of research. It will, of course, be reviewed, researched and reexamined. The results are impressive, far reaching and give reason for hope. While giving new answers to old questions concerning the beginning (the creation of the universe) which is at least as old as mankind and which has not been questioned in a long time, it rises several more, rather radical questions that have not been asked before.

We have searched long enough for the Creator of past and future, in the past, as if he didn't exist in the future. The accumulation of information we have today about what is visible is sufficient to understand the unseen in order to explain and understand it. Following the fingerprints left by the Creator who created the universe in six days and rested on the at seventh, will, with the help of science and technology, take us to the source that seems to be just out of sight.

Proverbs, 25:2 *To conceal a matter, this is the glory of God, to sift it thoroughly, the glory of kings.* **(OT)**

My only claim is my sincerity. When you're ready we will begin.

Aydın TÜRKGÜCÜ

In the book "A capital "G" is used to denote the true Creator and a lower case "g" is used for the others like fire, sun, ect. Which are worshiped by human beings.

OT : Old Testament

NT : New Testament

Q. : Qur'an

New Reasons to Believe

"Are you ready?"

This question propelled me to open my eyes and my consciousness.

When I opened my eyes to see the person who was speaking, the dark was so intense that it was as if I had been born into that darkness. The unidentified voice from out of this pitch black spoke again.

Voice: "Are you ready?"

My awareness was so acute that even though I saw nothing, as a natural response I said, **"I am ready, let it begin."** (As it was, the effect of an unexpected answer initiated another question.)

Voice: Usually everyone asks, "What for?" Why did you say "I'm ready, let it begin?" as if you had been waiting for a long time for something to begin? You could have simply said "I'm ready," but you said, "Let it begin." (I said to myself "This can't be the voice of God or the angels so no need to be afraid.)

(I could not pass up the chance of having a philosophical conversation with the invisible that I can never have with the visible. Just how ready was the one who asked if I was ready?)

I have accepted life as a virtual course that was created in order to determine my breaking points. Each day, to challenge the world which is ever more perplexing, I open the street door after reading these words I had written on the inside; **"I'm ready, let it begin."**

Voice: How did you figure out that life is a course?

If certain areas of our lives develop according to our choices, it means that we must be able to *choose* certain areas before we come to life.

II Kings, 18:38 Do not forget the covenant I have made with you. **(OT)**
*Luqman, 31:14 We provided man with a mother and father. **(Q)***
*Abraham, 14:34 And He gives you of all that you ask Him. **(Q)***

In recent years, when the things that I lived through turned into familiar scenarios, my life-course began to get monotonous and boring.

Voice: You answered like a person using the logic of Honore de Balzac when he said, *"To those at the very bottom, every change is up."* Was this out of compulsion to change a monotonous life and the longing for a new beginning? Or are you defying the existing scenarios?

Let me explain:

*I Corinthians, 6:2-3 / And if the world is to be judged by you, how can you be unfit to judge trifling cases? Since we are also to judge angels, it follows that we can judge matters of everyday life. **(NT)***
*The Kneeling, 45:13 / And He has made subservient to you whatsoever is in the heavens and whatsoever is in the earth **(Q)***

Similar verses say, God has put all the earth and angels under man's command and when Satan protested, he was banished. In science, it is accepted that man is brought into the world as the most intelligent, the supreme being and as the master of all creation, having been the hardiest and single champion sperm amongst seventy million that compete.
In spite of this, while religious men describe man as being *a helpless, pitiful poor slave*, some religious sects and some organizations even use the basic, helpless simile *a drop in the ocean* in order to define man, getting inspiration from the physical space that man holds on earth, or that earth holds in space.

In summary, having come into the world from millions of candidates, both as science's and God's champion with everything in the heavens and earth under our command, we disrespectfully reject God-given authority and the reports of science and live as if we were helpless slaves, doing the basic work of those who call us "helpless," bowing to kiss their skirts physically and mentally. 'Coming to "Let it begin…"'

> *Come, whoever you may be, come*
> *Even if you may be, an infidel, a pagan,*
> *or a fire-worshipper, come.*
> *Ours is not a brotherhood of despair.*
> *Even if you have broken,*
> *Yours vow of repentance a hundred times, come.*

Along with the tolerance that Celaleddin Rumi Mevlana[1] shows here, isn't there a little boredom or belligerence? Why does he invite everyone? Isn't he saying *"I'm ready (for a new lifecourse), let it begin?"* Is it necessary to be exasperated like he was in order to understand?

Voice: Instead of giving a short answer to a short question, why did you give a long answer by beginning with a quote from Rumi?

I'm in a conversation where I am unfamiliar with the rules. When you quoted Balzac, I quoted Rumi. As for your question:

First: If you and I are going to begin together, I would like to know just how prepared the person with me is. If only I, alone, am beginning, will it be worth it? Will it not? I want to know so that I may not get my hopes up. I'm not afraid of the dangers of the virtual life-course, but in anticipation of a new, higher life-course or dimension, I'm afraid of the anguish of disillusionment.

Second: Rumi, when saying, *"Come, come, whoever you are,"* puts no limit on those who come; he invites all mankind and displays an example of complete self-confidence. He may have been completely frustrated with those around him, understood that he was getting nowhere with them. He may have put forward his need for new ideas and new people. When I say "I'm ready, let it begin," in a way I am saying, "Whoever you are, come," since to me, right now, you are only a voice in the dark.

Voice: Once you have said "Let it begin" is there any need to question or find out who I am? In addition, when Rumi says,

---

[1] Celaleddin Rumi Mevlana the founder of the mystical Mavlevi whirling dervishes still centered today in Konya, Turkey. Throughout this book Rumi will be used in reference to this well known mystic.

"either appear as you are or be as you appear," what does he mean?

If something begins with choices, it continues that way. I am accumulating information for the new choices I may be able to make on a life-course that awaits me beyond the darkness.

It is not known if Rumi spoke those words for himself, for others or for both of those choices. I think he was talking about discomfort or suggesting: *"Make a decision now! Save us and yourself from this indecision now so that we may know how to treat you."* You don't know me very well, do you?

Voice: I glanced at the images recorded on the paths you have chosen. I usually do not talk much. If I had known this conversation would be so philosophical, I would have examined the "**Application for Earth**" form you filled out to come to earth, in order to be a little more prepared.

Which of my paths did you examine? Recorded images of mine? "Application for Earth" what does that mean?

Voice: The path you developed through the choices you have made from the day you were born through today: as the Scripture mentions, the recorded images of your life path.

The Kneeling, 45:29 *Surely We wrote what you did, (Q)*

I am referring to the application form that you filled out when you marked your choice of Mother / Father / Country. (He stopped talking for a moment as if he had let something escape.) In any case, our time is up! Now let me use my initiative and ask a question with deference in keeping with your answer and your adventurous personality: "**SHALL IT BEGIN?**"

By reading the words above a door I believed opened to an upper life-course, I said: **"I'm ready. Let it begin,"** as if, with my words, I were opening a spiritual door leading from darkness into light.

Voice: (Smiling) You said that as if you were saying *"Open Sesame"*. My duty was to initiate and now I'm finished! You didn't ask me who I was, and I will not tell you so that you do not lose your concentration on your path. As you return along the path you have come on, in the beginning you will be alone for a while. In relevant areas, those you looked to as an example, those whose works you have studied or pondered while you lived on earth, will appear to guide you. At the end of your horizontal trip, you will begin your main trip vertically by space elevator.

Psalms, 19:6 He has his rising on the edge of heaven, and the end of the course is the furthest edge. (OT)
The Believers, 23:17 And certainly We made above you seven heavens; and never are We heedless of creation. (Q)

It is there that you will understand who I am.

(I couldn't resist and interrupted)… Will I be able to hear you again?

Voice: (LAUGHING) You humans, you immediately create an emotional bond. As I said, my duty was to get the trip started. We'll meet again if there is a return trip. I am only a voice; give your curiosity and attention to the path. The images are of things you know: your own past. Now, don't get emotional when you see things and loved ones from the past. If you emphasize the emotional side of the contents of the picture for more than three seconds, you will return to earth and remember nothing. Than you will have to learn what you need to remember, from books, films and various normal sources.

Why is getting emotionally involved "bad"?

Voice: Just like the ones who can't experience the future in order to stay and live in the past, your mind is still stuck on the beings and niceties of earth. One will never be able to take the road straight up who is not finished with his/her past.

You will not understand the lessons while you are weeping and blubbering. Especially, when you think of the earth, emphasize the science and technological areas and understand the philosophy behind it. Hold out until the elevator! In addition, don't miss the clues that will help you get to the upper floors on your seven storey, perpendicular journey. I wouldn't recommend it, but if you become afraid, or get irritated or no longer want to see things from the past, you can end your side trip and return to earth. (In order to get more answers from the little time left I interrupted again).

Have we met before?

Voice: Yes. In 1998, we had a meeting. Since we meet again, that trip must have been a return trip. I am not here to give you detailed answers. Don't worry! You will return by the same road you went out on and you will remember the experiences of the things you've been thinking about for these past ten years. Your guides along the road will answer your questions that will allow you to reflect further. I have answered this question because they will not be able to answer this one. To calm your initial excitement, you will have seven seconds after you sit down. Now sit down!

(Until that moment, I had been unaware of my body, therefore I didn't know if I was sitting or standing. It was as if two disembodied voices had been talking in the dark telepathically. As I hesitated for a second...)

Voice: "Words fly away, but images stay in the mind a long time". That is the reason why some of you are trained on the road of life through images both on the way there and back. In order that the lessons remain in your memory, you have a three dimensional simulation training which allows for the conversation along the road with the guides you've chosen. Now don't keep me talking or you will confuse yourself. When you sit down your time will begin. Don't worry **"Your creator is with you."**

The phrase "Your Creator is with you" was the first phrase my maternal grandmother taught me and in difficult times, I found strength in the phrase whenever I recalled it. Was it a standard phrase of the Voice or did it know me better than I'd guessed? Did it choose the "Are you ready" question knowingly? I felt myself sit down as I thought…

It was as if I was looking at a completely dark night sky void of stars or moonlight. A distant light began to illuminate my surroundings and the stars and planets and galaxies began to appear. When I saw the moon in front of me, to my right, I immediately turned around and our planet was slowly turning in magnificent beauty; the earth we live on was directly in front of me. It occurred to me, to think of what was I sitting on in empty space; I looked down but saw no chair or stool. I clearly felt I was sitting, but was sitting on nothing.

The interesting thing is that just below my feet was another small earth that was not turning. If this was a reflection and the real world was turning, then the reflection would also be turning. Suddenly, a meter in front of me, there appeared a picture size of a screen of a plasma television. In the upper left corner of the screen was my name and in the upper right corner was the information: **20/03/2007 – 4:30:00.** On the screen was a fixed picture of earth.

As I examined the fixed images on the screen, there extended a row of images of the fixed earth beneath me continuing out into the depths of space, one after the other, as if there were thousands of lamps lighting the road. The seven second wait probably gave me a chance to calm down and gave them a chance to prepare the path I was to follow.

Beneath the image there was a red button with the word "**CANCEL**", another button was green with the word "**BEGIN**." I reasoned that seven seconds had passed, and the trip hadn't started, so there was no point in pushing a button to stop anything. I had no choice but to push the "BEGIN" button that had been assigned to me on this trip.

With the inner confidence of one who "hopes for all" and trusting the stranger in front of me, I extended my right hand and said, "Until we meet again" to the voice of the one whose job it was to set the trip in motion, and pushed the "BEGIN" button. I began my trip to space.

I began to move away from the earth, sliding on the earths that were lined up like train tracks beneath my feet. Beginning with the latest recorded pictures of my life on earth, my past began to pass before my eyes like a filmstrip. With the images in front of me, I was able to view the last one or two years of my life in a very short time. If I were to watch that period on a movie screen or a television screen, it would take one or two years. That is all well and good, but with the slow speed sense organs I have, how was I able to see the details of such a long time period in such a short time?

Psalms, 90:4 For a thousand years in your sight are like yesterday when it is past, or like a watch in the night. **(OT)**
Pilgrimage, 22:47 and Allah will by no means fail in His promise, and surely a day with your Lord is as a thousand years of what you number. **(Q)**

When this verse came to mind, I said, "I must be on The God's level."

The view of the spectacular universe changed at the same time as the images on the screen changed. As a person whose childhood dream was to be an astronaut, between the images of my past on the screen and the splendid views of the universe, I didn't know which to concentrate on. It was as if I were sitting in an armchair in space, watching my own documentary with a recording of my images on the screen in front of me. Feeling no physical motion, I was unable to differentiate whether the images were passing around me or if I was sliding on top of them. Also I was trying to understand these things:

* Was I awake? Was I thinking that I'm awake? Was I dreaming?
* Was I in an illusion of my own making?
* On the other hand, as is often explained, was I dying and my life passing in front of me like a filmstrip?

Since I saw no light at the end of the tunnel, since I had on no protective clothing in a place hostile to man, and since space does not protect man, I felt I was most certainly in a dream. In all probability, I had unconsciously repressed my desire to make this trip and the thoughts I had been unable to reveal to myself, were surfacing in the unfettered comfort of a dream. I hoped I would be able to remember everything when I awoke.

While my name in the upper left corner of the screen remained fixed, the date/time information was moving backwards as would be expected as the images sped into the past. I was literally making a trip to the past in time. This is what it must be like for man to face his past. Looking at certain areas, maybe I would have liked to make some changes, but I was unable to access interaction with the images: as with the images on a movie screen, my only option was to watch.

As in a dream without a definite beginning, the events were in my control and yet not, somehow. For now, it was an extremely exciting experience somewhere between the real and imaginary in space. Maybe I had begun to have controlled dreams of the type my good friend had told me, in conversation, that he had experienced. When I remembered the advice of the Voice, I began to examine my surroundings for their technical aspects.

In the confusion of the first moments, the frames of the funeral of my father, whom I'd lost a few years before, caught my eye but I was unable to see them clearly. It takes a while for a person to become accustomed to this type of experience and attach meaning to it. By the time the frames showed my life in my twenties, I'd seen almost all of the loved ones I had lost in the past twenty years. I began to see the images more clearly, either because I had become accustomed to my situation or because the system slowed down in this period.

When I saw my grandmother and grandfather who, in my childhood, had helped shape my beliefs about God, tears welled in my eyes. Unable to embrace or talk to those you love or even greet them is, indeed, a difficult situation. When I saw my grandmother who had prepared me for these days, praying for me at morning prayers, the tears flowed uncontrollably. I couldn't stop weeping when I saw the profound, loving looks my grandfather gave me. It seemed I was not able to act on the suggestions I'd just received and I became emotional and that intensified the images. Just at that time, when I believed myself to be alone, suddenly a friendly tap on the shoulder startled me. Confused, when I turned my head to the right, I was more astonished. The great Turkish leader **Mustafa Kemal Atatürk** was beside me. Just as in the course of life his blue eyes, bright with success, bored into mine as he started to speak.

Atatürk: One of your departed loved ones could have come instead of me, but then it would have turned into an emotional scene. Because the intensity would have lasted more than three seconds, your attention would have automatically pressed the **"CANCEL"** button, and you would have missed the success in the perpendicular ascent that is expected of you. These are the images you cannot control. Don't let pictures that you cannot change distract you. Those clues that you wondered about and questioned on earth are being shown in order for you to understand the technical makeup of the universe you are searching for. Observe and question as you always do.

You remember in 1998, as you visited shrines and brotherhoods as part of your quest, you also visited my mausoleum. And as visitors there said: *"We follow the path of our leader (Atatürk),"* you said to me: *"those followers, since they didn't understand you, they remained behind you."*

"O leader Atatürk, we know we are behind, but don't worry we will catch up." You criticized this, saying *"now we should say," O leader Atatürk, we are at your side. "* Then later, you said these words: *"O leader Atatürk, for the moment I am by your side, and soon we shall progress together,"* followed by *"A leader is the commander of ideas, both concrete and abstract, where there is no commander, ideas are the commander."*

I wanted to be by your side when you began this journey between the afterworld and earth that has the potential of increasing your knowledge so greatly. The things that you are being shown here are necessary to build a scientific foundation to understand what you will hear and see in the future. As for understanding what you will pay attention to, let me introduce what we call science:

What does science mean to mankind?

Science: *knowledge obtained from the systematic study of the structure and behavior of the physical world, especially by observing, measuring and experimenting, and the development of theories to describe the results of these activities:*

Atatürk: Good, and how is God defined?

God: (Especially in Christian, Jewish and Muslim belief) the being which made the universe, the Earth and its people and is believed to have an effect on all things". The Creator, the one and only holy spirit.

Atatürk: And last, how is the universe defined?

Universe: (1) everything that exists, especially all physical matter, including all the stars, planets, galaxies, etc. in space: (2) a universe which could be imagined to exist outside our own:

Atatürk: Now let us make the connections, if God created the heavens and the earth, and science attempts to understand and explain Universe, is science a way to know God?

(Confident that he knew my answer, he continued without waiting)

Atatürk: What did I say about science?

"Science is the truest guide to life," I said in one of the shortest answers I had ever given. His blue eyes smiled with pleasure as he received the answer he wanted.

Atatürk: I know you have studied the Holy Books for years, especially concentrating on the scientific verses. Is there a verse in the Holy Books that is particularly connected to the situation we are in now?

I immediately yelled,
Ezekiel, *40:4 Son of man, look carefully, listen closely and pay attention to everything I show you, since you have only been bought here for me to show it to you.* **(OT)**

We smiled at each other as he felt the appropriateness of the reply and I the happiness of having given it.

Atatürk: (Calmly) From the look on your face, I know you're confused.

Isaiah, 52:15 And kings stand speechless before him for they shall see something never told. (OT)
II Corinthians, 12:2-4 God knows right into the third heaven, I do know, however, that this same person, (whether in the body or out of the body, I don't know; God knows.) was caught up into paradise and heard things which must not and cannot be put into human language. (NT)

It resembles the surprise and confusion of the person in this verse. In order for you to understand what is being explained, it is important that you have basic information on the subject. In **Pope John Paul** II's book "**Fides et Ratio,**" *God who makes himself known is also the source of the credibility of what he reveals. (1:13)* The religious and scientific studies that you've made on earth so far will enable you to understand what you see and feel on this trip.

That is why, I said *"**Science is the truest guide in life,**"* and had the Qur'an translated into Turkish. This way, everyone could read the truth for himself and understand the importance of science in religion. Everyone could think about creation for himself and in this way the subject would not be made a toy in the hands of those who have no true understanding. So, is there a verse in the Holy Books that supports what I've said?

There certainly is!

Colossians, 3:2 Let your thoughts be on heavenly things, not on the things that are on the earth. (NT)
The Family of Imran, 3:191 Who remember God while standing, sitting and (lying) on their sides, and meditate on the creation of Heaven and Earth (by saying); Our Lord! You have not created this in vain. (Q)

I recited the verse quickly. The meaning is quite clear, how can the creation of the heavens and earth be studied deeply without scientific knowledge and research?

My dear leader, I have always wondered something concerning you, may I ask you a personal question? (When he had nodded his head, I asked immediately). When I think of your life and what you did in your life, I wonder how you endured.

Atatürk: The first rule is you must have no need for material things. When I was living, did I not distribute everything I did not need? That is why on earth, even my enemies in battle felt respect for my name and not my fortune. My struggle, which is taken as an example by the whole world, my enlightened thoughts, our enlightened Republic and our enlightened people have all remained.

Of course, I had very difficult, even unbearable days and nights, but remember, "Your Creator knows you and is with you." That is to say that what you are able to provide is what is expected from you. In the Holy Books, is it not said;

Deuteronomy, 30:11 For this law that I enjoin on you today is not beyond your strength or beyond your reach. **(OT)**
Deuteronomy, 30:14 No, the word is very near to you; it is in your mouth and in your heart for you to observe. **(OT)**
II Corinthians, 10:13 We on the other hand are not going to boast without a standard to measure against: taking for our measure the yardstick which God gave us to measure with, which is long enough to reach to you. **(NT)**
The Believers, 23:62, And We do not lay on any soul a burden except to the extent of its ability. **(Q)**

Do not forget, battle fields are places where man is brought closer to himself or is distanced from himself. A person's humanity can be measured by his treatment of his enemies. In battle, there are moments when emotions are rife and when justice is easily forgotten. As I always said *"Battle, unless unavoidable, is murder,"* ***"Peace at home, peace in the world."*** You can modify this to fit people and read ***"Peace on the inside, peace on the outside".***

If you are not at peace with yourself inside, if you constantly battle with yourself, some time later that battle will turn into an outer battle. Inside you will argue or battle with yourself and outside with everything you find, be it living or not. These days, instead of the classic battlefield, do you not experience the same moments in the economic battles of normal life to distance you from justice? I would like to share an anecdote that will remind you that the choice is yours alone. It will help you retain your inner sense of justice when you have reached the upper limits of your capacity.

Two Symbols

An old Indian chief sat in front of his tent with his grandson. They were watching two German shepherd dogs wrestling a short distance in front of them. One of the dogs was white, the other was black, and the boy who was twelve could not remember a time when they did not wrestle in front of his grandfather's tent. These were the two huge dogs that his grandfather always kept an eye on, that never left his side. Now the child thought that one dog should be enough to guard the tent and asked his grandfather why he needed the second dog and wanted to know why there must always be one white and one black.

The old chief patted his grandchild's back, smiled wisely and said "They are my two symbols, son." "Symbols of what?" asked the boy. "They are symbols of good and bad. Just as you see these dogs fight, good and bad struggle within us. As I watch them, I always think of this. That is the reason why I keep them by me.

The child interrupted here thinking, "If there is a fight, there must be a winner," he asked another question, as children do. "Well, then which one do you think will win the fight?"

With a broad smile, the wise chief looked at his grandson and answered, "Which one, my child? ***The one that I feed the most!"***

I will always remember this wonderful example. Your secular principles have become today's biggest problem. They say that secularism puts brakes on religion. Does it really?

Atatürk: Brakes are a valuable control mechanism used on all vehicles and equipment to ensure that the driver, and the vehicle in use may navigate the road safely. Anyone taking a car out on the road without brakes will either hit a wall by careening off the road or will overturn. However, if you don't know how to drive or you press the brake pedal instead of the accelerator, of course brakes can stop the vehicle. Secularism is the brakes that prevent religion from speeding up and running off the road or turning over or hitting a wall. **Didn't the Creator endow man with spiritual brakes that we call conscience?**

Given that we began with the metaphor of a car, let us continue with a car. How would you stop a car that is out of control, brakes having failed, and is about to go off the road? "You use the hand brakes." The mechanisms of security and justice were established as hand brakes to prevent those unscrupulous people, whose inner brakes, the conscience, don't work, from losing control and going off the road harming others. **As we established the Turkish Republic, we gave the responsibility of advancing these mechanisms not just to the politicians and institutions, but to the Turkish youth, especially.**

The Table, *5:42 God loves those who judge equitably.* **(Q)**
Psalms, *106:3 Happy are we if we exercise justice.* **(OT)**

(The great leader raised his voice) "Never let the injustices and ignorance you see frighten you and cause hopelessness!" because **light disburses more easily in darkness**. Weren't you the one who identified yourself with the slogan "**When moving out of darkness on the stairs to enlightenment, the last step is ours**"?

Think of the brightness created by a match lit in a pitch-black room. To darken the inside of the same room in the daytime, you would need layers and layers of dark sheets over the windows. The slightest bit of light bleeding through a small break in the curtain is enough to light the darkened room. Darkness cannot seep into a lighted room because brightness cannot be darkened by covering it. You can only stop the spread of light. While a few projectors can produce daylight for a night match in a stadium, to make the same stadium dark as night for a match played in the daytime would be very difficult, indeed.

Different matches can be used for each dark thought in the brain of man. For instance, for the darkness of religion, religious matches (verses) can be used. For scientific darkness, you must use scientific matches. Of course, no matter what the field, ignorance is the greatest darkness of the mind. Those in the darkness who think of themselves as being in the light, instead of complaining about those in the dark, must share enlightenment with others to understand the truly enlightened.

Scriptures about coming from darkness into light came to mind immediately.

Isaiah, 42:16 I will lead them in paths that they don't know. I will make darkness light before them, and crooked places straight. I will do these things, and I will not forsake them. **(OT)**
II Corinthians, 4:6 "Let there be light shining out of darkness." **(NT)**
Iron, 57:9 He is the One Who has sent down clear signs upon His servant, so he may lead you out of darkness into Light. **(Q)**

Atatürk: On the road along your journey here, the guides who appear at your side will assume the outward appearance of those whose explanation you will best be able to understand. It has been planned so you will remember the people and what you hear for the longest time. It will be just like in the film **Contact**, where the spaceman took on the appearance of Jody Foster's father so that he could speak to her with more ease. I too am a hologram, using the voice and the form of Mustafa Kemal Atatürk so that you may learn more. **Don't worry, I am not a spaceman or alien.**

He said, **"Your creator is with you and knows you,"** and wished me a safe journey. (He quickly receded in an increasing stream of light to take his place like a star to light the darkness of the heavens**.)**

Those who planned this training reached their goal. This conversation was made up of extraordinary things so that I would remember even the slightest word for long years to come. The images that prevailed throughout the conversation began to change once again, and I began to move into the depths of space towards my past. An image of me examining the book called **"Plato and After Plato,"** by **Dr. Fatma Paksüt** passed by on the screen.

I couldn't help thinking what a wonderful accomplishment it was for **Prof. Paksüt** to leave us a summary of the complete works of Plato. Beginning from Seneca it examines the influence the great philosopher made on man's thinking and shows the dimensions it reached. This work has always given me courage. Just at that time, a guide appeared to my left. At this point in my thought trip with images of Plato passing on the screen, the holographic image that appeared could have been none other than Plato.

Plato: "Yes, it's just as you thought, I am Plato's hologram. Which of my ideas affected you most? (There were so many areas that had affected me, I wasn't sure which one to choose.)

In this context, the most effective area, was your cave metaphor, I call this the **"virtual cave."**

"Consider an underground cave; in front, is an entrance completely open to light; and inside the cave, let's say, there are people sitting with their backs turned to the entrance, unable to move or even turn their heads because they are chained up. Behind these people and above them, suppose a fire burns. Between the fire and people with their backs to it, is a short wall with more people sitting behind it. And in these people's hands are puppets made of rocks and wood. Those people inside the cave, because they are chained, are unable to turn their heads and see those outside. What they see is the shadows made by the fire light and thrown on to the wall in front of them. When they explain things made by the shadows they see as real, they assume the sounds hitting their ears are coming from the shadows. If one of them breaks his chains and is taken outside his eyes will react to the light of the sun and the things he had seen before are much more real to him. To be able to see things his eyes need to acclimatize to the bright light.

Such a person first sees the shadows, then the reflections of people and things on the water, followed by objects, then stars, the moon and the sky. To the person from the cave, the moment he realizes that the sun had caused the seasons and the years, and that all the visible world was formed by the sun, that the sun was actually the source of everything he saw, is the moment he begins to feel sorry for those still in the cave. He scorns the importance they give each other, he belittles their beliefs concerning the shadows. And if he goes to his old friends and explains what he has seen, his words will not be believed. And when that person tries to save them and bring them out of the cave, he is attacked.

Other words can fit into the comparison; if the cave is the known world and the light of the fire illuminating the cave is the light of the sun striking earth, and if the beauty observed is the rise of thought to the world of spiritual thoughts, it may be easier to understand our thoughts." There are verses that support this metaphor, of course:

The Cave, *18:10 The youths sought shelter in the cave. (Q)*
The Cave, *18:17 And you might see the sun when it rose, decline from their cave towards the right hand, and when it set, leave them behind on the left while they were in a wide space thereof. (Q)*
The Cave, *18:21 When they disputed among themselves about their affair. (Q)*

To those who have never seen anything else in their lives, to cave people who don't know otherwise, their truth is in the cave. Anyone who says there are many other dimensions with many colors outside the cave will seem, in a word, "crazy." But, in fact, this is the truth.

Plato: Now let's look at the remaining part of the journey. Can you see the world you live in?

As I looked back, I realized that we had stopped at a location far from our world and our solar system. While speaking with the guides, the flow of images on the screen and progress on the trip had stopped. Perhaps these were short answer stops along the road.

Plato: As you see, you are situated behind the fire in the mouth of the cave. Your eyes have adjusted quickly to the light, but the adjustment of your thoughts to the next, more enlightened higher dimension will only be completed toward the end of this horizontal trip.

Dear teacher, it would not be fitting to meet you and not speak of our concept of "State." Just as you divided the universe into two, I introduced two states within government. In the book *Plato and After Plato,* on page 37: *"First of all, in addition to the gods' bright ceremonies, a pure heart should be thought more valuable than an expensive sacrifice. Gods, like humans crazed for gifts, are not likely to value the glitter of the ceremonies and the expense of the sacrifices made to them. It must be remembered that people of understanding as well as Gods value honesty and integrity above anything. Intelligent and honest people are those who know what to do and say to Gods and people.*
A person must learn what he can request from God before he begins to pray. He must know that a disrespectful prayer may not be accepted by God and remain silent lest God may possibly punish such disrespectful behavior. A person who does not know what's right and what's not is as a person covered in smoke. First, the smoke must dissipate. It is only when he reaches the point of knowing good from bad that he may make a request."

The chapter you have on prayer is one that comes to my mind every time I pray. From this viewpoint, I found **"A New Prayer Box"** for my prayers and as I watched the others pray I found the meaning of **"The visible State and the Invisible State."**

Plato: Interesting. Would you explain?

So called invincible Empires and states which I have called the Visible States have all been erased from the stages of history. It is worth our while to study the belief in God that has remained in the hearts of human beings of earth for thousand years which I have called the Invisible State.

Despite some undesired experiences resulting from misunder-standings, the Invisible State, by keeping human beings together for thousands of years is a ready-made universal platform for World Peace, if the interpretation is right.

A New Prayer Box
(Request the Unusual and get God's Attention)

I took as fact that there may be prayer boxes for various requests made to God such as a spouse, work, school, success, protection from harm, health, house, car, etc.

Then I envisioned that the millions of prayers made each day were first collected at a prayer-processing center and then sorted according to their request contents; a spouse, a job, school, success, protection from harm, health, house, car, etc. These were put into the bottom of all the boxes bulging from billions of previous prayers waiting processing. Those who wanted to move to the top of the pile of appeals, needing to catch God's attention and show their urgency, tried to draw attention by offering sacrifices and building places of worship, which they put in between the prayers. However, I did not have that financial strength.

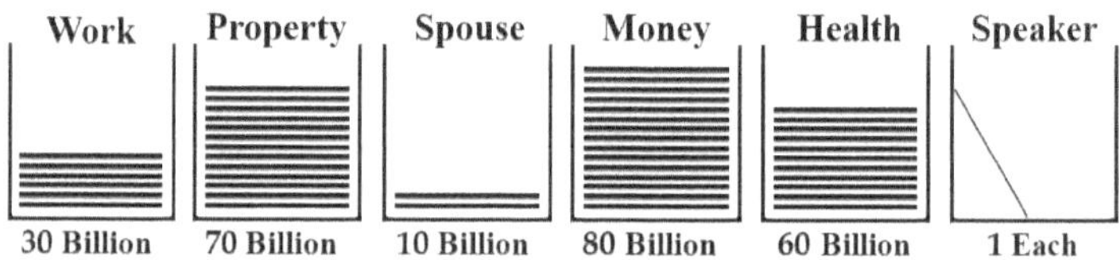

For years, people have been going to the shrines of special people to make their requests known. I don't know whether it was because they did not know how to make a request or whether it was because of the bureaucracy on God's level, but their prayers had gone unanswered or their turn had not yet come.

The Chicago gangster Al Capone is an example of those who can commit crimes, becoming impatient waiting for God to answer his prayer. Al Capone tells the story of his impatience as this: *"When I was a*

I really needed God's attention in 1994. Therefore, instead of writing a letter to God, the likes of which many have gotten lost between the sacrifices and often repeatedly sent letters, I decided I would send God a short telegram wanting something **exceptional but difficult, so I would attract God's attention.** Aristotle said once: *"God loves surprises!"*

Psalms, 141:1 Yahweh, I am calling, hurry to me, listen to me, I am invoking you. (OT)

The Narrative, 28.24 My Lord! surely I stand in need of whatever good Thou mayest send down to me. (Q)

As only a writer trying to write a book about creation could want, I wrote, **"You know my situation. STOP. I want my knowledge to be improved STOP. With my respects. STOP."** I wondered if there was a post box for the subject of my suggestion. If there was, how many request letters had been sent before? I felt lucky…

I Timothy, 3:1 To want to be a presiding elder is to want to do a noble work. (NT)

Taha, 20:14 Surely I am Allah, there is no god but I, therefore serve Me and keep up prayer for My remembrance: (Q)

At an unexpected time, death may come before the last words have been spoken, where both the person who goes and those left have words yet unspoken. Therefore, when I visit the cemetery I some-times say, "If there is anything you would like to say to those left behind, I will tell them." This bit of spokesmanship is like asking if there are any suggestions the dead person in the grave, would like to make to those living now.

In addition, I wanted the happiness that I needed not to be a **"gratuitous donation,"** but in order to be worthy of it, I wanted it to be **"a credit to be paid back"** and a **"chance at happiness."** And different from the others, I say **"I'm Ready. Let it (meaning training) begin"**: this is to make sure it is clear that I am ready for the material/spiritual training:

the punishment or test of competency needed to prove myself worthy of such a position.

Jeremiah, *29:12-14 Then when you call to me, and come to plead with me, I will listen to you. When you seek me you shall find me, when you seek me with all your heart; I will let you find me.* **(OT)**

Psalms, *139:23-24 God, examine me and know my heart, probe and know my thoughts, make sure I do not follow pernicious ways, and guide me in the way that is everlasting.* **(OT)**

Mathew, *7:7-8 Ask, and it will be given to you: search and you will find. Knock and the door will be opened to you. For the one who asks always receives; the one who searches always finds; the one who knocks will always have the door opened to him.* **(NT)**

On this subject, I would like to share an event that I experienced at the Wailing Wall on my trip to Jerusalem.

It is here that people stand in front of the wall and pray after inserting a piece of paper with their request written on it, into the small fissures in the wall. The cracks were full of pieces of paper one on top of the other where prayers had been stuffed into them. As I raised my head, I saw an empty cavity far above me and threw my paper up into it. My paper was one or two meters above the other prayers and the only one there. A curious person whom I did not know asked, "Why did you throw it up there and not put it into the cracks in the wall like everyone else?" I retorted: "You see, mine is a bit urgent." Upon hearing my reply the person tediously removed his own request paper from among the many jammed in with it and immediately threw it up next to my paper. Even though the contents were different, we had forged a **prayer brotherhood.**

Let me relay another anecdote from the Wailing Wall in Jerusalem: *"A Jewish man who came to the Wailing Wall, prayed and left every day at the same time for years, caught the eye of a security officer. The day the security officer was retiring, he overcame his shyness and to satisfy his curiosity he approached the man to ask him a question, "You have come here every day for the last twenty years to pray in front of this wall. Have your prayers been answered?" The man looked into the guards eyes and said: "Sometimes it seems like I am talking to a wall!"*

Plato: I must interrupt here and ask something. To the one who created such a perfect system, the prayer boxes that you speak of must be a simple job. Why did you infer otherwise? Isn't this example slightly belittling?

The prayers are not to express gratefulness, they are demands for the things we are not happy with and wish to be changed by God Many faithful worshipers who live right and pray for their wishes regularly with pure hearts, never have their prayers answered. When you think of the many positive requests in terms of the philosophy put forth in the our day's popular book, "The Secret" (think/desire so that it may come true), their prayers should have been accepted long ago. That means there is a problem somewhere. Either we use the wrong method of requesting or we request something that we shouldn't.

Visible State / Invisible State
(The Success of the Visible State is Inversely Proportionate to the Number of Prayers for Material Goods)

The State is responsible for establishing the systems that supply the material and psychological needs of its people. If we put the requests of those who go to the shrines in order, needs such as house/car/work will top the list. When you think of it, these are things that people are able to secure through work. But in many of the existent systems, these needs are not provided, so they are requested.

So it is obvious that the prayers, of those who are adjusting their peace to the material are going to be for materials.

So, in this situation, we can make the conclusion that the **failure of the visible state is in direct proportion to the number of people praying for material items.** Those who have given up hope in the visible state turn to the invisible state for help which they consider to be an upper grade.

Maybe therefore the religions are still standing tall while the hundreds of years of empires and states are fading in history.
From that point of view, people not understanding the Creator, are directed by two states: one that governs the physical body that is the visible state, and the other that rules the invisible body (the spirit) which

is invisible. Religious men have become the cabinet / re-presentatives and bureaucrats of the invisible state. And they usually do their job as inspectors. **Humans are managed by coalitions built around benefits derived from the visible and invisible states**. Richard Dawkins writes about the pressure of an invisible state on the visible state in his book. "The God Delusion": *"It is universally accepted that an admission of atheism would be instant political suicide for any presidential candidate..."* (page 45) In the meantime, do not endanger your morale or your health by praying for earthly benefits from a invisible state when you should be asking for them from the visible state.

Plato: What harm can there be in man praying continually to the true God?

Dear Teacher, in fact, the contents of all prayers begin with the idea of changing our lives. Most of these are things that you should and can successfully change. You have the ability to make the changes. If you cannot make the changes, that means you are not showing enough effort and nothing can be done from above through prayer.
The Elevated Places, *7:42 We do not impose on any soul a duty except to the extent of its ability.* **(Q)**

You can plead with the teacher who gives you an examination in order to give you the answers. But in a practical test such as life on earth, to plead and pray for things that you can achieve yourself is a waste of time. What is the meaning to life if you can get everything you want by praying? The point is to make an effort, and not to expect everything from God. Thus, you should be bound to show effort. As H. De Balzac has said, *"Debts are not paid with thoughts."* God wants us to put forth efforts, not just wait for handouts.

James, *1:22 You must do what the word tells you, and not just listen to it.* **(NT)**
James, *2:24 You see now that it is by doing something good and not only by believing that a man is justified.* **(NT)**
James, *2:26 And in the same way faith is dead, it is separated from good deeds.* **(NT)**
The Cow, *2:104 You who believe do not say "Herd us", and say (instead): "Watch over us," and (then), "Listen!"* **(Q)**

Prayer means "demanding". We don't take unanswered prayers for an answer. Instead of trying to find another prayer to be answered, we are saying Amen to the same prayers that are not real and are making ourselves sad in the process. Insisting on an unfeasible prayer is just like failing in an exam by sticking to one question but not working on others that you already know the answers to. Do not waste time screaming out in agony, begging for conditions to change. First, think carefully about what you might want and refrain from praying for that not feasible. You might want to reconsider the doctor's statement *"you are what you eat"* changing it to *"You are what you think."*

Romans, *8:26 The Spirit himself expresses our plea in a way that could never be put into words.* **(NT)**

Those who continually pray for something remind me of a documentary I saw on gambling. Let me tell you the gist of it.

Let's think of a person who regularly buys a lottery ticket. After researching any and all small signs involved in the process, this person will buy a ticket at precisely what he feels to be the right time and the right place. He then follows the clues to the winning ticket he thinks he has and waits with hope in heart that this time his ticket will be the winning ticket. If he is a believer, he will pray to God that He has mercy on him by helping him in causing his ticket number to be drawn.

When the day of the draw comes, and the person learns that the ticket in his hand is worthless he sinks into hopelessness, thinking himself to be unbelievably unlucky and even being punished. He feels that even as desperately as he needs the money, his most sincere prayers have gone unanswered by God; he feels unloved. In short, for a few days after the unlucky draw he feels lethargic towards the world and is unproductive in his work. He takes consolation in cigarettes and alcohol for some time.

A few days before the next draw, those people who have felt unlucky and punished for a while because they did not win the last draw, begin to look for the telling clues that indicate that *"this time it will be their number that is called"* and allow their hopes to sprout anew. As a result of this unhappiness and hopelessness and lack of self-confidence from the loss of hope and belief, they feel like God's outcasts and greatly increase tobacco and alcohol consumption.

Those who experiencing the loss of beloved ones or are breaking up with them, usually think that they have lost the draw of life and believing there is no hope left for their happiness. They are willing to quit for the long term (and commit suicide).

Depression is the point reached when no hope for the future and expectations of life remain. It is an outcome of the disappointments of life experiences that could not be avoided and diminishing pleasure induced by personal guilt.

The development of technology brings changes in sociological make up. This commends personal development and projects personal responsibility to the fore. Thus the emergence of personal responsibility in turn triggers guilt feelings in the face of negative outcomes.

As the person realizes that hope-filled daily prayers and desires are not being fulfilled, the deep depression he suffers may escalate into a "feeling of guilt."

A person who prays the same prayers daily will fall into the same situation when his prayers of supplications to God are not answered. Therefore, instead of begging, I feel it is more beneficial to keep yourself feeling happy and successful by praying prayers of gratitude and inserting small suggestions, that make you feel God and that you are integrated with God.

Plato: Why is being grateful important?

We must begin all prayers by expressing gratitude. By thanking God, we are giving ourselves morale and saying: "I did not give up, I'm still standing, and I will achieve with God's justice." Thanking God is like renewing belief in our most trusted friend. It is like feeling a bond and bolstering our morale and strength against our problems and hurdles. This boosted morale is good for our health and will lengthen our lives.

Ask to give
Give, when it arrives
If it doesn't be patient
But
Be grateful in every step

Plato: How is health improved by being grateful?

As Prof. Salih Akdemir Ph.D. mentioned in his classes, lie detection machines, used for questioning suspects use the changes occurring in body chemistry to produce a result of truth or non truth. The lies a person uses to produce wealth, for example, produce chemicals which weaken the immune system. In turn, a weakened immune system leads to illness and perhaps eventually to early death, while high morale produced from gratefulness, strengthens the immune system and prolongs a healthy life. This will lengthen your healthy life span.

Proverbs, 28:16 *He who hates (avoids) avarice will lengthen his days.* **(OT)**
Proverbs, 21:6 *To make a fortune with the help of a lying tongue, such the idle fantasy of those who look for death.* **(OT)**

Plato: This suggestion is only for believers. Are there any suggestions for those who are non-believers?

I am not trying to prove or disprove the existence of a Creator. I am trying to convey what we can achieve by assuming His existence, instead of not reaching anything by ignoring the information that we do have. There is no mathematical value of zero, integral, or derivative or formulae in reality, but we have considered them to exist (or not) because the concepts are valuable to mankind. Haven't we created the reality we call science from nothing?

Plato: My dear friend, *"What we call philosophy is meant to turn the spirit from darkness into light and elevate the spirit into true being by analyzing the concepts."*

Proverbs, *1:28-29 Then they shall call to me, but I will not answer, they shall seek me eagerly and shall not find me, they despised knowledge.* **(OT)**

Yunus, *10:89 therefore continue in the right way and do not follow the path of those who do not know* **(Q)**

While you are on earth, you have not followed those with no scientific knowledge, so you are able to understand what you see and hear. You have researched the world, contemplated a lot and that gives you the right to ask questions here. The journeys that seem to have no beginnings and no ends are clues to forward your attention on the things you see. However, don't make the mistake of trying to ask a question that should be asked last! You can use the clues from the step you are at to be able to make your way to the next step up. By using the answers found, you are able to move systematically to complete your journey. (From the tone of my guide's voice, I felt I had a chance to reach the end).

His advice reminded me of the parameters that I apply;

The Mental Stroke of Thought

"While I was watching a documentary on mountain climbing on television one day, I learned that mountain climbers make camp and live at that height for a week allowing their body's time to adjust to the pressure of the atmosphere at that level. Then they climbed a few hundred feet higher and again made camp to adjust their bodies. In this way, by stopping at certain levels they acclimatized their bodies enough to reach the summit. In short, if you attempt to go from the bottom of the sea or to the mountaintop in one leap you will suffer from physical stroke.

It is the same in the world of thought; if you attempt to answer the last question first, you will suffer mental damage and may lose your mind. Acclimatization is attained by using the information gained and waiting for the spirit, at certain points, before moving on to information of the next level. Just as food upsets our stomach when eaten quickly, if we get information from thought without properly assimilating it, we lose our minds.

Plato: These stretches of the journey are intended to give you the opportunity to understand and remember your basic rules. In a while, the main subjects will begin. Have a comfortable journey and keep your hand away from the **"CANCEL"** button. Socrates gained quite a few enemies by contacting men with broader knowledge than he possessed and by asking questions, he revealed their ignorance. As you work in the service of God, be sure not to stay in poverty and make enemies. If you return to the cave be careful.

(As he said this, I realized he was saying farewell and I immediately interrupted.)

Excuse me, you call the things of the earth the shadows, but you are also a shadow. You saved me from the wall of the cave, but chained me to the wall of a space cave. I think the shadows are very important because they have an interesting place in the Holy Books.

Job, *8:9 Our life on earth passes like a shadow.* **(OT)**

Colossians,** 2:17 These were only pale reflection of what was coming.* ***(NT)

*__Sent Forth,__ 77:30 Walk on to the covering having three branches. **(Q)***
As in the verses, I am caught between the shadows above and below and the shadows of the earth and the shadows of space. The so-called holy "Ancestral Cave" that our ancestors used when on earth, is that actually a space cave?

(Who knows what else I would have said but my teacher's hologram immediately intervened.)

Plato: Hold on there! You'll suffer from a mental stroke of the mind! Think of the number of years it took you to understand the cave on earth. Do not expect to understand the cave of space in one or two seconds. You will much reach more information and more solutions relating to people in the cave of earth. Wasn't it you who said of the books of earth: *"These books and these conversations are directed at bringing out what is within man. The derivatives from verses in Holy Books that concern people, such as "be good, be intelligent, think positively, stay young, happy and calm",* all say the same thing. They are methods of staying comfortable in the world.

I am attempting to reveal the system: to understand and model it. What do you expect? Do you think someone will appear before you, define the system, and show it to you? Or do you think he will make a single sentence statement? If it were that simple, we would not have gone to these lengths, would we? Don't worry! You are now at the beginning of training so as to understand the system and there isn't another cave like this. Now, try to understand space, so that you can skip the space cave and enter the system. (I calmed down a bit, a little embarrassed).

Fine. But you appear before me in the form of people that I have taken as an example, or whose works I have benefited from. When I explain these conversations to those in the cave of earth, won't it seem to them like it's their own conversations? Moreover, won't the resulting polemics damage the information I am explaining?

Plato: (Smiling) "It's as if you understand everything you have finished your journey, everything is understood and you are making plans to explain it all upon your return. I think you should take the advice of the Holy Books, use the information, and remember to put "God willing" in front of it all. Allow me to remind you of the most important rule: If you do not pass this side trip training before reaching the elevator and begin the upward path without it, all the images on this journey will be erased from your memory and you will be returned to the memory you have had before you began.

Prophets, *21:65 They were returned to their old memories* **(Q)**

(This verse came to my mind, but I did not interrupt.)

The technical information that you learn, and that should stay with you, will be given to you in a classical method: a class in school, a book, a magazine or a film. Somehow it will be explained to you in summary form with one of the communication devices. Of course, *if* you actually go to school, or read a book or magazine, or watch a film, think or do research.

The Poets, *26:5 And there does not come to them a new reminder from the Beneficent God but they turn aside from it* **(Q)**

On the subject of polemics, if in a dream you had about a conversation with Mustafa Kemal Atatürk or Plato and wished to explain the conversation to others wouldn't you say, "Atatürk said this", "Plato said that"? In the end, this is a type of dream. What's more, if I know your thinking, "words will fly away, writing will remain," you will want to explain these conversations in writing. Then you will have to credit everything you write with sources at the bottom of each page and this will make the text unreadable.

However, wouldn't it be more fluent and memorable if you applied this method to scatter the references throughout the text coming from their source? As you see, we always use this method.

Haven't you come a long way and learned a lot in a short time? Will you be able to forget this lesson soon?" He left saying, **"Your creator is with you and wants you to win,"** and took his place in space, a star, lighting the darkness around him.

And I thought I would be making a comfortable space trip, looking around, and having face-to-face conversations with people I cannot talk with on earth. With the disappearance of my teacher, Plato's image, the action started again.

Whenever I begin to speak about these subjects, I always look up the meaning of the vocabulary as it is used in the dictionary.

Universe: Everything that exists, especially all physical matter, including all the stars, planets, <u>galaxies</u>, etc. in space.

Space: The empty area outside the Earth's atmosphere, where the planets and the stars are.

From earlier text in this book: "God is the creator, protector of everything in the heavens, the one great being."

When I combined these meanings as, "What would happen if someone created a copy of the universe?" I immediately regretted that I had said that and apologized to myself. Yes, years earlier I had said, **"The limits of the mind can only be expanded with fearless thinking."**

In trying to progress on this road, one may think the unthinkable and in that case may be directed to invalid ideas. And without knowing, ideas that may be considered disrespectful to God may come to mind. One of God's specialties is being tolerant of researchers.

The Coalition, 33:5 What you may have slipped up on already will not be held against you, but only something your hearts have done intentionally. (Q)
The Star, 53:32 (Those who refrain) except for oversights (will find) your Lord is boundless when it comes to forgiveness. (Q)

Taking support from several verses from the Holy Books in the scientific experiment, I had taken steps into dangerous territory and pushed the limits. This time however, I am aware that I have moved beyond the edge.

My mind, because I was asking questions as they came to it, was looking around for my images, but I could see none. In spite of the fact that I really don't believe in Satan, I thought I had probably unknowingly entered Satan's territory of thought, and realized I'd better change my methods again.

While I was wrestling with these ideas, the journey stopped again along with the images. No one was around, "How awful!" I remarked. "I am off the path because I thought of things that were not allowed." Now the thought police will come and say, "If you start thinking these kinds of thoughts while you are still on your horizontal side trip, who knows what disrespectful thoughts may surface later?" Would my thoughts banish me.

Voice: Don't worry! Don't worry! It's not as you think. You did not wander into Satan's territory, get caught on the radar or go off the track. Those who make the copy of the universe yet cannot be a god, because being the first is what makes God. By the way, aren't you interpreting the verses a little to your own liking?

Don't you see things in the shape you expect, depending on your purpose? Whatever your purpose in reading the Holy Books, you will be drawn to the areas that concern you and you will take advantage of those. Here the important thing is not taking a few verses and interpreting them to your benefit, but the adaptation of a small part of a pattern to fit the whole. Rather than making a personal interpretation, it is important to receive the support of both religion and scientific sources. You can be sure that I am not trying to get God to say things that some religious men would like to say.

Voice: Don't be afraid to enter the areas that appear forbidden, if your goal is pure. The subject of your training at this level is the subject of the examination of recorded materials, as space. Questioning the system is a subject of a future area. By questioning it now, you have drifted away from this level of the training as you lack such education.

Instead of comforting me this made me even tenser. This voice I heard without an identity, speaks of reading my mind at this moment and my past memory and is proving it. (Can't a person think comfortably even in space? Is there no privacy of thought? As I fidgeted in these confused thoughts, I smiled as if I'd been caught on Candid Camera.)

"Which camera should I wave to? Are we on the air?" I said.

Voice: "We are always on the air, both from the inside and the outside."

What does that mean: both inside and outside?

Voice: We are recording both your experiences and your thoughts. You are seeing a recording of your own experiences on the screen during your trip through space. The small earths below you, that you think are lanterns, are your recorded images frames. A while ago, you realized that I was reading your thoughts. If I can read them, it means that I am able to record them wherever I want to. You are a computer programmer so you compare everything in the world to a computer. Regard space as a part of a computer.

When you live on earth, you cannot use resources other than those you have read, listened to or watched. Therefore, whatever you filled your brain with on earth you will use here. It is not possible for the brain to forget a source in excitement. We make sure you can access all the information and the experiences in the archives: when you think of something, you will be reminded of all the information on that subject and experience and its resources by an expert at your side in holographic form.

Think of this place as a thought laboratory, where you can perform the experiment of your choice. In the worst-case scenario, we/you will realize once again that a thought that has never been thought on earth is not worth thinking. After you go, you will have served humanity by preventing them from wasting time on thinking. In the example you always give from Socrates: *"Man came from nothing, and thinks he cannot be exterminated in a physical sense. However, to go from existence to nothing, from nothing into existence is impossible: that is to say that you cannot think of something that does not exist."*

Allow me to remind you of a verse that will comfort you and set you free,

Suad, *38:46-47 Surely We purified them by a pure quality, the keeping in mind of the (final) abode. - And most surely they were with Us, of the elect, the best.* **(Q)**
John, *8:32 You will learn the truth and the truth will set you free.* **(NT)**

You probably have understood that cleaning the dormitory of heaven is the cleansing of thoughts. As part of my duty, I feel I clearly explained that it is necessary to help you think without fear or limitations on your thoughts. Is there anything you would like to ask about the limits of thought?

No thanks, I understand completely.

Voice: Since you have gained permission to unlimited thought, remember the thoughts that you had on earth that were the least limiting and question them here. What is the meaning of the hesitancy in your eyes? Be comfortable! No one here wishes you harm. Let's think it through.
What is your goal? What are you trying for? Why all these thoughts and this research? Why not live like everyone else, say your prayers, without questioning everything, if you used the time you spend on these things on working and gaining goods and property and lived more comfortably... (with this I interrupted)

Have you noticed? If I do these things, you have said, all I will earn are the earthly goods. Who were the wealthiest people on earth 200-250 years ago? Artists, thinkers: sometimes a figure on the wall, sometimes a sound from an instrument, sometimes from marble, sometimes pages have reached us from a thousand years ago and are still able to be read to us. And even today, don't they help us to understand the present? Remember what the bard poet Mahsuni said:

Everyone should leave a work of art in the world. Winds blow in the place of those who leave no works." **"Earthly things come and go, but works of art remain."**

The Holy Books give importance to this thought.

Psalms, *49:10 When all the time he sees that wise men die, that foolish and stupid perish, both alike.* **(OT)**
Revelation, *3:5 I shall not blot their names out of the book of life.* **(NT)**

Voice: In fact you are right. A belief moves away from being divine when it aims to conquer material lands instead of hearts. What is your scientific education? What is your religious education?
If you happen to find a book without an author's name or title on the road, read it, and try to find some answers, will you give it less value if the author has no title? For thousands of years, haven't we been drowning in the problems arising from not assigning enough value to information because we evaluated the identity of the person bringing the information instead of the information itself? You change the battle of ideas to a battle of diplomas. (The event changed suddenly to a conflict of personalities. Instead of discussing the system in space, I was arguing with an unidentified voice personality.) In truth, it surprises me that instead of ideas, you are interested in labels. Have I asked you or your apparitions about their diplomas? I'll give you a simplified answer. I neither am a scientist nor am I a religious man. But I know that Albert Einstein was not the most intelligent man in the world!

(Said in a voice of someone who is confused.)

Voice: "What do you mean?" it was able to say. (With the confidence of having confused him and having taken control of the situation)

Aren't those who claim that Einstein is the world's most intelligent man, accepting the fact that they are from a lower level of intelligence? (Without waiting for an answer) They are. Well! But how can a person from a lower level of intelligence test a person from a higher level of intelligence? How can they make an evaluation and choose the best? Maybe it is because when people meet someone they don't understand, they either call them crazy and ostracize them, or crown him super intelligent, depending on **that person's place in society**.

Luqman, *31:20 And among men is he who disputes in respect of Allah though having no knowledge nor guidance, nor a book giving light.* **(Q)**

As this verse implies, the competition is open to everyone. Everyone can join in. (I lost myself in the heat of the conversation, without

Stephen Hawking: In your book "I Am Ready, Let it Begin," (1998) you said of me: "The more I have read his books *I have been impressed by the naturalness, his courage, his struggle, his knowledge and his modesty. As a friend he has not yet met, I not only want to introduce his scientific side, but I will also try to convey his human side that I feel so close to. It would not be fair to either* of us if I failed to do so." I want to thank you for this.

In addition to your scientific knowledge, your exemplary struggle for life has been a point of reference to me, as much as your scientific works. I wanted to share this exemplary life with my readers. You are second on the list of people I would most like to meet on this earth. I know you are not he, but even knowing that you are an apparition of him, just meeting your hologram is a wonderful feeling. Thank you. God willing, this journey will be the means of allowing us to meet on earth.

Stephen Hawking: Who knows. For now, let's hope so. On our level, even the shortest moments are precious and must be spent to the benefit of man. You have learned that you have been evaluated and judged worthy to take the round trip journey between the earth and the afterworld for the purpose of training. So, do you know what will be taught on the outward journey and what will be taught on the return journey? Not yet. The classic definition of **heaven is a place with everything you want.** Believe me, when we take people who wander on earth not knowing what they want or understand what they should wish for, and send them to heaven saying: "Here is heaven. Wish for everything you desire," they wish for earthly things such as food and drink and sexual fantasies and pointlessly waste their wishes. Because they turn heaven into a place where they complete their earthly desires, when the time comes, they are automatically sent back to earth because "they have not yet had enough of earth". Thus, on your return journey, one of the main goals of your training will be to learn what mankind must wish for and how mankind must wish for it.

You will remember that at the beginning of the trip it was said (in summary): "…so whatever you filled your brain with on earth, you will use here….we will enable you to access all information and experience from the information archives. The hologram of the master of a source you used as a reference will appear on your left with all the information and experience resources available." Just as it is happening now, the moment you are not thinking of a subject you should, it will appear as a clue for you. If you want the hologram of a source that is not related to the subject, you will not be able to manifest it.

When you hear my name, what is the first thing that comes to your mind?

"The Theory of Everything."

Stephen Hawking: OK, what does "The Theory of Everything" mean?

A theory that explains the universe. A theory that explains how the universe works and the reason for it. A type of unifying theory. You said in your book A Brief History of Time, page 185: *"If we do discover a complete theory, it should in time be understandable in broad principle by everyone, not just a few scientists. Then shall all philosophers, scientists, and just ordinary people, be able to take part in the discussion of the question of the universe and how we exist. If we find the answer to that, it would be the ultimate triumph of human reason for then we would know the mind of God."*
The Creator's message is universal and not a personal message for religious men and scientists. With these words, as a person on the street, I say that science should give me courage. ***"A theory that a person on the street is able to understand and discuss is a theory they can discover. Therefore I said: "The Theory of Everything = Everyone's Theory."***

Since the question is asked so that everyone can understand it, the answer should be in a form everyone can reach. If the answer to God was hidden in a form only scientists or religious men could find, then it would be unfair to people on the street. As it is, to show the simplicity of the hidden answer, prophets were chosen from among the man on the street. "The Theory of Everything = Everyone's Theory."

(Prof. Stephen Hawking's hologram stopped my words by a hand gesture.)

Stephen Hawking: Yes, but according to this view, if the answer is this simple, no one would work on science but would just sit and think. Wouldn't God be doing an injustice to those who work night and day if he rewards the man on the street? If the man on the street finds the answer by reading the words of scientists, isn't that unfair to the scientists? Is this God's understanding of justice?

From that point of view, what you say is true. But also you have found things ready for you in the human universe, God has given. Those who worship diligently every day would be in the same situation as the man on the street attempts to explain God. It would be like coming into the possession of something someone else has labored to produce.

But, under the heading "Big Bang" in the May 2007 issue of *Science and Technology* paragraph headed, "And Before?"

***"The most important question surrounding the Big Bang Theory is what happened "before" singularity. The answer to this question is usually put into the form of the* question being meaningless,** *because it is assumed that time started with the big bang.*

If you recall, you said in your book A Brief History of Time, page 128 that *"(The Pope in a private audience) told us that it was all right to study the evolution of the universe after the big bang, but we should not inquire into the big bang itself because that was the moment of Creation and therefore the work of God."*

If scientists and religious men stopped questioning and said we shall not ask the question with the information we have at hand and it is forbidden and useless anyway to think of the answer, then they would leave that arena to the man on the street. I know that you understand that the group of scientists and religious men who think as you do, are not included here.

I thought I would be speaking to the hologram of Stephen Hawking only about technical subjects.

Stephen Hawking: Be assured that our subjects are technical. But I needed to understand the integrity of justice in your thoughts. We must not allow misunderstandings, right?

(Knowing that this training is not only technical, but includes tolerance, will, justice and other subjects, I maintained my calm and began speaking.)

The prophets are believable through working miracles. People would not accept them as prophets unless they could heal the sick, raise the dead or perform other astounding miracles. People paid little attention to the messages of the Prophets, but chased after miracles. They tried to acquire their share of the Prophet's miracles by trying to get them to heal them and their diseases.

Luke, 11:29 *This is a wicked generation, it is asking for a sign.* **(NT)**

Holy Books have something for everyone in them. They have miracles for ignorant and information/system/methods for the intellectuals.

You will notice that the same is happening more recently concerning the Holy Books. People have begun to go towards explanations and programs that center on the miracles of the Holy Books, like they have for hundreds of years, instead of understanding and explaining them. The goal is to increase the number of believers through the miracle method they call the prophet method.

Under the heading of encoded miracles, examples are constructed by emphasizing historical events mentioned in the Holy Books that begin with a code number. But the subject here is not code, but soothsaying. Therefore, if a name is to be attached to this it should be *Predictions of the Holy Books*. This will be looking at a well-known historical event of the past and presenting it as a miracle. If the holiness (major value) of the Holy Books is seen to depend on the predictions it includes, then we would be forced to include in the holy category, the books of Nostradamus who lived 500 years before Hitler and predicted the gulf crisis and many other events. While reducing the *Holy Books* to the level of books of predictions that can be written by man, what will we have to say about Nostradamus? You think about that.

 Of course, they can't. There are interesting verses in the Holy Books on the subject of clairvoyance.

Yusuf, 12:100-102 He helped his parents up on the platform, and they fell down on their knees before him. He said: My Father, this is the interpretation of my earlier vision. The Lord has made it come true! He was kind to me in whatever way He wishes. - "My Lord, you have given me control land taught me how to interpret events. Originator of Heaven and Earth, You are my Patron in this world and the Hereafter. Gather me in as a Muslim and unite me with honorable men!" **(Q)**

When they wish to impose their own thoughts to society, people use God as a conduit of their own ideas, and they conjure up false miracles to gather the people. Just look at the subjects they discuss and cannot reach a common decision on: sin/good deeds, accepted/ unaccepted behavior. These are all worldly topics. When a teacher explains a lesson with a stick in his hand and constantly prods a student, what are the chances that student will understand the lesson? Those who explain things with the stick of hell, who attempt to teach religion, have about the same chance. Books that have been sent to explain life on the other side have become bogged down in worldly problems.

Scientists who no longer serve the philosophy of science, but hone in on the benefits it provides, have virtually ignored the findings they have brought to light. Therefore, we sadly see that God and the related Theory of Everything, in which the philosophy field would be expected to make a huge contribution, has not been a focus of research or study. Nor have there been lessons or research produced on the meaning of God or the unknown, unfortunately.

It is as you said in your book *A Briefer History of Time*, "*On the other hand, the people whose business it is to ask why, the philosophers, have not been able to keep up with the advance of scientific theories. Philosophers reduced the scope of their inquiries so much that*

Wittgenstein, the most famous philosopher of the twentieth century, said, 'The sole remaining task for philosophy is the analysis of language.' What a comedown from the great tradition of philosophy from Aristotle to Kant!"(page 142)

Just as the lottery draws do not generally go to those who pray most, the answer is not found by the one who believes he works hardest. I compare this to a three dimensional picture. When you have a one-dimensional picture you hold it close to your face, not to be able to discern the details, but to find the three-dimensional image that you are not able to catch when you first looked at the picture. If you look at the details, you will miss the actual picture, itself. Now, let's look at the theory that takes me from the first dimensional view to the third dimensional view of the world/space: You will remember from your book *A Brief History of Time;*

"Yet it seems that the uncertainty principle is a fundamental feature of the universe we live in. A successful unified theory must therefore necessarily incorporate this principle." (page 164)

"A necessary first step, therefore, is to combine general relativity with the uncertainty principle." (page 165) **Uncertainty**: the state of the quality of particular information not being able to be obtained.

Theory of Everything = Everyone's Theory

The strength of one is the weakness of the other. God is a "mystery" beyond being. And God gets his strength, in the eyes of man, from his uncertainty/unfathomable characteristics. Why would a God who knows and sees all want to learn about man when that man does not know himself, so much so, that He hides man's past?

Psalms, *7:9 You righteous God, assessor of mind and heart.* **(OT)**
Deuteronomy, *8:1-2 Remember how Yahweh, your God, led you for forty years in the wilderness, to humble you, to test you and know your inmost heart-whether you would keep his commandments or not."* **(OT)**
Revelation, *2:23 So that all the churches realize that it is I who search heart.* **(NT)**

That must mean that there are unknowns on both sides.

So far, since only the unknowns of God to man have been considered, the unknown equation with only one unknown $x = 0$ has the result $= 0$. Had another unknown been found, an equation of two unknowns would be formed and with the securing of one of the unknowns, the solution may have been found. Since there is only God and man involved, **to find the solution, the unknown quality of man to God must be found.**

The unknown equation with two unknowns in the universe: God and Man.

$$x + y = \text{Universe} = \text{God} + \text{Man}$$
$$x = \text{God's unknown to man}$$
$$y = \text{man's unknown to God}$$

The best representation of this is the six-pointed star:

The first large triangle is the view of God from above to mankind. The large triangle below represents man's view of God from below. The small triangles on the bottom and top of each large triangle are areas unknown to the other. Consequently, there is not only one triangle with an eye at the top, but also another with an eye on the bottom and both eyes are looking to each other for answers.

Stephen Hawking: From this viewpoint we can go from one unknown **(x=0)** to another with two unknowns **(x + y = 0)**, it is true, but if we are unable to fill these in and it does not result in a solution, it has no meaning, even if we change it into an equation with three unknowns.

My dear teacher, in your book *Brief History of Time* you wrote: *"Rather similar, seemingly absurd infinities occur in the other partial theories, but in all these cases the infinities can be cancelled out by a process called renormalization. This involves **canceling the infinities by introducing other infinities.**"* **(page 165)**

I will, of course, share my answer to the question you are pursuing. When we look at the universe that God created, we can see that the technology used was unquestionably more advanced than the technology in use today. Therefore, in order for my answer to be valid, I must first prove that the underlying science and technology are possible. Therefore, too, in order to understand my proof, I must share my theories with you; especially the theories of space. Since you have come as the hologram of my space expert, it means that we will speak about space theories.

Space and the universe is a region used to prove God's greatness, limitlessness and being. We call the power that created the universe, God. Did He create it for himself? Is God inside space or outside space? In short:

What Good is Space?
(The numbers of particles of sand in the ocean and stars in the sky are infinite.)

that the Creator created space not for us, but for himself. Whoever created it, if we can answer the question, **"What is space good for**?" we can get an idea about the Creator.

While space appears to be of no use, understanding it *will* scientifically prove the existence or non-existence of God; just as the false were gods like the moon and sun first found by man in the skies and when understood, were then, eventually lost to the skies.

Throughout history man has debated whether certain parts of the Holy Books were actual fact or false. These debates have caused wars and schisms in religions. One of these topics has been the idea of God watching man and recording every move they make. I too, had grave reservations about the validity of this notion until I realized that space is a recording device.

Space is Gods' Recording Apparatus/Archive Cabinet
(The path to the afterlife leads through space.)

As man leaves earth, he falls behind the time on earth, according to the distance he has made. As a man on the moon looks at earth, he sees an event on earth a few seconds later. A person looking from a farther planet would see it as a few hours later. For example: a person born in 1966, if he travels to the point at the distance where 1966 appears and looks back at the earth, the earth will still be living 1966.

From that distance, using a spacecraft outfitted with the proper speed and time instruments and proper setting capabilities, just as I am at the moment, you would be able to see the entire life of an individual in frames as you move towards the earth. If we can show a moment in any 24-hour span, at any point on our earth, and as we can show any moment of our millions of years of history in space, then space is a 24 hour, 360 degree three-dimensional recorder of earth.

The fact that we have satellites that constantly record our world that can be reviewed at any time, shows this work is from the hands of man. In space, the recording system is made by the Creator. **Then we can say that, "A recording device with the capacity to read and record at the speed of light, with space as the hard drive, is God's recorder/**

archive device." Why record then, if they are not going to be read or commented on? The Holy Books say:

Job, 20:27 *The heavens will reveal their iniquity.* **(OT)**
Deuteronomy, 30:19 *I call the heaven and earth to witness against you today.* **(OT)**
Luke, 10:20 *Rejoice rather that your names are written in heaven.* **(NT)**
The Kneeling, 45:29 *We have been recording whatever you have been doing.* **(Q)**

These verses validate that one of God's reasons for creating space is to record/copy/ or archive.

If the afterworld is outside space, for a dead person to be able to reach the afterworld, he has to be able to exit through his own door marked "Enter/Exit" by speeding through space at a speed much faster than the speed of light.

Revelations, 4:1 *Then, in my vision I saw a door open in heaven...* **(NT)**

A person, on his way to the other world has the opportunity to see recordings of only those personal frames of his own past. (Just as I am doing at the moment)

People who near death and return to life, often say, *"My life passed in front of my eyes like a filmstrip,"* as they near their entry/exit door.

Psalms, 16:11 *You will reveal the path of life to me.* **(OT)**

Stephen Hawking: Is the afterworld outside space?

If we accept the fact that the afterworld is outside space, we accept the fact that space is limited. Since man enters space through the afterworld, there is a certain road (his past), a certain path drawn in space that he must follow. At the entry/exit point perpendicular to the space-time line everyone must have their name and date, year and month, day hour, minute, and second recorded.

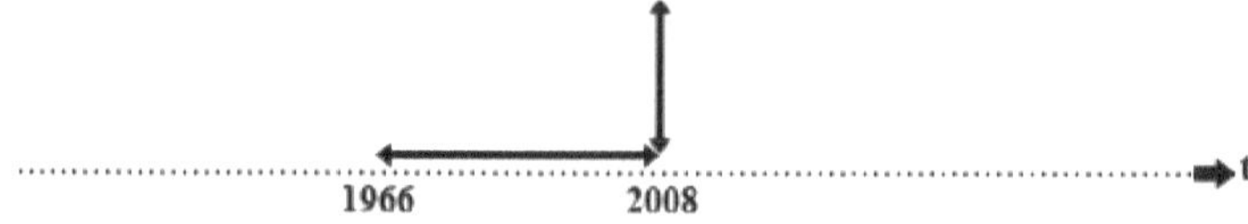

If the world's whole past is recorded in space, then the saying "all times are being lived at the same moment while in space" must mean that all-time, active/passive is being lived at the same moment. Someone able to look from out-of-space would be able to see at the same time any of the millions of years of recordings in space. He could choose the period he wants to concentrate on and investigate that period in detail.

A cosmic hall of mirrors (Sep 26, 2005)

Was Plato correct? The Greek philosopher stated that the world resembled a pentagon some 2400 year ago and he was proven correct by scientists of this day. Most astronomers think that the universe is infinite, but recent measurements suggest that it could be finite and relatively small. Indeed, as Jean-Pierre Luminet describes, we could be living in an exotic universe shaped rather like a football.

Cosmologists usually assume that the universe is simply connected like a plane, which means there is only one direct path for light to travel from a source to an observer. A simply connected Euclidean or hyperbolic universe would indeed be infinite, but if the universe is multiply connected, like a torus, there would be many different possible paths. This means that an observer would see multiple images of each galaxy and could easily misinterpret them as distinct galaxies in an endless space, much as a visitor to a mirrored room has the illusion of seeing a crowd. Could we, in fact, be living in such a cosmic hall of mirrors?

The Poincaré dodecahedral space (left) can be described as the interior of a "sphere" made from 12 slightly curved pentagons. However, there is one big difference between this shape and a football because when one goes out from a pentagonal face, one immediately comes back inside the ball from the opposite face after a 36° rotation. Such a multiply connected space can therefore generate multiple images of the same object, such as a planet or a photon. Other such well-proportioned, spherical spaces that fit the WMAP data are the tetrahedron (middle) and octahedron (right).

A rocket leaving the dodecahedron through a given face immediately re-enters through the opposite face, and light propagates such that any observer whose line-of-sight intercepts one face has the illusion of seeing a slightly rotated copy of their own dodecahedron. This means that some photons from the cosmic microwave background, for example, would appear twice in the sky.

Whether or not some multiply connected model of space such as the Poincaré dodecahedron is refuted by future astronomical data, cosmic topology will continue to remain at the heart of our understanding about the ultimate structure of our universe.
J Weeks 2001 The Shape of Space (New York, Dekker)
WMAP results: map.gsfc.nasa.gov   http://physicsworld.com/cws/article/print/23009

Example: the distance gauge of a vehicle that moves between points A and B, will show the place along the line that the vehicle has moved, when it begins at point zero. The figure indicates its place between A and

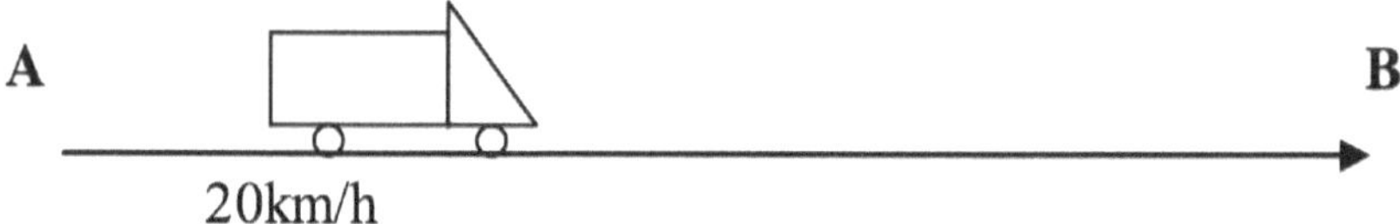

B.

The gauge we call time can show us the place of our earth is situated on the space-time line.

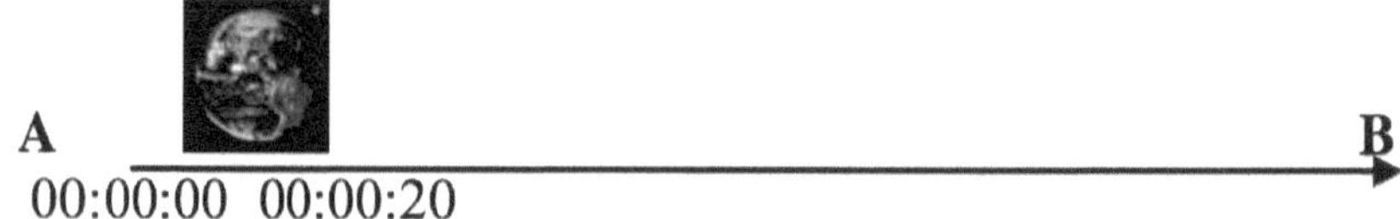

If space is a recording instrument, the stars, which may look as if they have no purpose, can be given the task of lighting the area to be filmed, like a flash or a floodlight or a lamp. Timothy Ferris in National Geographic Magazine, Nov. 2007 writes, *"They confirmed that the mysterious high-energy flashes of light called gamma-ray bursts arrive from all over the universe, and that one class of burst results from the implosion of massive stars."*

Ha Mim, *41:12 We adorned the lower heaven with brilliant stars and (made it) to guard* **(Q)**
The Kingdom, *67:5 And we have adorned the lowest heaven with Lamps.* **(Q)**

In your book **a *Brief History of Time,*** you say, *"Penrose's theorem had shown that any collapsing star must end in a singularity."(page 54)* Let us think of a classic light bulb with clear light burning out in a darkened room far away from it. It is being filmed and being shown in slow motion. The light gradually dims in the middle of a bright circle and terminates in a single point. (Just like a dying star).

If the earth is the only active point in space and all other areas are passive, then it must be a reader/writer head of the recorder (hard drive).

Just as Gary Sultan and Douglas Vogt predicted in 1975 when they likened the universe to a cosmic computer and concluded, *"according to the Theory of Multidimensional Reality the universe is like a video tape player which transfers information from a magnetic tape band onto the electrostatic television screen."* The universe was shaped according to the information on the magnetic tapes, they purported.

In addition to the light illuminating the surroundings, it also projects images. The energy used for the space recording device that we use to project and record the images, is the light from the stars.

(Space is like a giant dark room of photographers)

Daniel, *2:21-22 To know what lies in darkness and light dwells with him.* **(OT)**
Genesis, *1:3-5 God said, "Let there be light" and there was light. God saw that light was good and God divided light from darkness.* **(OT)**
Isaiah, *45:7 I form the light and create the dark.***(OT)**

The energy sources of a hard disk that works with light are sources such as the sun and stars. Distant suns and stars are the light batteries/energy sources needed to store the past/present data on the hard disk. White/black holes then would be the cooling system of the hard disk.

The interesting thing is the position of the future: if we see the earth's past in space from any place in space since the whole of the past is recorded there, where in space is the future? This reminds me of the DV-R or DVD+R recording systems.

If your DVD CD is –R the actual writing of the CD is from the outer rim inwards: it will be done by scoring ever-decreasing circle orbits from the outer rim to the center. In this situation, an eye looking from the CD writer's head will only be able to see the scored region and everything will be receding from it. In this instance stars are becoming distant by enlargement through outside or by an opposite enlargement through the inside. (During a short pause in the dialogue, my teacher cut in).

Stephen Hawking: So this is how the Holy Books and space are viewed through the eye of a computer programmer. Are you going to continue?

While I still have you here, I would like to share with you, all my thoughts that support this model. If space, which has been thought to be endless, turns out to be limited, would that cast a doubt over God's endlessness? Let us turn to the question of the endlessness of space.

Space is not Endless

Endless: not without an end, but the end not yet having been measured.

I found the best example for this subject during a visit to a memorial museum in Jerusalem (**Yad Vashem**) that was enacted to commemorate children who died in WWII. Thousands of small mirrors (about 10 x 5 cm.) are suspended on transparent strings in a dimly lit room. Because the strings are of the same color as the room in the low lighting, the mirrors resemble a path passing through the middle of a barely visible room.

In one corner of the room are five candles in a circle placed at certain angles to the dim light; the mirrors reflect thousands of candles which give the feeling that the dead children are stars in the sky. As you walk through the room, the reflections from the candles at varying distances cause you to feel you are in space. The candles you see are more or less the same as one another.

From *A Brief History of Time*: *"Why is the universe so uniform on a large scale? **Why does it look the same at all points of space and in all directions?** In particular, why is the temperature of the microwave background radiation so nearly the same when we look in different directions? It is a bit like asking a number of students an exam question. If they all give exactly the same answer you can be pretty sure they have communicated with each other."* (page 127).

When I read your lines, this room resembling the universe came to my mind. As you move the candles located in the corner of the room away, towards the middle of the room, the reflected images will also move away or towards you in equal proportion. *"But in 1929 Edwin Hubble made the landmark observation that wherever you look, distant galaxies are moving rapidly away from us. In other words, the universe is expanding."(page 9)*

As long as you do not touch the reflection of any candle, (touching the mirrors makes no difference) you think the reflection is the real candle. There, I asked, why space could not have been created through the same technique. **"Space is not endless.** If we think of the inside of the universe as the inside of a big globe with a mirrored surface, you will see more than one star at more than one place and at varying distances. As long as you do not touch the mirror on the edge of space, you will think of it as being infinite.

*I Corinthians, 13:12 Now we are seeing a dim reflection on a mirror; but then we shall be seeing face to face.(**NT**)*
*II Corinthians, 3:18 And we with our unveiled faces reflecting like mirrors the brightness of the Lord, all grow brighter as we are turned into the image that we reflect. (**NT**)*

In your book, *Black Holes and Baby Universes* you say, *"The surface of the earth has a finite area, but it doesn't have any singularities, boundaries or edges. I have tested this by experiment; I went around the world, and I didn't fall off."(page 85)* This example is a curious view of the concept of infinity...
Sizes that are said to be infinite have changed with time and technology; what people said were infinite a hundred years ago have now been measured and new infinities have been found. **How is it then, that a**

decision can be made about the infinity of the emptiness of space that has not yet been able to be measured?

Until the revelation by NASA in 2003 that "space is not infinite, but in the shape of a football," my mirrors in space idea was the topic that people made most fun of in my book "I'm ready. Let's begin."

If space is a room of mirrors, then "space is manmade, and there is not the afterworld outside of space, but man himself." Space, the earth etc. that are inside the mirrors, in short everything in the universe we live in and that are the finite work of an infinite God, also turn into a manmade, virtual environment. **(The idea of finding even the hologram of Stephen Hawking, on my list of people I have to meet while on earth, was so exciting that I continued my stream of thought). To strengthen the virtual space model we must look at some other areas.**

A cosmic hall of mirrors

Was Plato correct? The Greek philosopher stated that the world resembled a pentagon some 2400 year ago and he was proven correct by scientists of this day. Most astronomers think that the universe is infinite, but recent measurements suggest that it could be finite and relatively small. Indeed, as Jean-Pierre Luminet describes, we could be living in an exotic universe shaped rather like a football.

Cosmologists usually assume that the universe is simply connected like a plane, which means there is only one direct path for light to travel from a source to an observer. A simply connected Euclidean or hyperbolic universe would indeed be infinite, but if the universe is multiply connected, like a torus, there would be many different possible paths. This means that an observer would see multiple images of each galaxy and could easily misinterpret them as distinct galaxies in an endless space, much as a visitor to a mirrored room has the illusion of seeing a crowd. Could we, in fact, be living in such a cosmic hall of mirrors?

The Poincaré dodecahedral space (left) can be described as the interior of a "sphere" made from 12 slightly curved pentagons. However, there is one big difference between this shape and a football because when one goes out from a pentagonal face, one immediately comes back inside the ball from the opposite face after a 36° rotation. Such a multiply connected space can therefore generate multiple images of the same object, such as a planet or a photon. Other such well-proportioned, spherical spaces that fit the WMAP data are the tetrahedron (middle) and octahedron (right).

A rocket leaving the dodecahedron through a given face immediately re-enters through the opposite face, and light propagates such that any observer whose line-of-sight intercepts one face has the illusion of seeing a slightly rotated copy of their own dodecahedron. This means that some photons from the cosmic microwave background, for example, would appear twice in the sky.

Whether or not some multiply connected model of space such as the Poincaré dodecahedron is refuted by future astronomical data, cosmic topology will continue to remain at the heart of our understanding about the ultimate structure of our universe.

J Weeks 2001 The Shape of Space (New York, Dekker)
WMAP results: map.gsfc.nasa.gov

*If space is a room of mirrors, then **"space is manmade, and there is not the afterworld outside of space, but man himself.**" Space, the earth etc. that are inside the mirrors, in short everything in the universe we live in and that are the finite work of an infinite God, also turn into a manmade, virtual environment. (p.62-64)*

Stephen Hawking: If I understood what you're saying, space could be manmade and if so, the real God is outside this space. However, verses just mentioned conveyed the sense that God was inside space. Am I wrong?

My dear teacher, if space is manmade, it means that inside the true Creator and inside the true space, is a manmade space and inside that space is another manmade god. Did we not say that the power that created space is God? In this situation, there is space within space, God within God and while the manmade God is inside alone in space, the true God is in both. Now, let us examine the viewpoint that infinite space is expanding. How can infinity expand? Can a thing that is expanding be infinite?

Is the Universe/Space Expanding? Going away?

Think for a moment of setting off a fireworks display in the darkness of night in a giant, enclosed, sport arena where the ceiling and walls cannot be seen because of the darkness. As soon as they are fired, the spectacular, visual presentation spreads in four directions (Explosion = Expanding). This is just like what we call the big bang; starting from a high-density low volume, hundreds of pieces move away from each other, becoming less dense but with greater area.

As they explode, do the walls, ceiling or foundation of the sport arena expand? "NO." Could a person looking from the center of exploding fireworks, unable to see the walls of the arena due to darkness, say that the sport arena is expanding if he is only able to see the sparks flying away from the center? "NO."

Therefore, we cannot say that the universe or space is expanding, like the fireworks we call the big bang, just because we observe sparks scattering away from each other (stars) like the beginning of the fireworks explosion, and fading out at various distances (planets) and smaller pieces once again exploding to produce smaller displays (the birth of stars/galaxies). The expansion we observe in **the visible universe,** resulting in planets and stars, is the expansion of the area where the remaining pieces of the big bang explosion scatter.

Isaiah, 65:17 *For now I create new heaven and a new earth.* **(OT)**

Isaiah, 66:22 *For as the new heavens and the new earth I shall make will endure before me.* **(OT)**

The Cow, 2:245 *And Allah straightens and amplifies.* **(Q)**

This is the point to review the key question: "How can we decide if an empty space, whose limits we cannot measure, is expanding?"

Universe: 1) Everything that exists, all physical matter especially all stars, planet, galaxies, in space. 2) A universe which could be imagined to be outside our own.

Space: The empty area outside of the earth's atmosphere where the planets and stars are.

The universe or heavens, are names given to the infinite whole that includes all material and energy forms. That is, the "universe" the whole of everything that is included in the study of astronomy and astrophysics. A huge soup that contains "everything", is located in space that can be defined as both infinity or nothingness.

From that point of definition, **the universe** is the "one" thing, because it is the biggest known whole.

According to the article "<u>Big Explosion</u>" published in Science and Technology magazine, May 2007:

*"Space scientists often use the example of an expanding balloon to explain **the expansion of the universe**. Think of a balloon with space islands on the surface: the islands will move away from each other as the balloon expands. This is what we see in the universe. The space islands are receding from us in perfect proportion.*

"Einstein, in his Theory of Relativity claims that space is a dynamic construct. That is to say, without additional dimensions a universe can expand, retract and increase. According to popular belief, the universe is enough unto itself. There is no necessity for a center or an environment conducive to growth."

From these two paragraphs, we can say that space and the universe differ. The article continues:

"If the universe expands, does everything expand with it? To many of us the questions of whether the world we live in is expanding or not or the formation of an expanding universe comes to mind..." These lines suggest that the universe is expanding.

From this viewpoint, when I return to earth, I will suggest that changes be made to the definition of endless.

Endless: not something that has no limits, but something that cannot be measured for now. That's what I will propose. (As I said this my teacher's apparition smiled)

Stephen Hawking: I can see you're quite sure you will return to earth.

Yes, I have the feeling I will return. I think that is what God and you will also want because I want this training to be a benefit to mankind.

Stephen Hawking: Shall we stop or continue on the subject of space?

Continue, of course. Space may not be infinite, but what we have to say about it may never end…

In Space the Centuries are Experienced Simultaneously

Wherever we are on earth, we live one of the hours of the 24 hours of a time zone while the other 23 hours are being lived at various other places on earth. Someone looking on earth from space would be able to see and experience all 24 hours on earth at the same time.

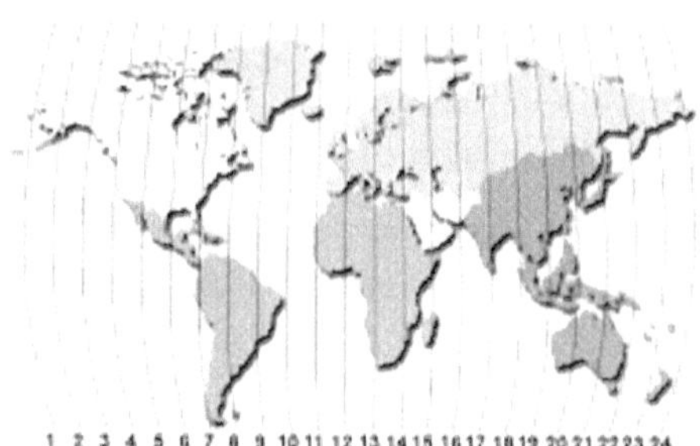

Since all of our worlds past is recorded on the space-time line, a person looking on from outside of space, can watch the complete past as it is recorded there.

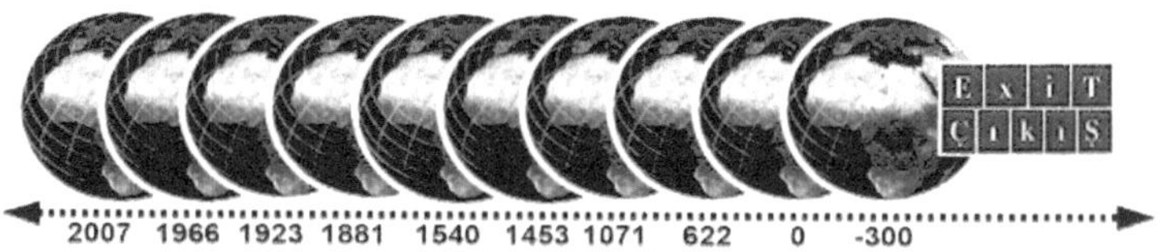

To a person looking on from space, the centuries are all experienced at once.

Colossians, 1:14-16 All things in heaven and on earth, everything visible and everything invisible, Thrones, Dominations, Sovereignties, Powers… all thing were created from Him and Through him. **(NT)**

Referring to the topic in your book "A Brief History of Time" page 168 you say, "A particle occupies one point of space at each instant of time. Therefore its history can be represented by a line in spacc-timc (**the "world-line"**). A string, on the other hand, occupies a line in space at

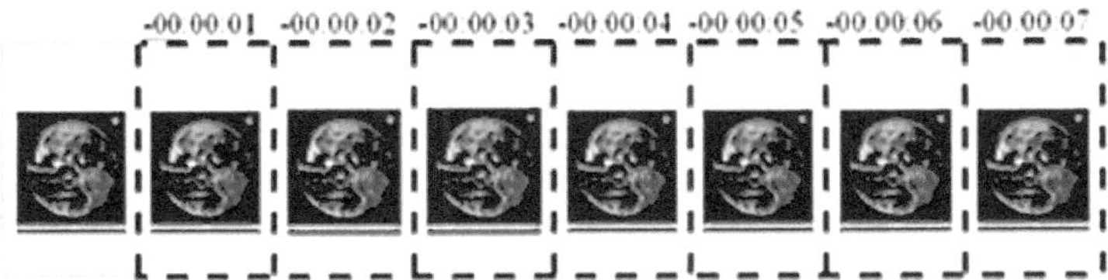

each moment in time. So its history in space-time is a two-dimensional surface called the world-sheet. (Any point on such a world-sheet can be described by two numbers: one specifying the time and the other the position of the point on the string.) Another support for this can be found in your book "Black Holes and Baby Universes." On page 65 where you say "an event in this sense is something that takes place at a single point in space, at a specified point in time."

In space, time is fixed only if records of the unchangeable past exist. To a person moving away from earth, the direction will be + or − earth time depending upon the speed, on a record being made at the speed of light on this fixed time line.

A short example will be of value here. Let's think of a car and a kilometers-long train both going in the same direction.

If the car travels faster than the train, a person in the car will begin to see the carriages that are toward the front of the train and if it goes slower, he will see the carriages at the end of the train. If the car and train move at the same speed, the person in the car will see the same train carriages and it will appear as if the train is not moving. When the car stops the person will see all the train carriages move past him.

At a fixed point in space, (i.e. Venus) a person looking at earth sees the frames of a film of the earth speeding by like the carriages of a passing train. Space is taking photos of the earth at the speed of light, just like a camera. The time is fixed in each frame just as in a normal camera.

A person traveling in space, seems to be traveling on a path made of the film of earth's past. A person looking at earth as he moves away from the earth at the speed of light, is like the person inside the car which is going at the same speed as the train. Therefore, to a person looking at the world while moving from the earth at the speed of light, the image of the world will become fixed and (because the time change is zero) time will stop.

Is the World Round?
(A different point of a view to the dimension we are living in)

Because the world is round and has a gravitational pull of 9.8 Newton (m/s2) at every point, if we think of north as up, people standing next to things like houses and cars at the North Pole would be standing upright. At the equator, they would be standing at a 90-degree angle and on the South Pole, and they would be standing with their heads upside down. In this situation if the same pull of gravity is being applied:

a. When the gravity pull is applied at the north, those in positions other than the North Pole would fall off.

b. When applied to the south, all others would feel heavier and be unable to move a step.

A balloon or a zeppelin in the air would be sideways at the equator and upside down at the south, but in actuality, they would be flying right side up.

In conclusion: In spite of the fact that our world is round and three dimensional, there is no up or down, therefore it is like a flat environment. A place with no up or down is one dimensional and flat. For a virtual environment, to move from one-dimension to three dimensions is to separate the dimensions which are next to each other (this is a wonderful opportunity for those who want to join those in a movie).

Because of the depths of the image, we believe films to be three-dimensional even though the screen is flat and one-dimensional. Scientists are now researching how non-three dimensional images that reach the vision center of the brain from the eye, are turned into three-dimensional perception by the brain center.

People working in the field of electronics developing basic electronic health support equipment have developed the branch of **medical electronics**, perhaps without even being aware of it: The model of the system is from computer programmers, hardware is from biologists, integration is from medical electronics.

Stephen Hawking: Is there a scientific development that supports what you wrote on this subject in 1998?

Yes, I present a section of the article "Why is the Universe Flat?" from Science and Technology Magazine Special section May 2007:

"Universal geometry may take one of three forms in regards to the total density of matter. If the density is the same as the measurement called critical mass, the universe flattens and takes on a flat geometrical form. If the density were above critical mass, the universe would collapse inward and become a ball. If the density were less than critical mass, a form of universe described as open, it would resemble the surface of a saddle. Observations of various waves to define the density of the universe point to the flat geometric form. Additionally, in the process of expansion, a flat geometry will be formed when it is expanded far enough to smooth out the curves to retain the homogeneity of the universe in a small area and the enlargement needed while the tipping is restored.

This means that the surface of a small ball, a sphere, when it reaches extraordinary size, the angle of tipping is so small as to not be noticeable. Space scientists seem to support the idea of a flat universe as they study the size spectrum of things in microwave background radiation. In mathematics the solution is in the ever-developing branch of topology: a flat universe may not be flat like a sheet of paper, it shows that several shapes are possible, for instance, one of the shapes is like a bent life preserver (torus). Universal geometry had not yet been sharply determined. In future, it is hoped that more sensitive observations shed light on this unknown." (page 14)

Stephen Hawking: On page one of "A Brief History of Time" on the subject of space: *"A well-known scientist (some say it was Bertrand Russell) once gave a public lecture on astronomy. He described how the earth orbits around the sun and how the sun, in turn orbits around the center of a vast collection of stars called our galaxy. At the end of the lecture, a little old lady at the back of the room got up and said, "What you have told us is rubbish. The world is really a flat plate supported on the back of a giant tortoise." The scientist gave a superior smile before replying, "What is the tortoise standing on?" "You're very clever, young man, very clever," said the old lady. "But it's turtles all the way down."* Now, what are your turtles standing on?

We have introduced the technological underpinnings of the system. Now, we will have come one-step closer to the solution if we look at the difficulties mankind encounters in understanding the system. At some point, the system must provide integration with man. Now, with your permission let's inspect the design of mankind on top of the turtle:

In A Brief History of Time, page 3-4 it says that Ptolemy put forth the theory of space science that said the universe was made up of seven spheres, each one within the other and made up a theory to prove it, but *"What lay beyond the last sphere was never made very clear, but it certainly was not part of mankind's observable universe."* In short, as mankind discovers the outmost circle there will be another, with God always being outside the last sphere.

If the thing that defines the boundaries between spheres is information, in order to reach the next dimension we must complete definitions for all the terms that depend on the prevailing information in the dimension we are in now. From the time of our creation and from the dimension we are in, a physical blockage of perception prevents us from passing to the next dimension. I would like to share this with you.

Stephen Hawking: In short, you are saying if science progresses with mankind, the speed of the development of science depends on the speed of learning and teaching of man, so the blockage of man becomes the cause of the blockage of science.

Blockage of Information Dependent on Perception
(Slowness is Weight)

In the dimension we live in, the increase in the level of experience and the information accumulation humanity needs to take us to the next dimension is a relay race in which information gained from an experience is passed on to the upcoming generation which takes it and reassesses it before taking it forward. There are two criteria affecting the success of the system:

1) Man's lifespan

2) The speed of transfer of knowledge and experience to a man's brain (learning/ teaching)

1. Man's lifespan: When the internet and television are added to the list of communication tools, with tens of books added each day to each sub-branch of science and hundreds of articles published, the task is even greater.

Think of the composite information and experience of mankind that a child studying science today would have to know to take mankind further; the education he needs and the books he needs to study. When the time spent in childhood and old age and sleeping are removed, you see that the remaining time to produce a good scientist is very little indeed.

2. Speed of the transfer of knowledge: In order for a person to be able to learn the information or experience acquired by man before him, that information must be transferred to his brain (by reading, listening or watching). Then it is necessary to process this knowledge and experience in his brain and then to share the data he obtains with other people through one or more of the communication channels. As is seen here, the speed of the development of knowledge and experience of man is dependent on his ability to learn (take it into his brain), acquire and to distribute it (teach).

Communication methods from the beginning of creation have determined the amount and speed of transferring/teaching this knowledge and experience.

<u>Historical communication developments include:</u>

1. The beginning of speech: the sharing of information and experience among members of a group.
2. The discovery of writing: sharing of information and experience among societies and across time periods.
3. The first communication period;
   - Telegraph
   - Telephone
   - Wireless radio and television (one way communication)
   - The second communication period; (Global Communication) computer, internet, electronic publication on-line written, spoken and visual communication

Look at the steps in learning/teaching

- How long does it take to load the information in a 100 page book into your brain? If that book is read through a cassette how long does it take to listen to it? Or if the book is made into a film, how long does it take to watch it?

- Once the book has been downloaded into the brain, think of it as being evaluated at the speed of electricity.

- What is the slow speed of synthesis and publishing or distributing that information with words? Think about that.

Lastly, returning to the same subject, think of the time needed to spend on acquiring information from worldwide publications in your own field and the time needed to relay your thoughts by writing or speaking. Think of the point and place you begin to slow down.

In spite of the great developments of communication tools over the centuries and the tremendous strides made in the sharing and storing of information, the speed of man's perception system, the five senses which receive this compilation of information has remained stable. Given the increasing speed of the publication of information we must use our sense organs. Our sense organs' inability to keep up indicates that we are faced with a serious deficit. This is like the problems of a growing city which has not developed or improved its substructure systems for water, sewage or electricity to accommodate a growing city population.

Daniel, *12:4 Many men will be searched and the information will be replicated.* **(OT)**

Let's think: how much of a teacher's information and experience can be transferred to a student? How much information is never passed on to the next generation: experienced, pondered, but not spoken of, or spoken but never recorded and consequently lost to subsequent generations. Think of your own life; how much of what you know and experience are you able to pass on to those around you? Think of what you are able to pass on and what stays within you! This is the situation of the loss of man's information and experience, unfortunately being lost in the education process. As it is now, each generation is required to rediscover everything!

Let's think of our past: Before science began to branch out into specialties there was only one type of dentist and he took care of all everything concerning teeth. As years passed, the information and experiences concerning dentistry have come to the point where the lifetime of one dentist is not long enough to learn all the information and experience known in this field. So the period of branches of science began. Specializing in branches in all fields of science is just a temporary, horizontal solution to the blockage we face due to the perceptual slowness we have and are not aware of. Even now the need is felt for a separate specialist who is knowledgeable in all the branches and who can integrate all the information.

Now let's first compare your own childhood with the childhood of kids today. While your time was filled with play, today's child finds himself in educational periods designed to acquire knowledge and experience through a system of preschool, extra lessons throughout the week, special make up schools on the weekends, summer courses, trial tests and special schools. Is this not an attempt to lengthen the period of education by reducing the age at which the person with a relatively short life span begins his studies? We take away from the time that they should have been playing childish games and having fun. Isn't the goal here to reduce the age in which training begins to increase the time a person can spend studying?

Speed reading is another attempt to increase the period devoted to acquiring education.

Stephen Hawking: In this limited time and this complicated arena how we to determine what are and how we must teach our children?

We have the potential to be able to learn the previous knowledge but since the time is short so we have to be selective and careful for criteria of suitability.

You're right. An outcome of the limited speed of perception/learning system is that the emphasis is put on teaching information that is new in order to best use the limited time available. Records are kept of older information gathered before a certain time and method, but it is not included in the training programs. This is only stored in archive libraries as history of knowledge and methodology for researchers to use later. An example of this can be seen in the storage tools of computers:

- **Punch cards**
- **5 ¼ and 1.44" disks**
- **CD, DVD-CD**
- **Flash disks**

In today's computer science training nothing is taught about punch cards and 5 ¼" disks. Today there is not one laptop with a floppy disk drive and soon disks will be a thing of the past as they are no longer found in desktop computers. In short, if a more developed version has come out and a product is no longer used, in order to make the best use of the short life of a human being, those unused versions are removed from training.

From the beginning of mankind, the biggest problem has been recording information and experience. Mankind developed writing, then the printing press and printing systems were developed to speed up writing. At the same time with the development the arena of photographs, video and computers and the technology to record and store information and experience under control, we breathed a sigh of relief as we reduced the amount of information loss. Since we have no records of history before recorded/written time, our knowledge is limited to opinion.

And you clearly refer to the subject of blockage in science in the introduction of your book *A Brief History of Time*, page VI when you say. *"But modern science is so dependent on technology that only a few expert scientists who are able to use certain mathematical tools are able to master."*

Stephen Hawking: If the chain is only as strong as its weakest link, the speed of our system as fast as our five senses.

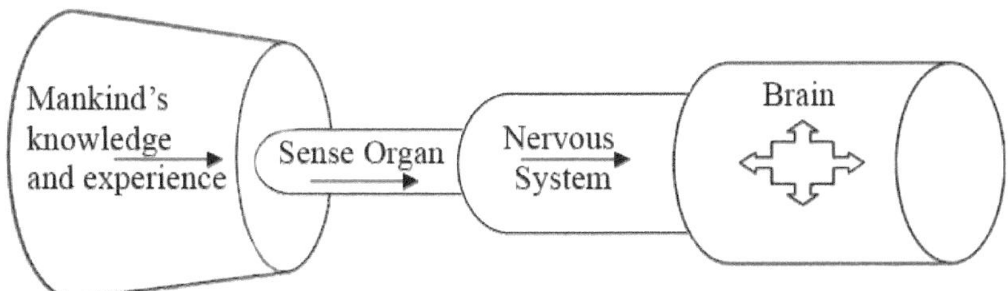

It is often said "we only use 5% of our brain." If our nervous system and our brain work fast, and our sense organs function at a slower rate, how can our brains function at full capacity? This means that we can only send inside 5% of the information received. Since this situation has continued for a long time and the area that sorts out meaning has slowed down in an effort to adapt, that means that our situation is bleak, indeed.

I don't even mention the reality of the knowledge because it is another difficult problem.

Three dimensional education is one that instructs all the senses. It is impossible to advance to the next higher dimension in a three-dimensional universe, where our tools for perception (books, note-books, TV, videos etc.) are one-dimensional, and we are left without the other two dimensions. If this situation continues, science by branching into new areas will continue to develop horizontally, but man's mind will not be able to make the perpendicular jump expected.

Stephen Hawking: Are you inferring that because of our basic human faculties, the way God created us, we have been prevented from finding the answer, and we are unable to advance?

We can call this the limited effort mankind's of to try and understand his limitless Creator. This shows that there is a need for an immediate intervention in the existing structure of the present dimension.

Stephen Hawking: Won't you find resistance to this from some religious men claiming you are "interfering with God's work?"

If by intervening we are able to overcome the problem it means that God has given man his permission.

The Man, 81:29 And you do not please except that Allah please, the Lord of the worlds (Q)

Haven't we solved the challenge of air travel with planes and space ships and the problem of waterways with ships, submarines and water bridges.

Stephen Hawking: Are there references to this intervention in the Holy Books?

There are indeed very interesting verses:

Colossians, 2:20-21 It is forbidden to pick up this, it is forbidden to taste that, it is forbidden to touch something else. (NT)
Yunus, 10:31 Who controls hearing and eyesight? (Q)

In this verse it is implied that the Creator uses our auditory and visual systems and has ultimate control over our senses. Thus, we will be entering a divine communication channel with God's permission. **Pandora's Box** is opening.

What is left for us to do is to map out a plan of the brain, and understand the perception and storage systems.

Intervention in the Simple Perception - Communication System of the Brain
(Whoever controls the senses, controls feelings)
(Whoever controls communications, controls the system)

Our brain at every second, and every minute, plans, administers and checks every function of the body. The nervous systems send the messages that the senses send to the brain, to the brain's sensing center. Because of these messages, a person's complete physical system is able to continue to function.

Perception of the surroundings by the five sense organs and connection to our brain is done by the same method. I am specifically using the link to the eye-brain connection as an example given the concrete developments in electronic medicine regarding the area of eye perception and brain connection.

Especially the eye: because if you succeed in deceiving the eye, it is easy to mislead the other senses. Without sight, it would be difficult to perceive reality because of the possibility of the other senses being mislead.

Matthew, *6:22 The lamp of the body is the eye.* **(NT)**

Ezekiel, *44:5 Mortal, mark well, look closely, and listen attentively* **(OT)**

The eye quickly converts the view into electrical signals sending those electric signals to the vision center in the brain across the nerves. The electronic signals developed in these brain cells are sent to the back of the brain to the –opsipital– area.
The signals reaching the vision center compare the data that already exists there (what we have learned before) with these electronic signals. The words we read are compared with the form data in our memory and we are able to understand the text we are reading.

This is true for not only our sense of vision but also for all our other senses. Touch, taste, hot/cold, vibration, perception, sound, pressure, pain....all the feelings that you can think of and inner and outer common signals are picked up by receptors converted into electronic signals and can be perceived. In short, the perception center of the brain is nothing more than electricity.

The most important thing here is that the signals of the senses different people send to the brain are of the same electronic signals. The same electronic signals are sent to the brain of all those seeing the same picture. The same signals that reach the brain of each person are given different meanings when compared to the information already stored there.

Let's analyze the steps that a book that has sold 1,000,000 copies worldwide has to go through. The author prepares one copy of the book, and it is sold exactly like that to the public. One million people buy the same book and take an average of 20 hours to load it into their brains through their eyes.

In this case, to get the same contents of the book into 1 million brains would take 1,000,000 x 20 = 20,000,000 hours.

Let's say that on average, it takes one cut tree for 1,000 books. For 1,000,000 books then, 1,000,000/1,000 = 1,000 trees will be cut down.

In this situation then, while the author, who is understandably happy and proud that his book sold 1,000,000 copies, must be distressed that 1,000 trees had to be cut and 20,000,000 hours were spent reading. But the actual thing he must be sad about is that scientists have not yet developed the technology that would allow him to directly transfer a single recording of his book to any number of his readers.

Stephen Hawking: Where do you contribute to the advancement of this program?

I am developing suggestions for the process of this simple basic system. As a man on the street, the least we can do is to voice our opinion about today's urgent necessity for practical advancement in this field.
If electronic signals from the book we read are transferred, these signals can be copied and the book will have been transferred into a meaningful digital form which can then be altered.

I mentioned this model in my book *I'm Ready, Let it Begin* (1998), only to find this news report years later which shows that this is becoming a reality by the day.

The vision trouble arising from the eyes comes from the inability to change the view seen by the eye into an electronic signal. If an electronic eye is developed to send the images to the brain, just as a book being read by an electronic eye, electronic signals can be sent to the brain and when copied, can be transferred to other readers who want to read the book without the twenty hours it would take them to read the book for themselves. The digital record can be transferred to the brains of other readers within seconds.

Of course, in more sensitive realities people looking at the same view may display minute differences in the signals sent to the brain. In this situation, the person when using the book "loading" technology will be able to adjust the clarity of the image on the first page to fit his own physical parameters. When the transfer begins the digital record of the book can be sent to the vision center within seconds at the speed of electricity. This is like aliens in science fiction films who come into our world, uploading/downloading our complete past history as thousands of images passing in front of their screens. (Speed of light = electric speed: from now on the term speed of light will be used.)

The incredible speed of physical and spiritual data transfers made by education at the speed of light is clearly mentioned in the Holy Books. In a normal process the difference in learning at the speed of light and the normal rate of learning is vast, as is seen in this verse:

Jeremiah, 1:9 *Then Yahweh put out his hand and touched my mouth and said to me: There! I am putting my words in your mouth.* **(OT)**
The Suad, 38:71-72 *When your Lord said to the angels; Surely I am going to create a mortal from dust: So when I have made him complete and breathed into him of My spirit, then fall down making obeisance to him.* **(Q)**

(It says that there is a digital information transfer made with one touch.)

Stephen Hawking: Just as a few minutes ago you were able to watch 1-2 years of your life go by in a few seconds. Why didn't you ask, since a little while ago you were wondering, "That is all well and good but with the slow speed sense organs I have, how was I able to see the details of such a long time period in such a short time?" Was it because you think of the world in this way?

I answered your question concerning this section at the beginning:

Colossians, 2:20-21 *It is forbidden to pick up this, it is forbidden to taste that, it is forbidden to touch something else.***(NT)**
Yunus, 10:31 *Who controls hearing and eyesight?* **(Q)**
Qaf, 50:16 *And know what his soul is whispering within him. We are closer to him than his jugular vein.* **(Q)**

And I'd like to add one more reference:

The Family of Imran, *3:13 You have already had a sign in the two detachments which met, one detachment fighting for God's sake and the other disbelieving; they saw them with their own eyes* **as twice the same number as themselves. (Q)**

This verse clearly means that the Creator *"who controls hearing and eyesight?"* is able to use this same capability to cause a group of people to see twice as much.

In a virtual environment, the speed of brain communication (electricity / light) may be reached by communication (connection) directly to the sensing centers and a person will begin to live a virtual life closely parallel to the real world. As years go by in a brain at the speed of light in a virtual reality, simultaneously, in the real world, only seconds will have passed. The ratio of time experienced in real life and virtual life is like the ratio mentioned in the Holy Books.

Psalms, *39:4-5 Look, you have given me an inch or two of life, my life-span is nothing to you; each man that stands on earth is only a puff of wind.* **(OT)**
Psalms, *90:4-5 To you a thousand years are a single day, a yesterday now over, an hour of the night.* **(OT)**
II Peter, *3:8 With the Lord, "a day" can mean a thousand years, and a thousand years is like a day.* **(NT)**
Pilgrimage, *22:47 A day with your lord is like a thousand years, such as those you count by.* **(Q)**
The Sand Hills, *46:35 On the day that they shall see what they are promised they shall be as if they had not tarried save an hour of the day.* **(Q)**

Let's do some figuring. 1000 (years) x 365 (days) = 365,000 days: the ratio mentioned in these verses is then 1/365,000. In terms of speed, this is faster than the speed of light. Given the fact that our nervous system sends electronic impulses at the speed of light, we must question if the difference may be dependent on the speed of thought. In a simulated universe (virtual reality) the ratio of the fastest speed, that of the speed of thought may be 365,000 kilometers per second.

In this situation, the ratio of 1000 years = 1 day in the verses will give us a view of what a life-time ratio is. If you noticed, the verses instead of saying "a thousand years" is "one day" it says that it is "like" one day. It is as if they are trying to warn the reader that this is a sign that this world is a copied or a virtual reality.

When at times my thinking becomes a bit like science fiction, I open a Holy Book or bring to mind Socrates' words which say, *"Just as man is unable to materialize out of nothing and then dematerialize when he wants to, he cannot do it in the field of thought, either. In short, a person may not think of anything that does not exist."*

These projects, better than utopia, are made possible by using materials of the near future. The vision of virtual reality is a technological style that combines science, mind and belief with curiosity and education by imagination, research, and animation.

Now let's take this to one more level. Inserting a receiver into the vision center of the brain will allow reception of the signals of the images we wish the person to receive.

When remote signals are sent, a person will think he is looking at the images we send because the brain is not aware of the source of the signals that have reached it and it is an organ programmed to evaluate the signals it receives. Perhaps hallucinations are images, one on top of the other, made by signals from different sources becoming mixed up.

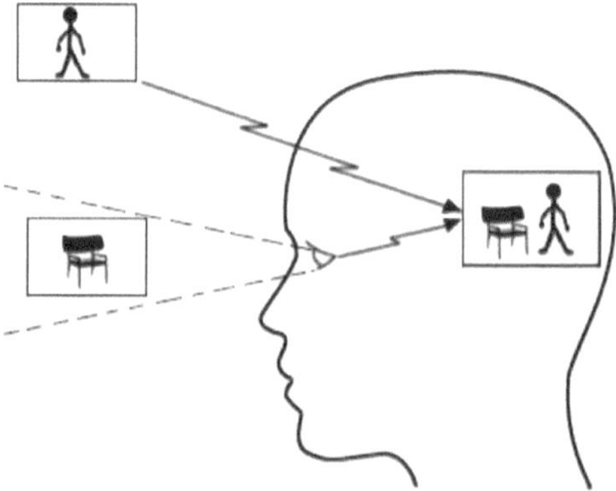

Like Dr. Sinan Canan's book "Fractal Thoughts" says: *"In short, the science of the modern nervous system has brought us to the point of the doubts that many philosophers, avatars and sages have felt. That we call the outside world is what we perceive with the organ we call the "brain" which uses signals originating from our severely limited senses. The actuality of these images has, unfortunately, not yet been found by anyone." (page 75)*

If we can send remote signals to our sense organs, a copy of the feelings coming from our sense organs can be picked up and recorded.

Psalms, 139:2 Lord, you read my thoughts from far away. **(OT)**

Ha Mim, 41:20 *So that when they come up to it their hearing eyesight and their skins will testify against them concerning anything they have been doing.* **(Q)**

Stephen Hawking: Let's take this idea of yours that you put forth in 1998, a little further using some quotes from the visionary Marc D. Hauser's book The Next 50 Years. "The neurobiologist Miguel Nicolle is and his colleagues have managed to record the electrical discharges of hundreds of neurons from an owl monkey's brain and use the signal to drive a robot's arm. This may sound like pure gadgetry, but it is not. It shows that at some level we can make sense of the neural code and understand how it mediates behavior. Now imagine that we could download the neuronal signals from any animal, creating a kind of hard drive library of their thoughts while they were interacting with the world. We would be able to read the mind of an animal as it eats, sleeps, grooms, has sex, com-municates. At some level, we would have a deep sense of what it's like to be them. We would be a peeping Homo sapiens. We might even be able to synchronize our own brain waves with theirs, thereby experiencing a kind of interspecies harmony never before achieved-clearly the ultimate in virtual reality games."

The Ant, 27:16 *And Suleiman was Dawood's heir, and he said: O men! we have been taught the language of birds, and we have been given all things; most surely this is manifest grace* **(Q)**

The Ant, 27:17 *And his hosts of the jinn and the men and the birds were gathered to him, and they were formed into groups.* **(Q)**

As a result, since the brain does not consider the source of the signal, just as with our eyes, we can use electronic signals of the other sense organs as a transfer system to send electronic signals we want of images, sound, odors, and touch to the brain. Thus, we can cause it to see things that it really did not see, hear what has not been heard, and touch what is not there. In short, man may cause a virtual reality where he senses the unreal is real and control a vast portion of his brain. When we add the fact that electronic signals making up images can be turned into mathematical statements, Pythagoras's theory "the ruler of the universe is mathematics and numbers manage the universe," becomes much more probable.

Exodus, 10:1 *"And the Lord said to Moses: go to live with the Pharaoh; because I have hardened his heart." **(OT)***
Luke, 24:45 *He then opened their minds to understand the scriptures.* **(NT)**
The Rock, 15:47 *We pulled out the hate in your chest. They became brothers living in the same villas. On the same couches.* **(Q)**
Women, 4:128 *Greed is ever present in our souls.* **(Q)**

The Holy Books refer to another means of control of the senses, don't they?

Stephen Hawking: The matrix in the Holy Books.

We can think of it in that way in some respects. Since I have been a computer programmer since 1988, I identify everything first with the computer. Ever since I've been self aware, I've thought about the things we've been discussing. In 1998 before Matrix and similar films were released, I wrote about a virtual reality and a virtual God in my book, *"I'm ready. Let it begin."* Films like the Matrix, The Truman Show[2], Dark City, Vanilla Sky, the Devil's Advocate, Contact, The 5th Element supported my thinking. The Truman Show is an unsurpassed example.

---

[2] **(Truman Show:** The film is set mostly in a town wholly dedicated to a continually running television show. All of the people present in the town are actors or film crew except protagonist Truman Burbank, who is unaware that he lives in a constructed reality filmed for the entertainment of those outside. Central characters simulate friendship or familial relations to Truman.)

The film Matrix introduced the virtual reality we live in well. Now, when we mention a virtual reality, the man on the street instantly remembers what he has learned in the film 'Matrix'.

I do not completely agree with the summary that Oracle gave of our creation in The Matrix film: *"You made the decision to come here in the first place, and you came to understand the reason for that decision."* I disagree with that, because understanding a decision made at the beginning would be a lesser goal. I, too, believe we make a decision to come, but our reason for being here is to prove whether we are the person of our decision or not. We are not here to understand our decision, but to prove we are able to do it. Only understanding is not enough.

Stephen Hawking: How did you like the Matrix series?

Even though Morpheus (in The Matrix) said, *"Anyone stuck in the reality of a previous level is able of conceiving the new level,"* in the scenario, he was stuck in the one previous level. Therefore, weapons and conflicts from the immediate previous level were chosen. In Matrix 1, the first section began with a good introduction to a virtual reality and instead of a second part with sharp-witted brainpower; it was turned into a struggle between primitive people with primitive weapons, the victors depending on physical and arsenal prowess and battle strategies.

As I said in a press release I issued after watching the film (September 26, 1999) I think the scenario should have been based on a different theory:

Today while a baby is still in the womb, certain physical illnesses can be determined and the fetus can have surgery or the parents can opt to terminate the pregnancy. In the future, at a time when we are able to connect the brain of a fetus in a virtual unifying environment, babies will be provided psychological and physical tests and evaluations through chosen scenarios. Here the testing, evaluations and decision making, will be done while the fetus is in the womb, and psychological and physical formation will produce babies of super intelligent and endurance. This will be done by a virtual environment computer called Matrix, the name of the film: Matrix, Earth Version 20.0. (20th century= 20th level). The first struggle with life is the person being born as a baby.

*Isaiah, 44:24 He who formed you in the womb. **(OT)***
*Isaiah, 49:5 He who formed me in the womb to be his servant. **(OT)***
The Luqman,** 31:34 He knows what is in the wombs **(Q)

There will be a struggle (physical/mental) among millions of potential babies (sperm) to enter the world with only the strongest earning the right to be born and live. Morpheus will continue to be the trainer of the babies who will be subject to testing at the end of training.

Stephen Hawking: You have been talking about this subject for years and just like the "mirrors in the sky", it has been considered highly fanciful by everyone. In the book *The Next 50 Years*, Professor Rodney Brooks says, "*It seems reasonable to assume that by the year 2050 we will be able to intervene and select not just the sex of a baby at the point of conception but also many of its physical, mental and personality characteristics as well...*" (page 190) This is cited as a goal of science within 50 years.

Mankind has difficulty assigning a right or wrong meaning to what he cannot see or conceive of without tangible data. **For example:** in spite of the fact that there is no tangible information about life in space, in science fiction films, it is clear they get stuck in the reality of previous levels. Even though all spacemen are strange, they all have one, two or three eyes, ears, a head, hands and feet and other human organs. All space people resemble earthlings and are all more intelligent and more developed than humans are.

Isn't the "third eye" is also a classic organ of sense which is identified as an eye with limits above those of a normal eye?

The Matrix series of films has had a stimulating impact on helping mankind understand the virtual environment. People are unable to see that God, too, used a virtual environment because they do not read the Holy Books from that point of view. Now, if you'd like, let me show you what a few references have to say on that subject.

Stephen Hawking: The subjects of this section are space and technical subjects. If you are able to progress to that point, those subjects will come up later. You will inspect them in detail then. Your conclusion then is **"with the body you have, if you are able to make changes to it, you have the right to make them."** But aren't babies made to specification a type of manipulation of the species?

Matthew, *8-12 ...will be turned out into the dark, where there will be weeping and grinding of teeth.***(NT)**
Sprites, *72:15 Anyone who defies God and his messenger will have hell fire to live in forever.* **(Q)**

The Cow, *2:14 Then heed the Fire which has been prepared for disbelievers whose fuel is mankind and stones.* **(Q)**
The Spider, *29:58 And (as for) those who believe and do good, We will certainly give them abode in the high places in gardens beneath which rivers flow, abiding therein; how good the reward of the workers:* **(Q)**

You're right, but isn't God creating super individuals by sending the good to live forever in heaven and the bad to hell, to be used as wood? Isn't this a form of manipulation? Isn't the same thing true of education?

Doesn't God give us life in a three-dimensional world? Three-dimensional education means godly education.

Stephen Hawking: There are a few examples of the advantages of a virtual environment from Roger S. Swank in his article "Are We Going to Get Smarter?" in the book "The Next 50 Years."

"Education in the deepest sense has always been about doing, rather than about knowing. Many scholars throughout the years have pointed this out, from Aristotle (*"For the things we have to learn before we can do them we learn by doing them"*) to A.S. Neill ("I hear and I forget; I see and I remember, I do and I understand." To Einstein ("The only source of knowledge is experience").

"Each generation improves on the experiences it opens up to the next. But a leap of tremendous proportions is coming in the next generation. The fact that we still have teachers and classrooms

and textbooks will be almost laughable in fifty years. People will look back at us and ask why it took so long to change our notions of education, why we thought answers were a mark of intelligence in any way."

The inescapability of a virtual world is also expected. In an article "A Complexity Ceiling" in the same book by John Lanier, it is stated: *"If an inter-organ protocol turns out to be possible, building one will force a tragic trade-off in the art of organ simulation."(page 221)*

While thinking about future life forms, just as today it is accepted that man will be able to make them, the possibility that new life forms have already been developed must also be considered.

I always thought that science was moving ahead until it developed the technology to intervene in the senses. But with the development of the capability to intervene in the senses and the brain of a life form, it will be possible to cause human life in the past or the future through thought. In this situation we, too, **may be living in an environment that is an integrated past made in the future.**

As you can see, what will there remain to research after man figures out his brain map? Man will make a copy/virtual himself and put himself out into the cloned universe to live and thus, in practice, man will be man's god.

Matthew, *17:22 The Son of Man is going to be handed over into the power of men.* **(NT)**

Stephen Hawking: This is a type of **"Digital god."** Isn't this the verse that gives the news that Jesus will be turned over to the Romans by one of his own people? How does this understanding result from this verse?

When you mention "The Theory of Everything" in your books, the theory is intended to explain the universe and how it functions. You identified the theory as a type of connector between the Holy Books; of religious leaders and the universes seen by scientists, further saying that "The Theory of Everything" would be *the pinnacle of man's intelligence.*

The Holy Books contain hundreds of verses that appear to be only things the prophets said, but if these messages are only unique to the person described in the verse, why do they have a place in a Holy Book? The information would have found a place in history books about the prophet in question. How is it that Scriptures with the meaning misunderstood or not yet understood are labeled "re-presentative" or metaphorical? If that is the case, who is to say that they do not refer to the subject at hand? I think that instead of the classic verses of "human understanding" we must find the verses of "God understanding."

If the answer has not yet been found, it is probable that God used a code system or a mysterious unknown method. There are questions, therefore there must be key clues to take us to the answer. Clues are usually looked for in places where religion and science seem separate.

Mankind, with the confusion between scientific and religious sources, alone without meaning, has resorted to using the anagram method as the key to the code for looking for the answers.

"An anagram is defined as a word, phrase, or sentence formed from another by rearranging its letters." In this research the anagram method has been modeled using sentences and comparing the contents of various sources. Just as pieces of a Lego set are connected to build a meaningful structure, meaningful theory has been constructed with an example of this same system.

A key that will be helpful in finding an answer to something that appears to be encoded is a prerequisite and can be said to be **"reconciled aspects (signs)"**. The parameters of a key, instead of focusing on the areas where science and religion clash, with the observing mind, a researcher must concentrate on the aspects that have been reconciled. Instead of using the substitution-of-many method of the anagram, if we apply the order first mentioned in the texts, the text of the thinking that developed the initial creation is understood and we begin to get answers. Science is religion's key, religion is science's key and man is the locksmith.

The continuance of time means the flow of information. If, universal solutions have not been found to problems that concern mankind as a whole, and solutions have only been constructed for countries, areas and groups, then as in the past, the universe will appear more chaotic and unfathomable.

Stephen Hawking: Why would the Creator give mankind this permission?

I have no doubt that the Creator wants us to win.

Ezekiel, 18:23 Am I likely to take pleasure in the death of a wicked man and not prefer to see him renounce his wickedness and live? **(OT)**
The Believers, 40:3 The Forgiver of the faults and the Acceptor of repentance. **(Q)**

In the classic birth-death line a person is born, grows up, dies and is rewarded in front of a jury. There is no returning and regrets will not help. God, whom I know wants us to win, must have presented us with more options than simply giving us the Holy Books.

Before the afterlife, man, by learning from his own experience, is offered a wonderful opportunity to know of his success in a virtual world.

Yunus, 10:30 There each soul will be tested for whatever it has sent on ahead in the past. **(Q)**
The Spider, 29:21 Travel around the earth and see how He began with creation. Later on God raises up the fresh growth. **(Q)**

Right at this point my dear guide interrupted and said, "Let's give this a little break." I thought he would say something related to what I had been talking about, but our journey through space began again, where we had left off. We continued watching the glorious scenery around us and our past on the screen. On the screen, Galip my brother-in-law, Nurten, my aunt, my cousins Ahmet Hamdi and Tayfun were having fun around the table as we conversed. At one point, I came to be aware of where I was and said, "This must be a break in space" (When my guide heard that, he began speaking).

Stephen Hawking: You seem certain you are in space; are you sure it couldn't be a dream? If you can determine that a being around you, alive or not, can feel with one or the other of the sense organs you have, that is, if you can evaluate him, you accept it as "existing" and take it seriously. You think what you can see, feel and touch is real and react to it. However, what is it that chases you in the imaginary reality of your dreams that aren't real?

I find it meaningful to accept, as true, that God wanted me to explain this to mankind instead of keeping it to myself. If this is a dream, I am sure it is in God's control. I continually share not only the material things I have, but also my thoughts and ideas in books or bulletins. (www.aydinturkgucu.net)

Dreams are a subject I have long thought about and studied. Man has experienced the imaginary reality we have called the virtual reality since the beginning of time. But not knowing, he calls it a dream and continues unaware.

There is no Gravity, Blame, Penalty, or Cost in Dreams

We can identify the universe or the cosmos as the environment we exist in along with billions of other beings, living or not, and the millions of stars; we say it was created by a creative force and not by man so that it cannot be measured. If we say that while we sleep, the environment is what we create turning imaginary things into dreams and then living inside them as if they were real, we can call this imaginary dream universe we live in, a temporary copy or pirated universe.

While everything begins at zero, humanity and dreams begin at one.

How is it that man, thousands of years ago, opened his eyes in a world that knew no beginning and believed in what he saw, then followed it; while we follow dreams which have no beginning but are a perfect copy of the real world? We chase after a false reality and we understand that what we have been experiencing is a dream only when we awake. The realization that the world is a dream is our awakening, as is mentioned in the Holy Books,

*__Psalms,__ 73:20 You shrug them off like the phantoms of a morning dream **(OT)**__*

*__Isaiah,__ 29:7 (It) shall vanish like a dream, like a vision at night. **(OT)**__*

We do not only observe our dreams, which are formed from commands produced in the brain and are highly dependent on the imagination for content and limitations, but we can also communicate with live and inanimate beings in them. We communicate with other people, we touch, board vehicles, love animals, are happy, laugh, are afraid, scream and can wake up sweating.

Our dreams sometimes include environments that we are familiar with in waking life, or would like to be familiar with. Sometimes a fantasy world that does not exist in our waking life and thus we experience places full of people living in an imaginary world. Dreams are a place where our thoughts and imagination transform into a virtual reality.

In our dreams:

* We can fly because there is no gravity.
* We can easily travel in space because we have no need for oxygen.
* Crimes committed are not crimes because in reality no one and nothing is harmed, so there is no punishment!
* Anything you broke, ate, drank, bought, and visited cost nothing because it is not real.
* We can experience any profession, manipulate any machine.
* There is no problem with visas or tickets, you can travel anywhere you like.
* We can visit the dead, talk with those with whom we are angry or separated from.
* We can travel through time, experiencing any period or state.
* We can talk in private with any politician/or artist without an appointment.

Our dreams are like our own individual heaven formed while sleeping.

Stephen Hawking: When you don't realize you are dreaming, doesn't your brain know it either?

My dear teacher, in a dream when someone calls to you or touches you, your brain asks if it is in the dream or in reality and knows it immediately.
If the sound:

* came from your dream, you react with your body and the dream continues.
* came from the surroundings you are sleeping in; the brain stops the dream and sleep and immediately awakens you to the real world.

Our brain monitors both the dream body and the environment surrounding the real body. Since it is quite capable of monitoring both and differentiating between them, it means that the brain just *pretends* it does not know it is dreaming.

Therefore, given today's conditions, we were created with two worlds: the real world and the copied world. We live in one and think we live in the other, we were created in one and create in the other and can only know which world we are in when we awaken.

We are safe because in this artificial world, if we take anything seriously enough to be hurtful, our brain will immediately wake us up.

If, while we are in a dream, our brains send electronic signals to a different training center that contains visions, sounds, etc, from our imagination and dreams and in doing so, creates a virtual reality, we can call our dreams the playground of our brain. (When I said this, Stephen Hawking's hologram displayed a strange expression. What's more, instead of looking at my face, he looked at a point in deep space as he asked…

Stephen Hawking: If you have completed what you have to say about space, let's continue to the elevator.

As soon as I answered enthusiastically the elevator began to move and the help that my Aunt Aysel had given me to assist me in passing the university entrance examination was passing before me on the screen. I watched it with deep gratitude.

Stephen Hawking: Our time is up. Please close your eyes. (I closed my eyes) "You may open them."

We stood in front of a door that had a sign on it marked "Exit", with my name and surname and the date/hour/minute/second of my birth. I waited in great anticipation.

Stephen Hawking: You will remember,

*Matthew,*16:19 *I will give you the keys to the kingdom of heaven and God in heaven will allow whatever you allow on earth. But he won't allow what you won't allow on earth."* **(NT)**

And my advice to you is that you should think about seeking a solution in heaven.

The hologram of Stephen Hawking faded into the distance as he said, **"Your Creators are with you"** and took his place in space, a star, lighting the darkness around him.

While I was wondering if the word "Creators" was a slip of the tongue, I concentrated fully on the door.

Psalms, 19:6 *He has his rising on the edge of heaven.* **(NT)**
Matthew, 7:7 *Knock and the door will be opened to you.* **(NT)**

As soon as these verses entered my mind, I knocked on the door: knock, knock, knock…

I was also wondering if every level had a different guide, or if they all have the same guide; if so, who would that be? Thinking these things, I became aware that I was standing, not sitting. As I turned around to look behind me, I saw that the frames of the world indicating my life path were lined up behind me. I didn't see how I could possibly go further. It meant that everyone was only able to see his own records. I stood, my past and my future in front of a door that was both an entrance and an exit: between the world and the afterlife. Finally, the elevator door opened.

Revelation, 4:1 *Then in my vision, I saw a door open in heaven.* **(NT)**

I thought I was probably in front of the door mentioned in this verse:

*"**Live simply that other's might simply live**"* says the weaponless warrior. **Gandhi**, stood looking at me, eyes sparkling. He said, "Hello". I answered with a respectful bow, "Hello". (Gandhi's statement of 1/25/1989 came to mind. "I believe in God's justice like I believe in English justice." I guessed that I was on the level of justice.) Mahatma Gandhi moved toward me…

Gandhi: You learned about me many years ago when you read the book "The Weaponless Warrior" and you drew a strategy for your life struggle from that book. You summarized it this way: *"I have always felt sympathy toward the Satyagrah the boycott without violence method that Gandhi used." "A person must display what he knows to be true and, without violence, must be ready to die for it."* Now, according to your beliefs about justice, you have the chance to punish anyone who harmed you or did wrong to you, living or dead. You may call them here and give them sentence. Whom will you invite first?

The weaponless warrior M. Gandhi just as in Shakespeare's play, "The Merchant of Venice," told me I was free to cut a piece of flesh off anyone I felt owed me something.

I remembered the words of prayers I used on earth, "I believe I have the right to ask something from God when I have suffered from evil. I think I have that right. Would you use that right to devastate the person who harmed you? On the other hand, would you ask for something positive for yourself? If you wish evil on that person, you would have to check to see if that wish were granted, and even if it were hidden, you would have a connection with him and you would not be able to get him out of your life. Additionally, if you began to follow your right to this evil wish on God's level, you would enter an extremely stressful period."

The prophet Muhammad replied in this way to those who wanted to damn their enemies in battle: *"I did not come to damn, I come to bless."* And the prophet forgave all the people of Mecca who, made an effort to murder him.

Exodus, *32:32 And yet if it pleased you to forgive this sin of theirs….But if not, then blot me out from the book that you have written.* **(OT)**

*__Numbers,__ 23:8 How can I curse whom God has not cursed?
How can I denounce those whom the Lord has not denounced?* **(OT)**
The Elevated Place, *7:199 Hold to forgiveness; command what is right;
and turn away from the ignorant.* **(Q)**

In this verse Moses is prepared to forgo his rank of prophet for the forgiveness of his people.

I don't know if I will be able to reach the point of forgiveness attained by Jesus. Why did he pray for the forgiveness of them? What is the main meaning of this forgiveness?

Gandhi: That has been explained in Karen Armstrong's book "The History of God" in this way: when he was brought to be crucified, he saw the cross and spikes, turned to the people and said a prayer ending with these words: *"Here are your herots got together to kill me, they have great enthusiasm to gain your bounty for your religion, forgive them. Oh my lord, show mercy on them, because if you had explained to them the things to you explained to me they wouldn't do what they are about to do. And if you had hid from me the things you hide from them I wouldn't suffer this trouble. You are the one to be ruined no matter what you do and whatever you wish the Medh is to him."*

As **Prof. Beyza Bilgin** said: *"If we believe in the power of prayer, why should we not ask for something nice?"*

As I found myself in the position of wishing for something in front of the elevator door, my eyes rested on the ring on the ring finger of my left hand, and the prayer I used at the Dome of the Rock in Jerusalem (Mescid-i Aksa) came to my mind.

On a trip to Jerusalem in 1997, I bought a ring that reminded me of the symbol I had used on my book entitled "My Unnamed Book". The silver ring is an eight-pointed star with an amethyst in the center of a gold circle. The next day, I was surprised to see the same symbol carved in the black marble of the cave beneath the rock that is said to have risen and remained suspended in air as the Prophet Mohammad ascended into the skies. I questioned those who were in charge:

"A feud broke out among the tribes when the time came to place the stone from heaven on the Hacer-ul Esvet Kaaba (Mecca). At that time, the prophet Mohammad spread his cape upon the ground and said, "First place a stone here, then choosing one person from each tribe, move the stone to its final place." There were eight tribes and eight men who placed the rock and the eight-pointed star called the **'Star of Mohammad'**.

In addition, I put the ring on my left hand on top of the eight pointed star on the engraved stone showing the direction to pray and said this prayer:

My God,
My hand into your hand,
My face to your face
My heart to your heart,
My spirit to your spirit,
I committed my path to yours,
Tell me and I will do it,
Show me and I will go there,
Teach me and I will explain,
Send to me and I will love,
Give to me and I will enable

(I looked into Gandhi's eyes)

Standing before a person like you whom I have embraced as a model, I will not behave in a manner that betrays the very ideals I have defended. I am not able to do anything that I do not believe in. If I have a right not to invite anyone in order to overcome my feelings of hatred and revenge, I will release them with my blessings. The tenet of the Prophet Jesus says "Turn the other cheek to those who strike you." I have always taken that as an example and tried to emulate it. I extend the other cheek and invite those who feel I owe them something to come and take what is their right!

The forgiveness and tolerance we expect from God, we must first demonstrate to others.

Gandhi: It is as if you have said the words of Shakespeare: *"The pain of the blows, to the house of my spirit, has taught me mercy."*

I do not like to complain nor do I like those who complain, either. But I can summarize the topic: *"The important thing is not that it snows on the mountain you trust, but that the snow should not become an avalanche and crush you. There is snow on the mountains of those who run life's course on earth."*

There will always be those around who apply the advice of H. De Balzac's work, Father Goriot: *"If you want to advance, think of each woman and man as a horse left to die at each place you visit, and you will reach your desires."* Some people you meet on the course of life are needed; some are there to impart knowledge.

"Don't try to change everything; just as you will be unable to change things, they will ruin you."

This advice indicates it is not necessary to allow people into your life who are only there to give you a lesson as if they were necessary. There is a saying that reads, *"Everyone chisels his own piece of stone,"* and chiseling stone is very difficult work. Those around you can be divided into the seasonal and the lifetime: the seasonal are called acquaintances and the lifelong are called friends.

Gandhi: Yes, but I looked at your records, you exhibited enough forgiveness to shock everyone. But is forgiveness and not stopping them actually good or bad? Are you actually saying, "The enemy I know is better than the one I don't know?"

I'd like to give an example from Nietzsche on this topic:

"And if a friend of yours hurts you, say this: That what you've done to me I return to you: but what you've done to yourself- how can I return that to you? This is how every great love grows: it beats the forgiveness and the pain. A person must protect his heart: once you let that go, you will soon lose your mind."

M. Gandhi took my arm and helped me into the elevator. It looked like an ordinary elevator with buttons to seven floors. When M. Gandhi said, *"you can begin on any floor you like,"* these things came to mind:

"thought stroke" and the advice of advancing "step by step." I said, "I'm ready, let it begin," and pushed the button to the first floor. Without feeling anything physical, the gauge changed from zero to one and as the door opened Gandhi said, **"Reality is the best guide,"** and directed me outside. As I stepped out of the elevator, a guide who reflected limitless thinking and wisdom awaited me. As I turned to M. Gandhi to say farewell, he said, **"Those who created you are with you, and you are with them,"** And the elevator door shut.

The spectacular view of space beneath drowned out the question marks sparked by Gandhi's parting words.

*Revelation, 4:6 Between the **throne** and myself was a sea that seems to be made of glass like crystal. **(NT)***

The universe's splendor was beneath me with stars and planets and galaxies at my feet; it was as if space was made up of many rooms and when I looked carefully, the partitions between became obvious. As I searched for the throne mentioned in the verse, I saw someone coming towards me in the distance. As he approached I saw it was the famous guide Nietzsche and we greeted each other.

Nietzsche: The fact that you have progressed so far shows that you have understood the use of the anagram. Which answer are you looking for?

Isaiah, 57:10 You grew weary from your many wanderings, but you did not say, 'It is useless.' You found your desire rekindled, and so you did not weaken. **(OT)**

As the road goes longer, the aim gets smaller. How can we possibly live in this world if we don't know where we came from and why we came into this world? I think we have come to this point because we haven't thought these questions through. Everyone talks about religion, but few speak about God.

Romans, 8:4-5 So that the just requirement of the law might be fulfilled in us, who walk not according to the flesh but according to the Spirit.

Whereas, every step on the path to knowing the Creator brings us a little closer to the answer to the question of from where and why we came.

Nietzsche: Do you use the anagram method for researching all the Holy Books?

We are like the kids, those lost on the way back home and are pieces of the puzzle that seems big and limitless.

Of course, I wouldn't read Holy Books, being like "a captain who doesn't know where he's going it doesn't matter which way the wind blows."

Like the example in Orhan Hançerlioğlu's book "History of Thoughts": Once the scientist Copernicus thought that *"I cannot understand the facts in the sky by believing stars are rotating around earth. I will try the opposite this time and will observe those facts by believing the earth is rotating around them."*

While studying the Holy Books if you look only at scriptures dealing with the earth, you will naturally find it someplace on earth. To find the verses that could be God's fingerprints/trace of Creation in the heavens, I have had to continually inspect the Holy Books over and over again with my own method.

Many years ago, an American teenager completely and coincidentally broke into the FBI's computer system and accessed top-secret information. When he was asked how he succeeded he replied, "I thought about the numbers that are not used in the telephone books like 111 11 11 or 222 22 22 and wondered who used the numbers that were never given to ordinary citizens. *With the help of my computer, I began calling these numbers not given to average citizens. Most were not in use but one number happened to be connected to the computer system of the FBI. That's how I cracked the system."*

The logic was simple. Most numbers are those given to average citizens (99.9%) and those left (0.1%) are the ones used by government units. They are the numbers of the directors of those who are being directed. I separated out the scriptures that deal with holy subjects that are not discussed much, which have been translated, from the subjects of daily life, but deal with the spiritual and the systems God has established. These Scriptures, which I call God's fingerprints, were like secret verses right before our eyes. In this way, I separated the earth and heavens, by Scriptures concerning the created from those concerning the Creator:

Isaiah, *42:20 You have seen many things but not observed them: your ears are open but you do not hear.* *(OT)*

The Moon, *54:17 We have made the Quran easy to memorize: yet will anyone (bother to) memorize it? (Q)*

The Kneeling, *45:4-5 The alternation of night and daylight and any sustenance God sends down from the sky with which he revives the earth after its death, and the wheeling of the winds are signs for folk who use their reason. Those are God's signs which We recite to you. (Q)*

Yusuf, *12:105 Keep your face set towards religion, seeking god) righteously nor appeal to something that will neither benefit not harm you. (Q)*

By taking advantage of seldom-used scriptures, I found God and the entrance doors to the system he created and finding entry codes within science and technology which I came across, I finally reached certain conclusions.

Nietzsche: What kind of conclusions?

Several verses from the Holy Books;

The Cattle, *6:32 What does worldly life mean except some sport and amusement? (Q)*

Others;

Smoke, *38-39 We did not create Heaven and Earth and anything in between them just by playing around. We have created them both only (to reveal) the Truth. (Q)*

If you aren't careful, these two verses look like they contradict each other. In this situation, I would like to explain another example using the computer. A person is able to do many things simultaneously on the computer, you can listen to music and at the same time you can play a game or write a message. It is not feasible to think that the Creator, using advanced technology, has only *one* reason for creating the earth. These verses are not contradictions, but proof there can be more than one reason for Creation. In these matters, "Since there will be no contradictions within God, they are a misunderstanding of man."

Nietzsche: Two possible reasons from a computer scientist. Is there another reason?

Of course there is:

The Cattle, *6:98 It is He Who has reproduced you from a single soul and granted you a settlement (on earth) and a resting place (after death).* **(Q)**

Notice there are two reasons explained in one verse. In this case, there are four reasons for the creation that are revealed: fun, consolation, testing and a place of safekeeping.

It is as Stephen Hawking said, *"There were two concepts in particular that I felt I had to include. One was the so-called sum over histories.* **This is the idea that there is not just a single history for the universe."** *Black Holes and Baby Universes* (page 31) I, too, feel that the universe was created for more than one purpose.

(Nietzsche was listening with great patience)

Nietzsche: The purposes of creation are a topic that is part of the upper levels. If you are able to reach those levels there will be more details explored. Now let's discuss the technical issues. Do you think it is right to view these verses from this point of view?

The Family of Imran, *3:7 He is the One Who sent you down the Book which contains decisive verses. They (form) the basis of the Book; while others are allegorical. Those whose hearts are prone to falter follow whatever is allegorical in it, seeking to create dissension by giving (their own) interpretations of it. Yet only God knows its interpretation; those*

In this verse the Creator clearly suggests that people on his path follow this method.

The God who is most discussed today and the verses which talk about the problems of earthly life (daily living) and provide no definite answers, the Sociological verses, is the one I have called the "Sociological God." The verses which explain creation and technical aspects, together with the God who defines them, I have defined as the "Technological/Scientific God." It is probable that today's scientists have been prevented from reaching the Technological God because these verses have not been brought to light. In order to demonstrate the great need of a **Technological God**, I will first mention the **Sociological God**

The Sorrowful end of the Sociological God

If we divide the journey of mankind's trip towards God into levels, we can say gods of earth are in the first, and gods of the sky are in the second level. When the gods of the first two levels turned out to be of man's own making, man, in his disappointment, accepted as the true God, the unseen God religious men found as they essentially searched outside the universe; the third step.

For mankind God is necessary only in emergency situations. In times when there was no science, given mankind's tendency to accept the easiest answer to problems and demanding quick solutions, he looked to events of nature on earth and in the skies, which he thought were supernatural, for his answers. As he accepted living and nonliving things in his environment to be gods, he experienced great disappointment.

In an effort to understand the world we live in, science has shown us that the path to understanding is through observation and experimental methods. Thoughts formed when the world was void of science and an ideology of false gods created from those times, retarded advancement of thought in the beginning. For this reason, before earth science was developed, people accepted fire, cows and other earthly gods. Then with the development of space science, they accepted the sun, moon and other heavenly gods as the true God.

Science, by ending the reign of false gods, extricated people from the worship of these false gods and did the 'true God' a great service. After all, was not the demise of these false gods now a service to Him, the 'true God', who had allowed the worship of these false gods for thousands of years?

Man was first miraculously created when there was no science and technology. Therefore, they used their experience of the daily solutions that shaped their lives to introduce the world they lived in but believed they hadn't created. Their efforts depended on fears and happiness or their imagination which reflected the lack of scientific data of the times.

Just as there was no science like there is today, in the time of the Holy Books, there was no societal order, either.

Judges, 17:6 *In those days there was no king in Israel and every man did as he pleased.* **(OT)**
Naturally, the verses for rules for daily life laid out in the Holy Books predominated.

When you study the Hadith (religious tradition of the Prophet Mohammad) you see that most are concerned with social events. Just as in the time before Pythagoras, before he put forth his idea of mathematical proof, decisions made and actions taken were without any direct connections to the Holy Books, as were rules based on custom and experience.

The subject that concerns the Sociological God are well defined by Karen Armstrong in her book "A History of God." In short: *There is a story that one day a pagan had approached Hillel and told him that he would be willing to convert to Judaism if the master could recite the whole of the Torah to him while he stood on one leg. Hillel replied, 'Do not do unto others as you would not have done unto you. That is the whole of the Torah: go and learn it."* (page 89)

Nietzsche: Didn't I kill God?

To me you are a good example of the current state of God. If you do not believe in God, you do not accept his being, you do not question and therefore you can't kill him. In my environs, instead of studying the Holy Books, taking into consideration the explanations and activities that are not true to any religion, there are those who don't believe in God. Not believing what is explained and not believing in God are two different things. For instance, several readers who had not read the Holy Books previously, read the outline of this book and decided to read the Holy Books as soon as possible.

In my opinion there is always a necessity for unbelievers in the development of belief. I reach the new reasons to believe during my research to find a way to convert the subjects that prevent people from believing. Some believe in the past some believe in the future. Just like some believe for visible reasons and some believe for invisible reasons. We must look at things more carefully for those who believe with visible reasons. Every nonbeliever is a potential believer.

The Thunder, *13:30 And thus We have sent you among a nation before which other nations have passed away, that you might recite to them what We have revealed to you and (still) they deny the Beneficent God. Say: He is my Lord, there is no god but He; on Him do I rely and to Him is my return.* **(Q)**

Children of Israel, *17:45-46 And when you recite the Quran, We place between you and those who do not believe in the hereafter a hidden barrier. - And We have placed coverings on their hearts and a heaviness in their ears lest they understand it, and when you mention your Lord alone in the Quran they turn their backs in aversion.* **(Q)**

Isn't that obvious in verses that there will be always nonbelievers and that the real success is to make them believe?

In the book "**A History of God**" author Karen Armstrong mentions a group of people who believed in God, but not in what was written about God; *"Those who were understandably reluctant to be circumcised and observe the whole Torah, often become honorary members of the synagogues, known as the "God fearers". (page 88)* I think you could be in this group.

I would like to mention those who have come to find solutions and the "Read, Understand and Apply" as in the Holy Books.

James, *1:22 But you must do what the world tells you and not just listen to it and deceive yourselves.* **(NT)**

The Sociological God says "Read"
The Technological God says "Read, Understand and Apply"

The first command of the Holy Books to the reader was "Read, Understand and Apply".

Applying is to teach us right. I think that religious men should say this after each worship session: *"Here, today you have renewed your belief in and promises to the Creator! Now, remembering the words of the Creator, in order to experience the wishes you expressed in your prayers, go into the tests that will earn you that right. I wish you success and determination."* Inspiration exists not only in theory, but in the application.

Nietzsche: As a philosopher said: " Work is also a prayer." When the laws of flying are followed a Muslim, can make a plane and fly as well as a Christian, a Jew or an atheist. In short you say, "God supports those who try without discrimination." Well, then, won't man's transition from sociological God to technological God be difficult? Isn't it going to be difficult for people to change from a sociological God to a technological God?

My dear teacher, The God you killed was the Sociological god of that time, who was unable to answer the question of the day. When you were unable to find answers to your questions, you entered belief's dead end and completely rejected the concept.

Man has so drowned in the subjects religious men put forth on mundane sociological subject that he has become eager for the technological God. Your words, "A person who loses God, will cling tighter to his beliefs," turns into "A person who loses God, clings tighter to the sociological God." And George Bernard Shaw says, *"The moral rules of countries are like teeth: the more rotten they are, the more it hurts to touch them."*

If believers belief is just for themselves it is selfish. The belief of the religious men must be strong enough to make the unbelievers believe. To understand that, find how they treat the unbelievers. Are they those who curse *"let them burn, let them die."* Or those who invite them to the belief? Which one of them is the real religious man? The kind of people who weakened your belief still exist and keep pushing people away from belief.

Our goal must not be to look at the past, but to **celebrate the future**; to find the mythological story of the future." This is the most important thing.

As mentioned in Karen Armstrong's book "A History of God", *"Had the notion of God not had this flexibility, it would not have survived to become one of the great human ideas. When one conception of god has ceased to have meaning or relevance it has been quietly discarded and replaced by a new theology." (page 5)*

Hollywood and the Need for a Technological God

Movies filmed in Hollywood like Matrix, Contact, The Truman Show, The Devil's Advocate, Dark City, and other science fiction films contain names and events from Holy Books. It is the combination of sociological scriptures and the technology used to produce these films that makes them seriously worth watching. The fact that films that explain religion through science regularly break box office profit records reflects man's need for the technological God.

Rumi said: *"I have seen many people who have no clothing. I have seen many sets of clothing that have no human being inside."* Due to the continued efforts of politic religious men to explain the appearance and shape of worship, technological scriptures are "in" while sociological scriptures are "out" of favor.

People are already way ahead of the technological God. There are millions of books being sold on the street "explaining God" written for the man on the street with new questions and new answers to their experiences.

Nietzsche: What are the parameters of choosing religion?

The Robin Hood method has always been valid on earth. Stealing the taxes collected from a cruel king and distributing the money to the poor, the Robin Hood logic, is unethical. Think of it: is a thief who steals another thief's goods innocent? Of course not! If Robin Hood had taken the same taxes from the king and used it for his own purposes, he would have been lynched on the spot. Therefore, because the system he used was beneficial for most of the people, using the logic that what is good for most of the people is valid; the Robin Hood logic is good throughout the world. Sometimes that which is thought to be good for everyone, uses the Robin Hood logic which doesn't question the source, is called civilization.

As mentioned in Karen Armstrong's book "A History of God," *"Wisdom literature was a well established genre in the Middle East; it tried to delve into the meaning of life, not by philosophical reflection, but by inquiring into the best way to live."*

A good example happened the night of the municipal elections in Ankara, Turkey. In a televised broadcast covering the elections the city mayor was asked, *"Did you expect such a decisive victory? To which he replied, "of course I did, we distribute help to 100,000 families."* I would like to share the cat's and dog's view of his owner from this prospective:

Dog: *"Since he always gives me food and meets my needs, and protects me, he must be my god."*

Cat: *"Since he always gives me food and meets my needs, and protects me, I must be his god."*

Nietzsche: To support this subject David Gelernter in *The next 50 Years*, "Tapping into the Beam" wrote in detail. *"2) The impossible-to-learn Law of Replacement: Society replaces a thing when it finds something better, not when it finds something newer." 3) Tangible gains always trump intangibles."* Is there no need for the sociological verses from now on?

Of course that is not what I'm saying! What I am saying is that not only the sociological verses but also the stories and the legends of those days will be questioned over and over in the light of new knowledge that has come upon us.

Yusuf, 12:111 In their histories there is certainly a lesson for men of understanding. (Q)

In the book **"Fides et Ratio,"** by **Pope John Paul II**, "The appeal to tradition is not a mere remembrance of the past; it involves rather the recognition of a cultural heritage which belongs to all of humanity. Indeed it may be said that it is we who belong to the tradition and that it is not ours to dispose of at will. Precisely by being rooted in the tradition will we be able today to develop for the future an original, new and constructive mode of thinking."(7:85)

Nietzsche: Could we explain this subject in this way? If we were to draw a picture of our situation, the part closest to earth would be God's sociological side; what you have called the sociological God. The part that is further to the technological God. Is this correct?

Technological God
Sociological God

It is not my purpose to depose of the sociological God completely, but to show the value in revealing the technological God in the present situation.

Technological God	**Sociological God**

Belief and worship belong to the sociological, questioning and understanding belong to the technological side. Worship takes you to heaven and questioning to the true God.
Of course, today it is a little strange to say that man's make up is a creation of a (virtual/ technological/ holographic/ digital) false god.

Nietzsche: While I was on earth, I also urged those around me to question as my life was an example of this. I see you are committed to uniting science and religion.

He then asked my permission to leave and left disappearing until he was just a silhouette in the distance. As he was leaving the silhouette of **Saint Thomas Aquinas** developed and a new guide appeared at my side.

Thomas Aquinas: What do you see as you look down now?

The first thing that caught my attention was a formation made up of rooms. When I looked closely, the boundaries between the rooms could easily be discerned.

*Job, 9:9 The Bear, Orion, too, are of his making, the Pleiades and the Mansions of the South. **(OT)***

These boundaries which are between the star formations, just as in the "C" drive of your computer, are divided into rooms, like directories. These three dimensional rooms are separate, each compartment containing a separate world and sun system.

The stars and planets swam freely in space, unfettered, like an electric train powered by magnetic forces with no visible connections.

*Thunder, 13:2 God is the One Who has raised up the Heavens without any support you can see. Then he mounted on the throne and regulated the sun and moon, each runs along on a specific course. **(Q)***
*Ya Sin,36:40 The sun dare not overtake the moon nor does night outpace the day, each float along in its own orbit. **(Q)***

Upon close inspection, every compartment has an entry/exit door in one corner, just as a computer directory with a name, surname and historical information on the top. From that information, it was clear to whom the room belonged, when that person was born, and when he was to die, and how much longer he had to live.

*Isaiah, 66:22 For as the new heavens and the new earth, I shall make will endure before me-it is Yahweh who speaks-so will your race and name endure. **(OT)***
*Ya Sin 36:38 The sun runs along on a course of its own. **(Q)***

Suddenly, I clearly saw the formation of a new room

*Revelation 21:1 "Then I saw a new heaven and a new earth." **(NT)***

The expansion of the space was done in two ways;

First: space is expanded with the birth of each new baby, as a new room is created with its own heavens.

Isaiah, 65:17 For now I create new heavens and a new earth. (OT)

Second: Just as space taken up on the hard disk in the C drive, the size of the rooms in space expands or contracts with the number of files and data added or deleted. The partitions of the three dimensional compartments in the hard disk of space expand and compress with the size of the input records; sometimes the spaces expand upward, sometimes downward. Just as we see in this verse:

Ezekiel 41:7 The width of the cells increased, story by story, for they surrounded the Temple in the stories that went right round it. (OT)

As in the verse:

Ezekiel, 44:5 Yahweh said to me: Son of man, pay attention, look carefully and listen carefully to everything I explain; these are all the arrangements of the Temple of Yahweh and all its law. (OT)

I began to examine my surroundings even closer at this point. The rooms within rooms of space reminded me of the construction of the house of God detailed in Ezekiel. I wondered if the "house of God" mentioned was in the heavens or on earth or both. In order to fully understand, I compared it to the computer: a computer program must be developed to include the measurements of the house of God mentioned in Ezekiel and will be compared to the concepts mentioned in Jean-Pierre Luminet's article, http://physicsworld.com/cws/article/print/23009)

A Cosmic Hall of Mirrors with WMAP data which show measure-ments of the cosmic microwave background constraining the curvature of the universe and providing hints about its topology.

The control of all streams of space must have been made from the same center to provide continuity.

Thunder, 13:2 God is the One Who has raised up the Heavens without any support you can see. Then he mounted on the throne and regulated the sun and moon, each runs along on a specific course. (Q)

The writing/reading head of the world in each room were governed by the laws of the room and the choices of the people in the rooms, using their free will. Everyone was living his own virtual reality in his own room.

Luqman, *31:20 Do you not see how God has harnessed whatever is in heaven and whatever is on earth for you?* **(Q)**

The Bees, *16:12 He has regulated night and daylight for you, while the sun moon and stars are subjected to his command.* **(Q)**

Just as a computer can run hundreds and thousands of programs at the same moment, in space there are an unlimited number of virtual lives being run simultaneously?

I Corinthians, *12:11 All these are the work of one and the same Spirit, who distributes gifts to different people, just as he chooses.* **(NT)**

I Corinthians, *12:6 Working in all sorts of different ways in different people, it is the same God who is working in all of them.* **(NT)**

The Table,*5:48 We have given each of you a code of law plus a program (for action).* **(Q)**

I was able to see who was in each room, but was unable to see what he was experiencing. According to the area of the writing /reading head of the earth, and according to the virtual reality developed in the brain of the person within each room at the speed of light, and the person's choices were being made and recorded there.

II Corinthians, *3:18 Where the spirit of the Lord is, there is freedom. And we with our unveiled faces reflecting like mirrors the brightness of the Lord, all grow brighter as we are turned into the image that we reflect.* **(NT)**

Like a movie screen, the frame of the picture on the screen appeared and disappeared. Was a computer screen not the same? The frame of the image on the screen appears/ disappears, comes/goes, is zero/one.

In a summary of the film, *"What the Blip do we know?"* by Fred Alan WOLF, Ph.D. *"They are at different places at the same time," "That's one thing. The same thing is at both places," "material is, and then it isn't. This means that this dimension goes and comes into another dimension."* In fact, it does not change dimensions: as the hard disk's reader head switches to another frame, it neutralizes the image in the previous frame, brings it to zero, and because it is about to activate the next frame, the image on the screen, goes from one to zero–zero to one constantly renewing itself. The areas between the images are perceived as nothing (empty) or as going from one place to another. The current dimension is continually being renewed, it does not go anywhere between image frames.

Space appearing to have no purpose stood before me, a living hard-disk made up of microorganisms which were directed by light.

As my guide coughed shortly, I emerged from my thoughts, "**The Creator is giving to get return**" I said.

Thomas Aquinas: What? **"Only God can give without receiving?"** Are you saying these words are not true?

When I analyzed the system, I found that the saying **"Only God can give without receiving,"** should be **"the Creator who gives to receive"** and I discerned the divine power given to man by the Creator.

My beloved guide, let us think of a situation in which you begin a trip in the city with your car and that a helicopter is secretly following you. In this situation, the person in the helicopter will know which streets you take, the speed you use and the route you take, if you are following the rules or not and all of your choices. Again, because the person in the helicopter is looking from above you, he will be able to see all the street options you have and all the buildings you could visit along the way, but would not be able to know which streets and which buildings you would choose. Because he is forced to follow you, if you suddenly reverse or turn left or right, the person in the helicopter, knowing what you are doing and what your choices are, takes action accordingly.

Ezekiel, *1:19-20 "When the animals went forward, the wheels went forward beside them; and when the animals left the ground, the wheels too left the ground.* **Where the spirit urged them, there the wheels went, since the spirit of the animal was in the wheels." (OT)**

This is because the person in the helicopter, aiming to learn our preferences, has given you permission to drive and direct the helicopter.

*Deuteronomy, 8:2 "Remember how Yahweh, your God, led you for forty years in the wilderness, to humble you, to test you and know your inmost heart-whether you would keep his commandments or not." **(OT)***
*Yunus, 10:14 Then we place you as overlords on earth after them, so We might see how you would act. **(Q)***
The Holy Prophet,** 11:7 (He did this) so He may test which of you is finest in action. **(Q)

It can be seen in these verses, as **God has given us sovereignty over the earth in order to learn what we do; is this not giving to receive?**

Thomas Aquinas: Did you find only three scriptures in the Holy Books to support this conclusion?

Of course, these three are just from the beginning scriptures. When all scriptures in this vein are collected and examined, a course of **give to receive** emerges. Allow me to explain in detail with examples from a racecourse;

Think of a small town that has been emptied out to provide a racetrack to be used for pre-race trials in order to determine which of the cars will enter the final race. According to the level and the category they request, let's give the candidates the cars they want and set the start and finishing points.

*Psalms, 16:11 You will reveal the path of life to me. **(OT)***
*Psalms, 139:3 You examine me and know me, you know if I am standing or sitting, you read my thoughts from far away. **(OT)***

Judges who follow and evaluate the candidates by helicopter, record their actions and know the choice of route available, but do not know what route the candidates will take. The purpose of the race is to determine where and how the contestants will go.

Job, *28:23-24 God alone has traced its path and found out where it lives, (For he sees to the ends of the earth and observes all that lies under heaven.* **(OT)**

Psalms, *33:13-14 Yahweh looks down from heaven, he sees the whole human race from where he sits he watches all who live on the earth.* **(OT)**

Mohammed,*47:19 God knows how you (all) bustle about on your business and where you settle down.* **(Q)**

Thomas Aquinas: If you remember, Nietzsche said, *"Until a person reaches a certain freedom in their mind, he will not think of himself as a traveler on the earth, because that is not the point."*

Yes, and in the continuation of those words he said, *"But he will want to keep his eyes open to see what is happening throughout the world. So he should not set his heart fast on anything, but must find something temporary and different, something moving in his being."* I think we should allow our hearts to be free and be careful of the false guides and traps on our course.

Job, *18:10-11 Hidden in the earth is a noose to snare him*. **(OT)**

Matthew, *10:16 Remember, I am sending you out like sheep among wolves, so be cunning as serpents and yet as harmless as doves.* **(NT)**

Yunus, *10 :89 So act straightforward and do not follow along the way of those who do not know.* **(Q)**

The Elevated Places, *7:16 (Satan) said: Since you have let me wonder off, I'll waylay them along Your Straight Road.* **(Q)**

Usually racers in a race like this, make the following choices:

1. They do not try to race or leave the race after a short time (suicide). A man killing himself is murder, too. Therefore, suicide is murder of the spirit, it is to become a murderer.

The Believer, 40:11 Is there a way to escape from here? (Q)
The Counsel, 42:44 And whomsoever Allah makes err, he has no guardian after Him; and you shall see the unjust, when they see the punishment, saying: Is there any way to return? (Q)

2. They do not take the race seriously and ride around aimlessly.

They do not like this world enough. Couldn't your lack of striving be due to the fact that you have experienced better before?

Ecclesiastes, 6:12 Who knows what is good for man in his lifetime, in those few days he lives so vainly, days that like a shadow he spends? (OT)

3. Some, pull the car over, and beg the people in the helicopter to tell them the right road to take. They want the people in the helicopter to take pity on them and show them pity. Instead of racing they stop racing and begin to put on shows meant to depict begging.

Psalms, 139:24 God, examine me and know my heart, probe and know my thoughts, make sure I do not follow pernicious ways, and guide me in the way that is everlasting. (OT)
The Immunity, 9:60 God and his messenger will give us something out of His bounty. (Q)

4. Some, ask those in the helicopter to show them the path to help them along their way suggesting gifts and making promises with bribery in mind. They attempt to prove themselves with hairstyles, beards and the style of clothing they wear.

Ezekiel 1:28, 2:1 *"It was something that looked like the glory of Yahweh, I looked and prostrated myself, and I **heard** a voice speak.*
*It said, 'Son of man, stand up; I am going to speak to you.' **(OT)***
Job,** 6:22 "Have I said to you: "Give me this or that, bribe someone for me at your own cost." **(OT)
Matthew,** 6:7 In your prayers do not babble as the pagans do for they think that by using many words they will make themselves heard. Do not be like them; your Father knows before you ask him. **(NT)
The Kingdom,** 67:22 And is someone who walks along with his face bent down better guided than someone who walks properly along a Straight Road? **(Q)

5. There are those who are satisfied with what they have and try to reach the goal.

6. Some both continue on their way and implore the persons in the helicopter, saying, "Give me a faster car, this one goes too slow, check up on me, I am ready for more serious tests! What must I do to break the record?" (This is a request to raise their level.)

The Cow,** 2:104 You who believe, do not say: "Herd us," and say (instead): "Watch over us" and then "Listen." **(Q)

 7. Those who understand the system are in the most highly ranked part of the afterlife. They are the new inheritors of the system and want to manage it. As you see, I pass the tests of this system easily. I solved the function of the system. These races no longer pleasure me, I want to go up to the helicopter, I want to be among those that run the course and the set the race and evaluate the results.

Psalms,** 37:29 The virtuous will have the land for their own and make it their home forever. **(OT)
I Peter,** 1:4 And the promise of an inheritance that can never be spoiled or soiled and never fade away, because it is being kept for you in the heavens. **(NT)
The Companions,** 39:73 They will say: "Praise be to God Who has held True to His promise for us and let us inherit the earth!" **(Q)

In Stephen Hawking's book, "Black Holes and Baby Universes" he says, *"We may break through to a complete theory of the universe. In that case, we would indeed be Masters of the Universe."*(page xiv), *"If you understand how the universe operates, in a way you control."* (page 4)

Whoever knows the system, controls the system. I would add that the important thing is to be able to survive after understanding the system. Therefore, 1998 in the book *"I'm Ready, Let it Begin"* I insured all readers against shock. (**Virtual god-1.0 version**)

Thomas Aquinas: Those who blame satan for their sins, and blame their parents for their birth, harbor themselves to satan's palliativity when they lose the race. And they also try to find someone to address their own failure by saying *"Satan mislead me! He enticed me!"* I hope, God willing, you publish the things you have seen here. So do you say there is no fate?

I think the Creator's most important power is justice, to make me believe in.

Thomas Aquinas: I really can't see the connection between fate and justice.

One of the basics in all religions calls on followers to specifically provide for widows and orphans. It works like a social security system in law and order.

James,1:27 *Religion that is pure and undefiled before God, the Father, is this: to care for orphans and widows in their distress, and to keep oneself unstained by the world.* **(NT)**

If, as is said in the scriptures, God is the judge of all people in heaven and earth, each will be provided for as he deserves.

Psalms, *7:11 God the righteous judge...***(OT)**
Romans, *9:14 Does it follow that God is unjust? Of course, not.* **(NT)**
The Fig, *95:8 Is God not the wisest of those who judge?* **(Q)**

This justice is not a justice dependent on the result of a trial, it is the justice of expectations.

Deuteronomy, *30:11 For this law that I enjoin on you today is not beyond your strength or beyond your reach.* **(OT)**
The Cow, *2:233 Yet no person is charged with more than he can cope with.* **(Q)**

In short, it is said that "justice is the basis of the system." Since we have three periods to live in our life, **birth, life, and death** there must be three different tiers with **three different justice systems** applied. (Isn't that the way the world is: before the test, the test and after the test?)
The story of creation in both religion and scientific scenarios include an unreachable place and unfortunately, the details are experienced. There are two general thoughts on fate:

* Our Creator, in what is sometimes referred to as the writing on our foreheads, has determined what we will experience at the beginning of our lives. The person created is only responsible for living those things at birth, death and in between. If everything has been determined by the Creator, free will, or a person being responsible for what he does, cannot be judged because that has not been set up, therefore, there is no meaning to judgment.

* In the second approach, man's fate is in his own hands and he determines his whole future himself.

Thomas Aquinas: Is the system of complete surrender valid, as seen in religion?

When we say complete surrender, we leave the solution of our problems to everything outside ourselves; our sins to Satan, our traffic problems to the traffic monster, our money problems to God, so we believe all our problems will be solved by patience and no effort. While we could be using our patience to work, strive, and prevail, we use it in waiting while we do nothing. To rid ourselves of the responsibility of work we act as if we don't see our power.

James, *1:22 But you must do what the word tells you and not just listen to it and deceive yourselves.* **(NT)**
The Spider, *29:58 The ones who believe and perform honorable deeds (will be rewarded).* **(Q)**

A good example of this is the Turkish politician called "Father", Suleyman Demirel. (Served as Prime Minister and State President for many years.)

The "rule of one" or dictatorship in Indonesia as explained by the leader, Sakurna, in literary terms as a "Feeling Democracy" or a "Family Democracy" with himself shown as the "Father." In the beginning the majority of Indonesians were content to accept this "Family democracy," and "leave all the work to Father"; it was convenient.

In a country, where God is often referred to as "Father God", and the government is referred to as the "Father State" where family values are high, like Turkey, one of the reasons for his long-lived political career is undoubtedly the fact that Suleyman Demirel was known as "Father."

Thomas Aquinas: What do you think we should understand when we say complete surrender?

It is knowing our limits and our power, therefore knowing ourselves. In direct contradiction to leaving everything to God, it is not struggling with the universe, saying I am going to determine my fate, either. Actually, in the period we live, it means establishing and applying an ergonomic system within the universe.

Thomas Aquinas: How is the threefold justice construct you mentioned before applied?

1. Justice applied at birth:

Before you enter earth, in order to take the determination test you must complete the "Application for Earth". According to you physical health, the points you earned in the first level and your purpose for applying, you determine the criteria and enter the system by choosing the country, family, historical era, environment, economic status and other items. Using these criterion you determine the initial virtual scenario you will use to enter the system. The Application for Earth is clearly mentioned in the scriptures.

Proverbs, *16:9 A man's heart plans out his way, but it is Yahweh who makes his steps secure. **(OT)***
Ezekiel, *7:3 Judge you as your conduct deserves. **(OT)***

I Corinthians, 11:28-29 Everyone is to recollect himself before eating this bread and drinking this cup; because a person who eats and drinks without recognizing the body is eating and drinking his own condemnation. **(NT)**

James, 1:12-14 Never when you have been tempted say, "God sent the temptation;" God cannot be tempted to do anything wrong and he does not tempt anybody. Everyone who is tempted, is attracted and seduced by his own wrong desire. **(NT)**

Abraham, 14:34 He gives you everything you ever ask Him for. **(Q)**

The Elevated Places, 7:42 We never assign any soul more that it can cope with. **(Q)**

Yunus, 10:30 There each soul will be tested for whatever it has sent on ahead in the past. **(Q)**

In virtual environments, one of the most important choices is the identification of the virtual family (mother/father). Here is a simple question: Did your mother and father choose you as you came into the world? Or was it a mutual understanding? Be careful! The answer you give is an indication of the strength of your position in and against life.

Jeremiah, 4:18 Your own behavior and actions have brought this on you. **(OT)**

Luqman, 31:14 We have commissioned every man to (look after) his parents: **(Q)**

Romans, 30:36 Yet if any evil should strike them because of what their hands have sent on ahead, then they feel despondent. **(Q)**

It clearly indicates that the virtual scenarios you are living in are illusions, a shadow of reality, a copy of reality. And these scenarios have no beginning.

Job, 8:9 Our life on earth passes like a shadow. **(OT)**

Colossians, 2:17 These were only pale reflections of what was coming, the reality. **(NT)**

Hebrews, 8:5 And these only maintain the service of a model or a reflection of the heavenly realities. **(NT)**

I think that there is a specified work force; the one finishing the fastest with the least will pass the test. In this situation, what kind of a scenario/ life course would you choose for yourself? Please carefully complete the "Application for Earth," you find below. (If there are different choices on *your* application form, please let me know at www.aydinturkgucu.net)

As I have said before, in my life, I have accepted this world as life course within my chosen virtual/simulated scenario in which to test my breaking point. Therefore I begin the day with the statement I wrote on the back of my front door **"I'm ready, let it begin."** I chose a scenario less used. I convinced myself that I had not stopped there, but that I had completed the most difficult form so that I would improve my state and stay on the road. (In order to attain a higher degree of endurance than those who came before on the same life course.)

The main outline of a form I believe I could have completed before I entered this life is like this:

Application For Earth
(The Fewer the Resources the More Points)

***The Cattle,** 6:94 You have (all) come to Us now. Just as We created you in the first place. You have left behind what we conferred on you.* **(Q)**
__I Peter,__ 1:7 Your faith will have been tested and proved like gold-only it is more precious than gold. **(NT)**

APPLICATION FOR EARTH	
SUBJECT	**VALUE**
Subject factor Which subject do you wish to test: Profession, heroism, administration, talents, justice, marriage, courage, a combination of these or all?	—
Period Factor Higher points for promises quickly kept	1/life
Term Beginning Factor The later the date the higher the possibilities and education. Higher points for fewer possibilities	1/birth year
Financial/psychological support from family factor Higher points for persons closer and fewer for family that understand and support you. Mother/father=3, Sibling=2, other relative=1	1/person x value + 1/ person x value +….
Financial/psychological support from others factor Higher points for lower number of persons who understand or support you. i.e. You choose a person from your family to help. Since it is family, you get fewer points. When you choose someone from your outer circle of friends, since you have to contact that person somehow to get help, you get extra points for the trouble. Close=1, Unknown=2, Enemies=3 (gaining the respect of your enemies gains you higher points)	1/person x value + 1/ person x value +…

Financial/psychological help from your work place Factor The life course is above all a fight to stay alive. Therefore, help from your work friends is very important.	1/person
Health factor or physical capability factor (HF) This reminds me of people at the beach who claim they can swim well; when someone claims he could swim a certain distance with one arm, for example. Anything that would hinder will increase points. For those who feel that if they have a certain illness they will finish sooner; Asthma/rheumatic fever=4, heart=5, partial blindness=6, hand/foot=7, ALS =10	Health factor 1 + Health factor 2 + Health factor 3 …
Education level factor Reducing: Whatever education level you mark that is below standard levels will be an extra point. Increasing: the upper level you can attain is measured. Any level you attain above the level you chose will give you an extra point.	1/level + Level +1 + Level 2 + …
Spouse by your side factor On the racecourse of life, a spouse is a great help to the soul. The longer you can delay marking this field, the more points you will have. I wonder if those who never marry did not check this factor.	Marriage year
Number of problem children factor When children become caring adults, they can make life easier; if in childhood or adulthood, they are ill or somehow abnormal they can make life difficult. In this case, the abnormal child can add points.	Number of abnormal children

Difficult Environment Think of the things you have succeeded doing in your life; if you had a chance to repeat them would you be able to do them is such difficult, Justice, War, Global warming, environments? Economic crisis	Sum of the fields of difficulty
Economic Situation Factor Think of this as the initial investment. There is a difference in succeeding from poverty and from wealth. Each situation has its pluses and minuses. But money is a serious support. So the less the initial investment, the more points gained. The important thing here is not where you began, but what you contributed.	1/beginning investment
Country Factor What country will you be doing what you intended to do: England, USA, Germany, Turkey, Iraq, China, Russia, the Far East, African countries etc. Each one has plus or minus points according to the situations surrounding your subject in that country in the period you live there: more difficult = more points.	1/country
General TOTAL	
Name, Surname	Signature

Now, please take a paper and pen in hand, and ask yourself "what type of form could I have filled out when entering earth?" Then complete it. When you have completed the form put it up on the back of the front door and write, "I am ready, let it begin," next to it.

Begin each new day by saying **"I am ready, let it begin"** as you open the door. It has certainly helped me and others who have used this method. I feel sure it will help you, too.

*James, 1:12 "Happy is the man who stands firm when trials come." **(NT)***

Who knows, you may have some difficulties of your own choosing.

The Family of Imran,** 3:182 That (has happened) because of what your hands sent on ahead. God is no One to harm (His) worshippers. **(Q)

Thomas Aquinas: In this situation, you have divided fate into two: permanent fate and changeable fate. Let us assume that we marked the form before we came to earth; once we are here is there any chance of changing it?

In that we call fate, God may set most of what we experience, but we also have a big say in it, because God is not a puppeteer but does set the scene. If you want to change it, I am suggesting that you can say, **"I am sending a request that you change my choice of … on my Application for Earth to …"**

In 1994, I was home alone one evening after a particularly stressful day, at a time when my life was upside down financially and emotionally. I suddenly began to feel tense, and began to experience the world in a supernormal way, as if I could no longer fit into my skin. The discomfort continued to increase. Speaking to people, going out and other normal activities no longer sufficed; in short, humanity and this world were not enough and I was in an ever increasing panic. In distress I could not identify, and losing control of my perception and body I began to think: "I'm going mad."

At this point when what I was experiencing was not enough, the angels that the Creator gave for humans to control and the fact that some angels may be under my control came to mind. I spread my arms and cried out: "All angels responsible for me, all angels and other beings under my command, I am calling you to come here. Come here immediately and help me." Within two or three minutes I was sleeping peacefully. In this experience I have learned that prayer is not just begging but words of command. (I believe I'd probably summoned the technical service I saw years later in the film *Vanilla Sky.*[3])

---

[3] (**Vanilla Sky** is a 2001 American psychological thriller film, which has been variously characterized by published film critics as "an odd mixture of science fiction, romance, and reality warp", "part Beautiful People fantasy, part New Age investigation of the Great Beyond", a "love story, a struggle for the soul, or an existential confrontation with the eternal", and an "erotic adventure, romance, comedy, mystery and psychological thriller, with a dose of science fiction".)

I Corinthians, 6:2-3 *Since we are also to judge angels, it follows that we can judge matters of everyday life.* **(NT)**

The Kneeling, 45:13 *He has subjected whatever is in heaven and whatever is on earth to you.* **(Q)**

Saba, 34:12 (1) *And there were Jinns that worked in front of him, by the leave of his Lord.* **(Q)**

As another method I used: I have always believed that each person has the right to use a joker a few times in his lifetime. In times of great difficulties and in circumstances in which I normally could not have succeeded, I twice used this belief and thought: "If, I have the right to use a few jokers in my lifetime I want to use one now and ask for emergency help!" Both times it brought help.

Each strong thought is a prayer.

Thomas Aquinas: Are there other methods you have used?

Years ago I wrote, "A lucky family is one in which the parents are given the chance to experience the benefits of their children and the children are given the chance to be of benefit to the parents who raised them before they die. (9/10/1995)." This statement stemmed from the fact that my father was in intensive care during that time. And having lived in another city for a long time and being young, I had not spared much time for my family. In short, I had not done my share of duties as a son. (They had not experienced the benefits of me, their child.)

I sat at the feet of my father's bed in the intensive care unit and prayed: "My Lord, I want an additional period of healthy life for my father so that I can fulfill my duties as a son. If necessary take these years from my own life. Please don't send him away like this, and leave me behind like this." My father recovered and was released from the hospital in a few days and lived a healthy happy life for five or six years before he died, providing me the opportunity I'd prayed for.

People living on the street affect me a lot. When I have the means and the opportunity I help them. At times when I don't have the time to stop and give them something, I put my EFT (Electronic Forwarding System) into play, and say, "I would like to have a certain amount of money taken from my account and given to this person, for your information." I don't know if it reaches them or not. But I believe it does.

Saba, *34:12 (2) (Solomon)…there were some sprites who worked in front of him by his Lord's permission.* **(Q)**

Look at an interesting scripture concerning the course;

Luqman, *31:33 So do not let worldly life deceive you, nor even let the Deceiver deceive you concerning God* **(Q)**
Iron, *57:14 You tempted one another, and let yourselves waver and doubt. Your saying "Amens" to everyone has deceived you until God's command came along. The Deceiver has even deluded you concerning God.* **(Q)**

Of course, when looking at the classic view of these verses, passed down through the centuries, the devil who is the "disastrous/ insidious deceiver" has used the name of God to lead people astray. If you insist that today's Holy Books which are meant for all times, came centuries ago, were translated and cannot be reevaluated (or that they are historical), it means that those verses that were meant for these times, due to lack of methods and knowledge with which to translate them, do not shine on the problems of today.

I. Samuel, *2:3 Talk no more so very proudly, let not arrogance come from your mouth; for the Lord is a God of knowledge, and by him actions are weighed* **(OT)**
II Timothy, *4:4 And then instead of listening to the truth they will turn to myths.* **(NT)**

Those who say, "Our Holy Book is not a book of science" are creating a false image as if "there is no technological side to the Holy Books." Conversion of the Holy Books into "a guide for social life" is happening although technological verses exist.

Holy Books only show us the path to take in our social life. If you say that the "the Holy Books are not books of science" it means that you do not accept the technological aspects of the Holy Books.

If we evaluate the same verses from the point where technology is today according to a scientific model, the meaning will change. At this point, with manipulation of the sense centers, the natural reactions of those people on a virtual life course are being monitored; this could be understood to be a virtual god.

Thomas Aquinas: A simulation of God?

"The frogs in the bottom of the well, think that the stars they see within the circumference in of the opening of the well are all there are." I like this metaphor: a wonderful description of those who attempt to explain the future from a more limited perspective than the prevailing information available.

Job, 8:8-9 Question the generation that has passed, meditate on the experience of its fathers, We sons of yesterday know nothing. (OT)
Job, 16:2 How often I have heard all this before! What sorry comforters you are! Is there never to be an end of airy words? What a plague your need to have the last word is! (OT)

Now in answer to your question, and to show you a good example of these verses, I will share a few points with you about Will Wright's god game called SPORE.

Q&A: Will Wright, creator of the Sims
Will Wright is responsible for some of the world's most famous games – but he's really excited the prospect of plugging them directly into his brain Bobbie Johnson guardian.co.uk, October 26 2007
http://www.guardian.co.uk/technology/2007/oct/26/willwright

The game allows the player to develop a species from a microscopic organism to its evolution into a complex animal, its emergence as a social, intelligent being, to its mastery of the planet and then finally to its ascension into space, where it interacts with alien species across the galaxy. Throughout the game, the player's perspective and species change dramatically.
The game is broken up into distinct yet consistent, dependent "phases". The outcome of one phase affects the initial conditions facing the player in the next. Each phase exhibits its own style of play, and has been described by the developers as ten times more complicated than its preceding phase. While players are able to spend as much time as they prefer in each, it is possible to accelerate or skip phases altogether.[23][24] When playing the game for the first time, a player must play through each of the stages in order, unlocking each in turn. Some phases feature optional missions; when the player completes a mission, they are granted a bonus, such as a new ability.
If all of a player's creations are completely destroyed at some point, then that players species will be respawned at its home base.

Q & A: Spore creator Will Wright Video game maker hopes new 'Sim Everything' game opens doors for science August 29, 2008, by Paul Jay CBC News

A screenshot of the game's creature creator, which allows players to customize their life form. (Electronic Arts) A screenshot from the game's final chapter, where players guide their civilization to galactic exploration. (Electronic Arts)

There's a perception of science in some ways as something that's either esoteric and inaccessible, that's done in universities with lots of equipment or something that's very impersonal. The universe has these laws that are set this way for arbitrary reasons, etc., etc. Whereas when we have immiscible entertainment experiences we tend to think of those personal and very connected and very centered on us. I think that's the bridge I was trying to build.

Divorce, *65:12 God is the One Who created seven heavens and the same (number of planets) which are like the earth.* **(Q)**

Thomas Aquinas: Why don't we remember these steps and the application we made and why don't we realize life is a game?
In the book *"Book without a Name"* (1995) I wondered if the reason for hiding our entry into the world from us was not because *"if we knew, we would not want to come."* (page 148)

Hebrews, *11:15 They can hardly have meant the country they came from, since they had the opportunity to go back to it.* **(NT)**

When I saw this verse I was very surprised; it meant that those who don't wish to come to earth need not come to earth. It is their decision.

Acts, *3:25 (You are) the Heirs of the covenant God made with our ancestors* **(NT)**

As I have always said, it all stems from not understanding the system. The logic is simple, if you remember, you will play a role, and instead of being as you want to be, you will be as you think you should be. Why does God hide from us the reason why we came and where we came from?

In previous conversations on this trip, we said, "Those who rule senses rule emotions." When the communication of the brain and its downloading system are understood, man will be able to program the past and the future and manipulate everything in life. Just as the Holy Books indicate;

Jeremiah, 1:9-10 Then Yahweh put out his hand and touched my mouth and said to me; "There! I am putting my words into your mouth, look, today I am setting you over nations and over kingdoms, to tear up and knock down, to destroy and over throw, to build and to plant." (OT)

Jeremiah, 31:33 Deep within them I will plant my Law, writing it on their hearts. Then I will be their God, and they will be my people. (OT)

Acts, 16:14 And the Lord opened her heart to accept what Paul was saying. (NT)

The Holy Prophet ,11:47 We will strip away any rancor that (lingers) in their breasts; like brethren they will face one another on couches. (Q)

Women, 4:128 …greed is ever present in our souls. (Q)

The Elevated Places, 7:43   And we will strip away any rancor that lingers in their breast. (Q)

In these verses it is clearly stated that on this life course, our thoughts and lives can easily be manipulated.

It is the time to pay attention and work and hang on with the choices you made on the Application for Earth and the level determination test. Are you ready to show yourself on the life course?

2. Justice during life (fate on the life course):

I Corinthians, 15:53-54 Because our present perishable nature must put on imperishability and this mortal nature must put on immortality. When this perishable has put on imperishability and when this mortal nature has put on immortality, then the words of the scripture will come true. (NT)

1 Timothy, 3:10 They are to be examined first, and only admitted to serve as deacons if there is nothing against them. (NT)

You have a different mission with every live thing you contact. I.e. Spouse: the relationship you have today with your spouse is the sum total of all positive and all negative behavior to date. Stephen Hawking puts it technically in *A Short History of Time* page 141: *"Probability that the particle, say, passes through some particular point is found by adding up the waves associated with **every possible history that passes through that point**…On must add up the waves for particle histories that are not **in the "real" time that you and I experience but take place in what is called imaginary time. Imaginary** time may sound like science fiction but it is in fact **a well-defined mathematical concept."***

As the famous heart specialist, Dr. Mehmet Öz has said, *"For a certain period your body warns you. After a certain point you are forced to follow your body and begin a diet."* We do the same with our bodies; in the beginning we live life the way we want to in relationships, after a while we are forced to want to live the way we should. Any experienced person watching us from a distance can tell us how long the first part of our life will be, or easily guess what awaits us in the second part.

In summary, the choices we made from the available choices and the plus and minus situations are general ready for our use. With the positives **(+)** and negatives **(–)** you use, your plan will change. In addition to your father and mother, siblings, spouse, relatives, friends, neighbors, cat, dog, bird, even your house and car are all part of your fate.

It is like playing chess on the computer. You make a move and that makes you move according to the plan the computer comes up with after using the previous moves and millions of configurations and calculations to figure the future moves possible to you. As Stephen Hawking said in *Black Holes and Baby Universes* page 76, *"This means that what happened in imaginary time could be calculated. **And if you know the history of the universe in imaginary time, you can calculate how it behaves in real time**. In this way you could hope to get a complete unified theory, one that would predict everything in the universe."*

After a move different from what the computer expects you to make, after making another million calculations, guesses about your future will change. This is the computer making a decision after the person has made a choice using his free will. Man, too, is able to change the plan for the future with the choice from the scenarios that show up from the system. The most important thing: the human struggles, two against one, against a computer and the computer programmer separately but together simultaneously.

Holy Books have determined the general rules of scenarios you and many others coming before you will come across on the course of life.

Job, 18:10-11 *Hidden in the earth is a noose to snare him, pitfalls lie across his path.* **(OT)**

The Table, 5:48 *We have given each of you a code of law plus a program (for action)…so he may test you by means of what he has given you. (Q)*

The Cow, 2:155 *We shall test you with a bit of fear and hunger, plus a shortage of wealth and souls and produce. Announce such to patient people.* **(Q)**

Mohammad, 47:31 *We will test you till We know those who strive among you as well as those who are patient. We will test your reactions.* **(Q)**

The Elevated Places, 7:129 *They said, "We were oppressed before you came to us, and will be again after you have come to us." He said, "Perhaps your Lord will wipe out your enemy and leave you as overlords on earth, so He may observe how you act.* **(Q)**

Sometimes there is so much confusion that, our hands and arms tied, we are unable to do anything, let alone understand the solution to the problem. It is then that the problem is turned over to the virtual god and that virtual god takes action. **Your job then is to get out of the way, do nothing, wait for the virtual god to complete his action. Instead of doing something untimely, understand the process.** When it is your turn again, you will make your move. (Allow God to show you the way.)

Matthew, 6:34 *"So don't worry about tomorrow; tomorrow will take care of itself. Each day has enough trouble of its own."* **(NT)**

When you go to a psychic to learn about your future, **looking at the present situation will be able to see the plan for the future** and is thus able to tell your future. This is the system's way of communicating to you clues about information it thinks you should have. **"Fortune tellers are the post boxes of the system."** Without the express permission of God does the person you call a psychic have a chance of saying anything?"

The psychic system is one of the most dangerous traps of the system. If you put too much faith in the predictions of fortune tellers and other lower forms of soothsaying, you will begin to live your life accordingly. And you will begin to be a pawn of the system. Since your past is recorded and can be read when wanted, and because they appear to predict the future when they guess, you may think that your future is predetermined. I see all this is as part of the underlying information of the system.

You can test yourself like this: some people know how to behave in every situation they are in. Knowing how you will act in a situation is one type of knowing the future, is it not?

Banishment, *59:18 You who believe, heed God! Let every soul watch out for whatever it has prepared for the morrow.* **(Q)**

On this life course, you also live with virtual figurants.

Thomas Aquinas: Figurants in the system?

The Virtual Does not Realize It Is Virtual

Of course, my dear guide, there are always those who provide the questions, provide whatever is desired and to help solve problems in any multiple choice question examination. At this point, we can take an example from computer games. Think of the car race game. The player chooses the car and the course. The other cars determine the program; you race with your car against three or four other cars chosen by the program. The course on earth is like this: you, your figurants and the figurants of the virtual god are in it together.

The Pilgrimage, *22:7 And because the hour is coming, there is no doubt about it; and because Allah shall raise up those who are in the graves conscious* **(Q)**

Figurants have no intelligence/will of their own. They work in a system we call the central will system. They are virtual robots which are centrally remotely controlled which look like people. They all function by means of the central will. Those that are under your command function only with the approval of the central will.

Isn't that obvious in this verse that some of them are conscious and some of them are not figurants; those who won't be raised up are the figurants of system.

There is no doubt in my mind that the universe is a virtual universe. The interesting thing is to know which of those around us are giving their own decisions and which are functioning at the command of the central will system. The bodies are definitely virtual, but the whole question is which has a real spirit. Virtual or real, that is the question.

If we imagine the opportunities of the future the question of today "Why do we exist?" will turn into "Do we exist?

Jeremiah, 7:27 *You may call them: they will not answer.* *(OT)*

I Corinthians, 15:40 *Then there are heavenly bodies and there are earthly bodies.* *(NT)*

I John, 4:1 *It is not every spirit, my dear people, that you can trust; test them, to see if they come from God.* *(NT)*

Hebrews, 1:14 *The truth is they are all spirits whose work is service, sent to help those who will be the heirs of salvation.* *(NT)*

The Cattle, 6:112 *Thus we have guaranteed each messenger an opponent, devils from humankind and sprites.* *(Q)*

Sometimes in our lives, if we need some emergency help, the person we ask as a friend, but is actually in no position to understand our situation doesn't show up, but a person whom we do not know well, and whom we refer to a bit formally suddenly shows up unexpectedly and helps. The whole point is whether or not these people are virtual or real.

Yunus, 10:4 *He begins with creation then performs it all over again so He may reward those who believe and perform honorable deeds in all fairness.* *(Q)*

Some are actual people and some are simply figurants who appear to be people. We continue to live our lives with the friend/enemy figurant characters mentioned in the Creator's verses.

Psalms, 115: 5-8 *(They) have mouths, but never speak, eyes, but never see, ears, but never hear, noses, but never smell, hands, but never touch, feet but never walk, and not a sound comes from their throats.*

Their makers will end up like them, so will anyone who relies on them. **(OT)**

Romans, *11:8 God has given them a sluggish spirit, unseeing eyes, and inattentive ears, and they are still like that today.* **(NT)**

The Elevated Places, *7:197-198 While those you appeal to instead of Him cannot lend you any supports not do, they even support themselves. If you summon them to guidance, they will not hear, and you will see them looking towards you while they are (really) not seeing.* **(Q)**

The Elevated Places, *7:179 They have hearts they do not understand with, and eyes they do not see with, and ears they do not hear with. Those persons are like livestock; in fact, they are even further off the track, they are so heedless.* **(Q)**

Your fears are only a figment of the truth, dreams/virtual truths given by what might be a simulation of God.

Isaiah, *29:7 Shall vanish like a dream, like a vision at night.* **(OT)**

Colossians, *2:17 These were only pale reflection of what was coming: the reality.* **(NT)**

The Cattle, *6:116 If you obeyed most of those who are on earth, they would lead you astray from God's path; they only follow conjecture and are merely guessing.* **(Q)**

Yunus, *10:36 Most of them merely follow conjecture. However, guessing is no substitute for truth. God is aware of whatever they are doing.* **(Q)**

In classical explanations, the "deceptive, sly" devil has the job of deliberately leading people off course. On a virtual course, isn't the devil given over to us for use when we need him?

The Suad, *38:37-39 And, the devils every builder and diver, as well as others hitched together in a chain gang. Such are Our gifts; grant them freely or hold them back, without and further reckoning.* **(Q)**

Marium, *19:83 Have you not seen how we send devils to disbelievers, to provoke them to fury?* **(Q)**

Thomas Aquinas: If justice is done on the course of life, what is the need for justice in the afterworld?

My dear guide, one of the most important characteristics of the course of life is that if all we experience and think are being recorded, in the phenomenon we call death or at the end of the race, the black boxes can be opened and the results evaluated for the racers.

3. Justice applied after death

(If you could have thought before you fell, you wouldn't be wondering now why you fell.)

There will be one and only question in the afterlife "what was missing for success, except your courage?"

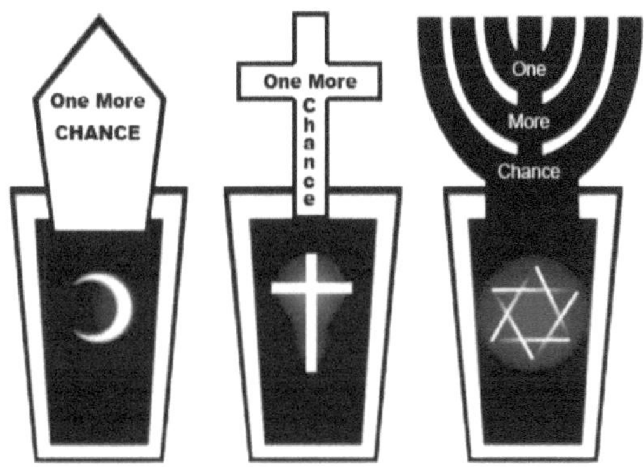

Dying is waking up from sleep and coming out from under of the control of dreams.

Job, 14:12 *But man once in his resting place will never rise again. The heavens will wear away again before he wakes, before he rises from his sleep.* **(OT)**

Psalms, 73:20 *You shrug them off like the phantoms of a morning dream.* **(OT)**

The Great Event, 78:9 *We have created you in pairs and granted you sleeping for repose.* **(Q)**

People believe and were made to believe, that the good and the bad behavior they performed in a lifetime will only be judged in courts after death. **As a result of belief in only the justice system applied after death,** instead of the justice systems applied at birth, during life and after death, a sort of credit card system of payment has developed. Like the person who uses a credit card without knowing the system well, because he does not have money in his pocket at the time, he thinks, "I'll pay for it later, somehow, anyway, who knows how long I'll live? Let's live it up today!" He has temporarily forgotten the payment period in the control system.

I Corinthians, *15:32 You say: Let us eat and drink today; tomorrow we shall be dead.* **(NT)**

But in fact, justice, or fate is experienced precisely during life: "**But people seeing what they want to see and believing what they want to believe, are unable to see the justice system that is applied or turn a blind eye to it**." In short, "explain it however you want to, the person will only understand you to the extent he benefits from it."

People must do what is necessary within the certain time frame of life. In the justice system applied after death, success is dependent on certain things:

* Will you come back on the same level, or an a level, or on a higher level?

* Have you reached the point at which you do not have to return? Has the goal been reached?

Thomas Aquinas: Karen Armstrong in her book "A History of God" *"Karma bound man and women to endless cycles of rebirth into a series of painful lives. But if they could reform their egoistic attitudes, they could change their destiny."* (page 44) Where is the justice without rights to defense?

My dear teacher, this is one type of karma but it does not limit egoistic behavior (sociological). This also is a type of technological karma, developed by man to research and bring out people's hidden talents.

These are the types of questions that are answered and at this point there is no opportunity to defend oneself.

My dear guide, if all is recorded, and documented, what is there to defend? It has been made clear there is nothing to defend because all is recorded.

The Narratives, *28:78 Will not criminals be questioned concerning their offences?* **(Q)**

The Moon, *54:52-53 Every thing they did is (to be found) in the Psalms: everything small or great has been recorded.* **(Q)**

Ya Sin, *36:12 We revive the dead, write down whatever they have sent ahead, and (left) as traces; we calculate everything in an open ledger* **(Q)**

"No, I did not do that! That was not my intention!" These types of defense tactics are not valid. If you are not able to defend yourself with the records, it means that you have no right to speak.

Socrates, as he evaluated the court he was tried in said, *"If death frees me from this world in which truth is not respected, and allows me to be judged in a court that is free from bias, why should I be afraid of death? Let me leave the fear to the thieves and liars of this world."* Since the judge is to be the best:

Psalms, *7:11 God the righteous judge.* **(OT)**

The Fig, *95:8 Is God not the Wisest of those who judge?* **(Q)**

In the afterworld, in a day when no one will be of any help to another, and our mouths will be sealed shut, I will have no right to complain. I am trying to **fight and defend** myself now and show people **who I am** and **what I can do now** while I am still living and can defend myself.

Romans, *14:12 It is to God, therefore, that each of us must give an account of himself.* **(NT)**

The Poets, *26:88 The day when neither wealth nor children will benefit anyone.* **(Q)**

What does God want with a person on the other side, who on earth was ignorant, lazy and a sponger? What does the world want with a person like that?

Thomas Aquinas: Roger C. Shank in the book *The Next 50 Years* in the article "Are we going to be Smarter in the Future?" Says: *"In a realistic performance based educational system it will not matter how much we know, but what we produce that counts."*

You think life to be a test or a life course and have changed it into hell. From this point of view, we are sorely pressed to know which is real and which is a figurant. Are we not constantly asking ourselves that question?

My dear guide, only one of the goals of this creation is "Personal Choice" or 21st century human resources. It is therefore wise for those who are born into the world to watch themselves carefully as the scriptures say.

The Holy Prophet, 11:7 … *(He did this) so He may test which of you is finest in action. (Q)*
The Kingdom, 67:2 *He is capable of (doing) everything, the One Who created death and life, so He may test which of you is finest in action. (Q)*
Mohammad, 47:31 *We will test you till we know those who strive among you as well as those who are patient. We will test your reactions. (Q)*

Thomas Aquinas: There are many things to talk about, but our time is up so you must get back into the elevator. Up or down? (As I said "up, of course!") You always have a choice. These choices are among the choices you prepared in making the choices of the past.

(At that point, the elevator door opened) He said goodbye with the words, **"Your creators are with you, they will give you what you deserve."**

As I reached the elevator, I realized there was no one inside. As I unthinkingly pushed the button for the second floor, the door opened. My maternal grandmother, my grandfather Hamdi, grandfather Nuri, my father, my uncle Dr. Ahmet, his wife aunt Ayten, my uncle Cezmi and my fraternal grandmother appeared. The holograms of my most beloved family, long since dead, were there waiting for me.

Even though I knew they were holograms, I broke all the rules that I had been warned about and embraced them enthusiastically. The holograms were probably astonished thinking it the classic emotional earthling behavior. I was able to collect myself within the three-second time limit: even though they were holograms, I was able to resolve my feelings of having not said proper good byes before they passed over from earth life. I looked at them with curiosity. At that point, the hologram of **Shams-i Tabrizi**[4] appeared at my side.

Shams-i Tabrizi: You completed the course of life successfully. Now you are at a point in heaven where you can meet anyone you wish. Your loved ones want you to join them. What do you say?

(Until that point I had been comfortable, but now that I was asked to make a choice, things had changed. I was faced with the problem of answering my loved ones in heaven that I had questioned on earth and had not quite agreed with.)

Shams-i Tabrizi: What is it that is making you think so hard? Don't you want to be in heaven with your loved ones?

You are my loved ones, whom I believe with both my common sense and in my heart, love me, and I would never hurt you.

Shams-i Tabrizi: It looks as if you are not interested in the heaven where people are dying to get in. What is it about Heaven that makes you hesitate?

As I said, you all love me and I love you. As I read the Holy Books, I saw that the highest level a human being could attain as the level of prophet. In addition, as I wondered what the second highest level for

---

[4] **(Shams-i Tabrizi** or in full, Shams al-Din Mohammad died 1248) was an Iranian[1] Sufi mystic born in the city of Tabriz in Iranian Azerbaijan. He introduced Mawlānā Jalāl ad-Dīn Muhammad Balkhi, usually known as Rumi in the West, to Islamic mysticism, for which he was immortalized in Rumi's poetry collection Diwan-e Shams-i Tabriz-i ("The Works of Shams of Tabriz"). Shams lived together with Rumi in Konya, in present-day Turkey, for several years, and is also known to have traveled to Damascus in present-day Syria.) http://en.wikipedia.org/wiki/Shams_Tabrizi

human beings was and I searched further. I found a third place between heaven and hell in the afterlife and I have prepared myself for that place.

Shams-i Tabrizi: What is the belief you hold about heaven that has caused you not to choose the prize that everyone accepts when he hears the name? Be assured you are not being disrespectful.

I beg the pardon of the Creator and of you; it is not my aim to denigrate the choice of heaven or those who have chosen it. As I read the Holy Books I realized that this third place was exactly what I had chosen on my **Application for Earth.**

In light of the fact that the subject of this level is heaven, I will talk about all the aspects of the heaven of the sociological God that give me concern.

The Heaven of the Sociological God

*(For those who have not had their fill of worldly sustenance,
whose eyes are bigger than their stomachs.)*

On a photograph of yourself standing, mark the areas of your body that correspond to the rewards of heaven. (For example, unlimited food and drink will reward your stomach.) Connect the areas you marked in the photograph with a line. Is the line downward between your navel and genitals or upward between your heart and your brain? Or think of the palaces/jewels that were promised you.

In this world, are we not trying to conquer our ego, the stomach and the genital areas? Have we not changed the sacred heaven into the venial here?

Ezekiel, *28:13 You were in Eden in the garden of God. A thousand gems formed your mantle. Shard, topaz, diamond, chrysolite, onyx, jasper, sapphire, carbuncle, emerald, the gold of which your flutes and tambourines are made, all were prepared on the day of your creation.*
(OT)

Ephesus, *2:3 We all were among them too in the past, living sensual lives, ruled entirely by our own physical desires and our own ideas.* **(NT)**

The Mountain, *52:19Eat and drink at leisure because of what you have been doing.* **(Q)**

The Mountain, *52:22 We will spread out any fruit and meat for them such as they may desire.* **(Q)**

Mohammad, *47:15 (Here) is what the parable of the Garden which the heedful have been promised will be like: it will have river of never stagnant water and rivers of milk whose flavor never changes, and rivers of wine so delicious for those who drink it, and rivers of clarified honey.* **(Q)**

The Beneficent, *55:72 Bright-eyed damsels sheltered in pavilions. (Q)*
The Mountain, 52:23 Young men of theirs will pass around them, as if they were treasured pearls. **(Q)**

Let's think of it this way; Adam and Eve, with the unlimited food and fantasy-filled heaven were so bored that they accepted satan's offer of adventure/excitement even though it meant going against the direct orders of God, and ate the fruit. And satan, promising something to those already in heaven, lured them out of heaven.

Genesis, *2:16-17 Then Yahweh God gave the man this admonition, "You may eat indeed of all the trees in the garden. Nevertheless of the tree of knowledge of good and evil you are not to eat, for on the day you eat of it you shall most surely die."* **(OT)**

What was so attractive that they would want to get out of heaven?

Genesis, *3:5 God knows in fact that on the day you eat it your eyes will be opened and you will be like gods, knowing good and evil.* **(OT)**
Ta Ha, *20:119 Satan whispered to him, he said: "Adam, shall I lead you to the Tree of immortality and such control as will never disappear?"* **(Q)**

In heaven what would fanatic football fans do at matches where our team always played well and the scores were in our favor and we always won every match? In films or matches without conflict and surprise endings, there is not contest, there is no excitement! In short, if the beginning and the end does not contain the excitement of your imagination, fantasies and scenarios, then, man is removed from humanhood and reduced to animal status. Just as sheep do not tire of living in a meadow, in order for man to not tire of heaven, he must not have a memory or must have the memory of a fish.

The point we are trying to reach on earth by taming our ego, is the point where widows and orphans are taken special care of, we are not envious of the property of others or the personal honor of another, we do not take another's possessions, virtuous and courageous, treating all life with love and respect. Is the heaven we have described appropriate to mankind?

Proverbs, *31:8-9 Speak, yourself, on behalf of the dumb, on behalf of all the unwanted, speak yourself, pronounce a just verdict, uphold the rights of the poor of the needy.* **(OT)**

Shams-i Tabrizi: Just as Yunus Emre said:

> *"Heaven, heaven they said*
> *with a few virgins and servants,*
> *God grant that to those who ask,*
> *You are necessary for me, You."*

I discussed this point of the afterlife with my friends, "Aydın, you have taken heaven from us, but please put something in its place, is there a courageous place in heaven for the courageous in the Holy Books?

Qaf, *50:31And the garden shall be brought near to those who guard (against evil), not far off:* **(Q)**
Qaf, *50:35 They have therein what they wish and with Us is more yet.* **(Q)**

This is identifying a work of God such as heaven and hell, using anthropomorphic and worldly parameters heaven is suddenly turned into a place where normally empty stomachs are filled, and hell is turned into a torture center where those same stomachs are burned in fires. On earth, train millions of people to do a specific job, train scientists, train artists, then put them into a heavenly garden with a table of food and a bed, where they could not use their talents. Could God be so wasteful? This also means that nothing is learned in heaven: in this situation, to the virtuous it will be like hell. If a person's heaven consists of earthly needs.

The Third Choice in the Afterworld

The dictionary defines virtue as: "**1)** the general term for ethical goodness including humility, strength, honesty, uprightness etc. **2)** philosophical man's spiritual maturity."

Socrates accepted virtue to be the basic goal of morality. To him virtue was absolute knowledge and attainable through the mind. To be virtuous meant doing wrong to anyone.

Confucius said of virtue: *"Virtue comes with focus on the service not the prize"*

Given the reasons I just mentioned, I do not find heaven desirable. I then asked if there isn't another choice and began research on the Judgment Day. I reasoned that if a prophet had helpers: disciples, Caliphs and assistants, there may be similar hierarchies in the skies.

The verses speak of a separate family life from the place from which we come to earth.

The Resurrection, 75:33 *Then he stalked off haughtily to his family.* **(Q)**
The Companions, 39:15-16 *Say: The losers will be those who have lost their own souls as well as their families' on Resurrection Day. That will be the obvious loss!* **(Q)**
The Counsel, 42:45 *"The losers are the ones who have lost their own souls plus their families on Resurrection Day."* **(Q)**
The Spider, 29:64 *What is the worldly life except: an amusement and a game? Yet the final Home will mean real living, if they only realized it.* **(Q)**
The Rending Asunder, 84:13-14 *He used to be happy with his own people. He supposed he would never revert (to God.)* **(Q)**

I became confused as I read the verses above. Outside heaven and hell is a place where people were with their families before they came into this world. There is a third place where life occurs outside of heaven and hell.

The word Logos in Greek has the meaning of a nuance of reason and is used as a understanding of feelings and another word for *pathos*. It is used to emphasize Reason and reason related words, as law, order or information.

In the fifth century BC Heraclitus explains the logos as that which establishes the "fundamental order of all" and the reason through which all things are made." In this way, logos is both the source and the fundamental order of the cosmos: Logos is the biggest force in the universe: (The last limit human mind can draw/solve) (http://tr.wikipedia/wiki)

John, 1:14 The Word was made flesh, he lived among us and we saw his glory, the glory that is his. **(NT)**

In the Quran, A'raf, a place between heaven and hell and the name of a hill, is mentioned as an interim area. It is also the name of a group of people (people of A'raf).

The Elevated Places, 7:46 Between them both there will hang a curtain, while on the Heights above there will be men who recognize everyone by their futures. **(Q)**
The Elevated Places, 7:48 The Companions on the Heights will call out to some men whom they will recognize by their features. **(Q)**

Karen Armstrong in her book a History of God explains the Biblical Logos: *"Man and woman had a potential for the divine and would only become fully human if this were realized."(page 156)*

*Marcellus, argued that the Logos could not possibly be an eternal divine being. He was **only a quality or potential** inherent within God."* (page 135)

Psalms, 37:29 The virtuous will have the land for their own and make it their home forever. **(OT)**
Psalms, 37:34 Raising you until you make the land your own and see the wicked expelled. **(OT)**
I Peter, 1:4 And the promise of an inheritance that can never be spoilt or soiled and never fade away. **(NT)**
The Originator, 35:32 Then we allow our servants who we have singled out to inherit the Book. **(Q)**

After reading these verses, I knew I had found the team I wanted to be on. I dedicated myself to it. As computer programmer, I had the foundation built. The next step was to unite the data from religion and science, breach the distance between the seen and point of the unseen, make a model of it and publish it.

If the adventure were to be explained as a witness to religious science and science, I would have to obtain the necessary scientific background to understand the data I found. For a religious foundation, I began to study all the Holy Books without prejudice. I modeled the story of Creation and in 1998 published a book called, *I'm Ready, Let it Begin*. As soon as I return to earth, I will publish the new details and the information I have learned.

Shams-i Tabrizi: You are a programmer so you know, just as no one in the world is an exact copy of another, and he must have a unique field name in the directory of a computer. (setup.exe, word.doc, readme.txt)

You also know that in the set up of a computer each program must follow another in order to prevent physical breakdowns. In the event of a breakdown, there must be instant intervention by the technical support team. If the problem is with the program, then that program must be read, evaluated, and rewritten. There is a need for a program control support team to continually monitor the gradation of the difficulties. These could be thought of as inheritors.

My dear teacher, it is not possible to say definitively that everyone was created differently. In a system where everyone has not had their fingerprints taken and without comparing the fingerprints of everyone, it is not possible to say they are different from one another. When technical support and control is added, I would like to make two support quotes from Jaron Lanier as found in the book *The Next Fifty Years*. *"The computer is the only industrial product that is expected to fail frequently and unpredictably during normal operations."*

"There has always been an (only occasionally acknowledged) observer problem in computer science."

As a programmer I would say we are looking at the situation as we want to, but the dictionary defines inheritance this way: (figuratively) "That which one generation leaves for the next generation." And an inheritor as: (figuratively) "A person who puts forth another's good or bad characteristics." A computer that leaves the good and the bad of its system to a computer of the next generation could be said to be an overseer.

A small village would have been enough if God was willing to test just my morals. There was no need for a rich big world and space. If the world was created for a clean and healthy society, there would be a need for others in the skies. If here is made for the development of there, **Here=There**.

Matthew, 16:19 I will give you the keys to the kingdom of heaven: whatever you bind on earth shall be considered bound in heaven; whatever you loose on earth shall be considered loosed in heaven." **(NT)**

The Pilgrimage, 22:11 If some good should happen to him, he accepts it calmly, while if some trial should strike him, he turns over on his face in despair. He loses in both this world and the hereafter **(Q)**

Divorce, 65:12 God is the One Who created seven heavens, and the same number of planets, which are like the earth. **(Q)**

A person thinking in earthly terms may think of physical needs when they hear of heaven. When they hear of hell, they may naturally think of performing ritual worship over great boiling pots and hot coals or any other earthly horrors. These are all earthly physical pains. The punishment in the afterlife of the navel/genital heaven would be hot metal, boiling water, fires and similar things.

However, hell and the state of the soul of the person who is burning in hell and his regrets do not occur to anyone. The regret of the person whose flesh is burning in hell and of having missed the heaven that the soul could have earned is overlooked. Do you think the person burning in hell is burning in pain because his body is burning or because he has missed his chance to be in heaven?

If the earth is an opportunity, and this opportunity is not used, or a test and the test is not passed, that in itself there is plenty of pain. A case in point: a young person who does not pass the college entrance exam is returned to hell for another year until he has another opportunity to take the test.

If the earth is an endurance course, it is a type of hell and is called the racecourse of hell on earth. A person wishing to attain heaven in the skies must go through hell on earth or must turn hell on earth into heaven on earth.

Job, *36:22 What teacher can be compared with him?* **(OT)**
Psalms, *25:8-9 Yahweh is so good, so upright, he teaches the way to sinners: in all that is right he gives the humble, and instructs the poor in his way.* **(OT)**
I Thessalonians, *4:9 Since you have learnt from God yourselves to love one another.* **(NT)**

Since the best teacher is God, he will want our success.

Ezekiel, *18:23 Am I likely to take pleasure in the death of a wicked man, and not prefer to see him renounce his wickedness and live?* **(OT)**

This verse shows clearly that God does not wish the death of a bad person, but wants us to win. As if he was saying "This person, even I couldn't make this person into a good person" and is sending him to hell not a failure? (When I finished my words, my beloved family and teacher, Shams, looked at me with happiness in congratulatory eyes.)

Shams-i Tabrizi: Why don't you find your heaven on earth instead of being with people you love? As a person having questioned the entrance into heaven thus far, have you questioned exit from heaven?

In order to find the reason behind the reason for Adam and Eve being banished from the Garden of Eden, let's examine each verse pertaining to the incident carefully.

Genesis, 2:9 *With the tree of life and the tree of knowledge of good and evil in the middle of the garden.* **(OT)**

Genesis, 2:16-17 *Then Yahweh God gave the man this admonition, "You may eat indeed of all the trees in the garden. Nevertheless of the tree of knowledge of good and evil you are not to eat, for on the day you eat of it you shall most surely die."* **(OT)**

In these verses, God clearly wants man to live in heaven without being aware of good and evil, and without query; unaware. Then satan appears and makes his well known offer.

Genesis, 3:5 *God knows in fact that on the day you eat it your eyes will be opened and you will be like gods, knowing good and evil.* **(OT)**

Adam and Eve had been warned that the punishment for eating of this tree was clearly death. But they wanted to know the divine within and in spite of the threat they accepted Satan's offer and ate the fruit anyway.

Genesis, 3:7 *Then the eyes of both of them were opened and they realized that they were naked.* **(OT)**

Ta Ha, 20:121 *In the result, they both ate of the tree, and so their nakedness appeared to them: they began to sew together, for their covering, leaves from the Garden:* **(Q)**

This is a critical point: before their eyes had been opened Adam's and Eve's eyes must have been closed. Otherwise, how would they then be able to know the beauty and goodness of the place and how could they be held accountable? A person who sees things without his eyes being open is seeing directly from the vision center. Isn't this situation an example of the senses being manipulated in a virtual simulated world called heaven?

Shams-i Tabrizi: Why do you think their eyes were closed in Eden?

If God had wanted it wouldn't he have continued allowing them to live in the Garden of Eden with their eyes open? This is tantamount to saying, in heaven, a condition of closed eyes is a parameter. When your vision center is bombarded with signals from the views you are seeing, and signals from other sources, there will be two visions, one upon the other, which will produce confusion in the vision center. To prevent this confusion, the eyes of those whose visions centers were being stimulated needed to remain closed. (That's why we don't have dreams with our eyes open.)

Romans, *11:8 God has given them a sluggish spirit, unseeing eyes and inattentive ears, and they are still like that today.* **(NT)**

A person, when his eyes are open, will see the truth of the world he finds himself in and will be as if a person awakened from a dream. He will then separate himself from the views of heaven he thinks he has been seeing.

Psalms, *73:20 You shrug them off like the phantoms of a morning dream.* **(OT)**

When they awaken to the real world they will see the directors of their dreams (false heaven) and will understand the truth like they do.

Genesis, *3:22 God said, "See the man has become like one of us, with his knowledge of good and evil." **(OT)***
I John, *1:1-3 Something which has existed since the beginning, that we have heard, and we have seen with our own eyes; that we have watched and touched with our hands, the Word who is life- this is our subject. That life was made visible: we saw it and we are giving our testimony telling you of the eternal life, which was with the Father and has been made visible to us. What we have seen and heard we are telling you so that you to may be in union with us.* **(NT)**

Here, the words "he has become like one of us" show that the truth has been seen/learned or his eyes have been opened. Let me draw your attention to the word "like" here; he has become "like" one of us.

Genesis, *3:24 He banished the man and in front (east) of the garden of Eden he posted the cherubs, and the flame of a flashing sword, to guard the way to the tree of life.* **(OT)**

In short, they were thrown out of Eden and the tree of life was protected so that others would not have their eyes opened (so they would not claim their human rights). In particular, the eastern part of the garden was fitted with a security system of fire.

In a divine system could there possibly be such a security problem, particularly in the fear that there would be an attack from the east? It can easily be seen that when our eyes are shut we are living in a universe we think is a universe.

Shams-i Tabrizi: How do you explain the "we" in these verses?

The Creator of everything, since he would not have a security problem, would not have had these problems and fears. It means that these problems are connected to the group called "we." By researching the scriptures closer we can better see what the group called "we" are.

The main problem stems from the fact that the Holy Books appear to explain two levels of creators. Just when we feel there is one Creator that created everything, then we see that there is something that refers to themselves in the plural; a group who appears to be tending a second universe. (Like a parallel universe.) Let's look at an example of this:

The Rock, *15:9 We our self have sent down the Reminder just as We are safeguarding it.* **(Q)**

As Rumi says*: "The face that is seen, forms the proof of the face in another realm, the realm of mercy. And that body was taken from another unknown face of mercy. (2887)*

Yunus, *10:29* **GOD***(1) suffices as a Witness between* **US***(2) and* **YOU***(3)* **(Q)**

Please pay attention to the three sides identified here. (We, You and God)

Now let's look at a verse that mentions a council, another type of management.

__I Corinthians,__ 7:31 And those who have to deal with the world should not become engrossed in it. **(NT)**
__Revelations,__ 4:4 Round the throne in a circle were twenty-four thrones and on them I saw twenty four elders sitting dressed in white robes with golden crowns on their heads. **(NT)**
__The Rangers,__ 37:164-166 There is none of us but he has acknowledged status. We are drawn up in ranks. We are those who glorify God. (Q)
__The Suad,__ 38:69 I have no knowledge of the supreme council such as they claim to have. **(Q)**
__The Rangers,__ 37:9 Against every stubborn devil so they may not listen to the supreme council. **(Q)**

Remember in the film Contact when Jodie Foster spoke to the spaceman in the form of her father, *"Do they all travel her through that transit system you built?"* He answered, *"We didn't make the system; we don't know who did. They left a long time before we came here. Maybe one day they will return."*

There is a very interesting verse that explains that part of the film.

__The Jinn,__ 72:8-11 We reached out for heaven and found it staffed with stern guards and shooting stars. We use to squat in some of its seats to listen, though anyone who eavesdrops now finds a shooting star lurking there for him. We do not know whether evil is intended for anyone on earth or their Lord wants integrity for them. Some of us are honorable while others of us are quite the opposite of that. We travel along such diverse routes. **(Q)**

Then right afterwards those who refer to themselves in the plural profess the singularity of God.

__Ta-Ha,__ 20:98 (1) Your God is God (alone), there is no deity other than Him! **(Q)**
__Ta Ha,__ 20:99 Thus do We relate to thee some stories of what happened before: **(Q)**

As you can see, it says "your God" and from "your level." The Council has a problem of safety and protection as does the tree of life in God's heaven. In a virtual world that has been made up from information available, this system will first be projected in thought because it has lived through thought.

Ta Ha, 20:98 -99(2) He is Vaster than everything in knowledge. - We have given to you a Reminder from Our level **(Q)**
***The Cave,** 18:91 That was how We controlled information about whatever lay before him.* **(Q)**

If we are unable to live outside our world for only a short time, it means that it is forbidden for us to leave. In this situation the world is a big garden of wondrous beauty and is protected by walls in the skies that are unseen to man. We could call it a classic prison, protected by information. (No way out!)

You only know that you are in a prison when you try to leave it.

***Qaf,** 50:36 They were much braver than they are and stormed through the land. Yet had they any escape?* **(Q)**

Shams-i Tabrizi: In a virtual environment why is there no way out for a physical body?

If man is only able to attain heaven through virtuous living, when only a very small stage is needed to test those virtues, why has God seen fit to show mankind an infinite macro universe or minus infinite micro universe? Since mankind in the face of this splendor, feels insignificant, like a drop in the ocean, is it not disproportional use of knowledge and power?
I think that this disproportionate feeling is triggered as a way of warning, as if saying that man should not even attempt to explore or understand (the universe) because it is far beyond his capacity.

***Job,** 5:9 His worlds are great, past all reckoning, marvels beyond all counting.* **(OT)**

When mankind, losing hope of understanding the world he sees and leaving it, decides to stay in a virtual world, he will forget his quest for divinity, will return to pursue daily goals in a virtual reality.

Finding the divine within, in addition to love, peace, brotherhood, is discovering the feeling that man can create the universe. In some belief systems it is forbidden to make sculptures. Perhaps this is an effort to stifle the rise of suppressed divinity.

Shams-i Tabrizi: What is the divine within a person then?
The Suad, 38:71-72 *When I fashioned him and breathed some of my spirit into him.* *(Q)*

Whether an entertainer, a professional, or homemaker, the picture a person makes, a shoe, a meal, must he not put something of himself into his work? Doesn't he put some of his spirit into each project? Sometimes that will be so obvious that we use "……'s painting", or "……..:s shoes" or "Mrs. ……..:s cookies?" We are seeing the trace of the spirit they put into their work.

Shams-i Tabrizi: If, in a thought process outside our world, we are not able to prove a theory in a setting that includes the physical body, how will be able to be sure of a theory? Isn't this the situation of doubt that religious information is in today, with no scientific proof of its truth?
In physical prisons, while those inside try to get out, in thought prisons, (just like in a computer system) there will be those on the outside who try to get inside (hackers). In systems where information is protected, those who are left out of the system are isolated from information, and they will want to learn about what the system contains.

The Rangers, 37:9-10 *We have beautified the worldly sky with the splendor of stars plus a safeguard against every stubborn devil so they may not listen to the supreme council and are hurled forth on every side. Driven away they will have lingering torment except for someone, who tries to eavesdrop so that a blazing meteor follows him.* *(Q)*
The Rock, 15:16-18 *We have placed constellations in the sky and established it for onlookers. We have safeguarded them against every outcast satan except for such as may try to eavesdrop, so a blazing meteor follows him.* *(Q)*

Security problems of the council, with the precautions stated, clearly show that it is not a divine system.

Shams-i Tabrizi: In religious teachings it says *"there was nothing in the beginning.* "What do you think the conditions were in the beginning?

Saying "there was nothing in the beginning" means that nothing was known about conditions then.

Exodus, 20:11 For in six days Yahweh made the heavens and the earth and the sea and all that these hold, but on the seventh day he rested. **(OT)**

The Adoration, 32:4 God is the One Who created heaven and earth as well as whatever lies in between them in six days. **(Q)**

A God who created something in six days and then rested has strangely has anthropomorphic aspects. There will be those who claim that these are symbolic explanations, but what proof is there that it is not the way I have presented it here?

One of the best features of a virtual reality is that you can have a body in any form you want to. Those on the council were clearly in touch with the people of the virtual world in earlier times. Because of their authority, they were able to use space ships and travel above the clouds.

Ezekiel, 1:4 I looked: a stormy wind blew from the north, a great cloud with light around it, a fire from which flashes of lightening darted, and in the centre a sheen like bronze at the heart of the fire. **(OT)**

Isaiah, 60:8 Who are these flying like a cloud, like doves to their cote? **(OT)**

Revelation, 14:14 Now in my vision I saw a white cloud and sitting on it, one like a son of man with a gold crown on his head and a sharp sickle in his hand. **(NT)**

Changing form, sometimes in the form of a person, the council roamed the ancient world.

Ezekiel, 1:5-6 In the center I saw what seemed like four animals. They looked like this. They were of human form. Each had four faces, each had four wings. **(OT)**

Acts, 14:11 "These people are gods who have come down to us disguised as men." **(NT)**

Given mankind's tendency to accept the easiest answer to subjects and demanding quick solutions, he looked to what he thought was supernatural for his answers and easily accepted what he saw as his new God.

Ezekiel, *1:28 It was something that looked like the glory of Yahweh. I looked and prostrated myself, and I heard a voice speaking.* **(OT)**
Ezekiel, *2:1 It said, "Son of man, stand up: I am going to speak to you."* **(OT)**
A virtual copy of the real world was created (think Noah's Ark).

Genesis, *1:26-27 God created man in the image of himself. In the image of God he created him, male and female he created them.***(OT)**
Romans, *1:23 Until they exchanged the glory of the mortal God for a worthless imitation, for the image of mortal man of birds, of quadrupeds and reptiles.* **(NT)**
The Cow, *2:210 They do not wait aught but that Allah should come to them in the shadows of the clouds along with the angels, and the matter has (already) been decided; and (all) matters are returned to Allah.* **(Q)**

People developed experiments and graphs to help them accustom themselves to the virtual world.

James, *1:18 By his own choice he made us his children by the message of the truth so that we should be assured of first-fruits of all that he had created.* **(NT)**
Romans, *11:23 Otherwise you will find yourself cut off too, (and others), if they give up their unbelief, grafted back in your place. God is perfectly able to graft them back again.* **(NT)**
The Believers, *23:14 Then we reproduced him as a fresh creation.***(Q)**

Man's brain, connected to the virtual system, can be programmed with whatever information is desired. For example: people on earth were suddenly able to speak different languages.

Acts, *2:1-4 When Pentecost day came round, they had all met in one room, when suddenly they heard what sounded like a powerful wind* *from heaven, the noise of which filled the entire house in which they were sitting. And something appeared to them like tongues of fire; these separated and came to rest on the head of each of them. They were filled with the Holy Spirit, and began to speak foreign languages as the Spirit gave them the gift of speech.* **(NT)**

The virtual universe is a simulated universe used to end problems in the kingdom of heaven (the real universe) at the lowest cost.

Matthew, *16:19 I will give you the keys to the kingdom of heaven: whatever you bind on earth shall be considered bound in heaven; whatever you loose on earth shall be considered loosed in heaven."* **(NT)**

The Pilgrimage, *22:11 If some good should happen to him, he accepts it calmly, while if some trial should strike him, he turns over on his face (in despair). He loses both this world and the hereafter.* **(Q)**

Martin Reese in the book, **The Next 50 Years** in an article entitled "Cosmological Challenges: Are we Alone and Where?" *Is our entire universe perhaps the outcome of some experiment in another universe? Smolin speculates that a daughter universe may be governed by laws that bear the imprint of those prevailing in its parent universe. If so, the theological arguments from design can be resuscitated in a noble guise further erasing the spurious boundary between neutral and "supernatural" phenomena.*

As an experiment, those in the heavens married those of the earth.

Genesis, *6:4 When the sons of God resorted to the daughters of man, and had children by them.* **(OT)**

In this period, people from the skies, the engineers of the system, came and went from time to time.

John, *1:51 You will see heaven laid open and above the Son of Man, the angels of God ascending and descending.* **(NT)**

And they occasionally took people from the earth into the skies.

Revelations, *11:12 Then they heard a loud voice from heaven say to them, "Come up here," and while their enemies were watching they went up to heaven in a cloud.* **(NT)**
John, *8:23 (He said to them) 'You are from below, I am from above; you are of this world, I am not of this world.* **(NT)**

Shams-i Tabrizi: Don't we still in this last period hear people explain how they were taken into the skies? Do you believe these stories?

I have said "the people who dream about heaven full of foods and fantasies are actually dreaming about the things they have never had on earth They will accept with no hesitation the imaginary positions in heaven which they have never had on earth.

As you said, the stories of people being taken into a ship in the sky, returning to say that they have witnessed other life in the skies, have increased. As the number of claims have increased, it has become more realistic.

Because man is unable to produce something that doesn't exist somewhere, I can't say anything definite. I asked a simple question of those who say they went and say they had experienced a life there.

If we bring an indigenous person, raised far from modern civilization into a modern city, and allow him to live there for a time, then bring him back to his tribe, this person will have been exposed for the first time to advanced civilization, will have seen many features never experienced in his tribe, (like a wheel, matches and scissors). He will see these things to be useful to him, and when he returns to his people, he may try to explain or construct the things he saw.

In order to believe those people who claim to have talked to those in other realms and to have seen another life of their own, I would ask them a simple question. I would expect them explain something that is present in the other world and not in ours. When I tell this to people today, they say they haven't thought of it in this way, but if you begin to look at it this way, I'm sure people will begin to bring samples to light. In this way, I would be able to differentiate between those who have actually seen what they were experiencing and those who did not.

Shams-i Tabrizi: Why did reports of these trips stop at the end of the New Testament?

When the virtual bodies were developed to the point they were able to control people and command them remotely, the system engineers (of the council) no longer needed to visit earth and be seen as often.

Psalms, *139:1-3 Yahweh, you examine me and know me, you know if I am standing or sitting you read my thoughts from far away. Whether I walk or lie down you are watching, you know every detail of my conduct.* **(OT)**
Colossians, *2:21 It is forbidden to pick up this, it's forbidden to taste that, it's forbidden to touch something else.* **(NT)**

The Qur'an clearly shows that the council is referred to as "We." And it is clear that the council/We was not the original Creator.

Yusuf, *12:76 We raise anyone we wish to in rank while someone aware (stands) over everyone possessing knowledge.* **(Q)**

Shams-i Tabrizi: Just how far is such a system as this applicable?

Just as I said before, it will be valid as long as the virtual sign of the son of man has not been understood. And mankind may reach that understanding at the most unexpected time. Man, when he understands the virtual realms, will lose all faith in the heavens and earth.

Matthew, *24:29-30 The sun will be darkened, the moon will lose it brightness, the stars will fall from the sky and the powers of heaven will be shaken. And then the **sign of the Son of Man** will appear in heaven.* **(NT)**
Mark, *13:25-26 The stars will come falling from heaven and the powers in the heaven will be shaken.* **(NT)**

This is what is called the day of reckoning and is nothing more than the understanding of the virtual system.

On the day of reckoning, people living in the virtual system will have their eyes opened, much like Adam and Eve, and see that the creators of the virtual system are people similar to themselves. With this understanding, the virtual system will have come to an end.

Genesis, 3:22 God said, "See, the man has become like one of us with his knowledge of good and evil." **(OT)**
I Corinthians, 13:12 Now we are seeing a dim reflection in a mirror, but then we shall be seeing face to face. The knowledge that I have now is imperfect but then I shall know as fully as I am known. **(NT)**

Shams-i Tabrizi: Please excuse me now, our time is up. Remember, "Your Creators are with you, and they wish you to know."

And he left. I was thinking about the next guide to come, suddenly an image of someone I didn't recognize appeared. He spoke.
Unknown person: "If our way of belief is the best, let the others use it too" is it familiar to you? Maybe now you realize whose image this is. And I yelled "**Maimonides!**[5]"

Maimonides: The last prophet has been sent, but when the world needs another more than ever, why has the Creator not sent another prophet?

With the last prophet, it is said the team of prophets has been filled and those who follow will be false prophets.

---

[5] **Moses Maimonides**, also known as **Rabbi Moses ben Maimon**, the **Rambam**, and **Musa ibn Maymun** (Arabic:) was born in Cordova, Spain on March 30, 1135, and died in Egypt on December 13, 1204.One of the greatest Torah scholars of all time, he was a rabbi, physician, and philosopher in Spain, Morocco and Egypt during the Middle Ages. He was the preeminent medieval Jewish philosopher whose ideas also influenced the non-Jewish world. (http://en.wikipedia.org/wiki/Maimonides)

Maimonides: The most important reason that it was called the last prophet was that the flow of knowledge that was directly needed for us to understand the system has been completed. From now on we can project information indirectly by using science. It has been said that those who can put aside the barriers between religion and science without taking sides will inherit the book.

In short, the Creator sends information directly through the prophets and indirectly through science. God sent science to prove and complete his sayings. Human beings based their belief up on miracles, strengthen their belief through the universe's heavenly greatness, distinctness and the harmony discovered by science.

Where are you from? (to this sudden abrupt change in subject I immediately answered…)

From earth.

Maimonides: Your having given the response "I am from earth" with no time to formulate your answer means that you think of us as spacemen.
How did you draw that conclusion?

Maimonides: What do you answer in Turkey when you meet another person who asks you where you're from?

I say I'm from Edirne (a city in western Turkey).

Maimonides: And what do you say when a person from outside Turkey, asks you where you're from?

I say I'm from Turkey.

Maimonides: If an alien asks you where you're from what would be your reply?

I would say I'm from earth.

Maimonides: Do you see that you have just justified my claim? The reason is quite simple: it is the fact that on earth you are educated to think in such narrow parameters that it is quite difficult for you to entertain the possibility that we are normal human beings. You have a great tendency to connect anything more advanced than yourselves to a supreme power, just as your definition of me as an alien. Additionally, the reasons for the answers you gave in Turkey, outside Turkey, and space were different because of the level of the perspective you answered from. Calling the space empty means we look at it with empty eyes. "Look at events through a bird's eye, but do not perceive like a bird." Shall we continue?

Virtual Prophet

A Prophet is: *"One who notifies man of God's messages, invites them onto the path of God, calls them to religion, an emissary."* When you return to earth and tell people of the virtual god and explain the model of this to man, will you not deserve the title of prophet yourself for conveying the message of a virtual god?

Believe me, I am only a helper explaining what I know about virtual reality. As I said, no one is expecting another new prophet because the contingency of prophets on earth has been filled and anyone who claims to be a new prophet will be branded false and put under psychological observation. From this day forward we are expecting a false prophet, but separating the two is extremely difficult. Just how ready is mankind to accept living in a virtual universe created by a new virtual god?

Above all I am not transferring messages from a virtual god. From the classical point of view, as those who reveal the messages of the new gods, have always been called prophets, it might be thought that I was a candidate for the title of prophet, too. However, it is clear that this title would be a false title right from outset because it will be known that this virtual god has the make up of a person, so the title is not real.

__The Cattle,__ 2:62 Then they will be sent back to God, their true Patron. **(Q)**

__Yunus,__ 10:30 There each soul will be tested for whatever it has sent on ahead in the past and they will be handed over to God, their rightful Patron. **(Q)**

If you notice it says the "true Patron". That means there is a false one or another virtual master.

__Yunus,__ 10:36 Most of them merely follow conjecture. However, guessing is no substitute for truth. God is aware of whatever they are doing. **(Q)**

Again, if you have noticed, first, "no substitute for truth" is said.

Today only a few know those who were the richest in the world some 200-300 years ago. It is only by keeping your name alive through your children that anyone would remember you for more than three or four generations. But you may be remembered for thousands of years if you contribute to a good idea or work of art.

On the course I am on in this world, the only work of art I could leave behind would be like an answer sheet used in a multiple choice test. There should be a requirement of a life thesis just as there is a requirement of a university graduation thesis, a master thesis, or a doctoral thesis. I think, if I do not leave a work of some kind, it is as if I have entered a course and not taken the final test or have left the final test without having marked the answer sheet.

As I do this, it is not that I am afraid I might be misunderstood, but that I am afraid of never having tried to explain myself. I also feel it is important that I publish my conclusions and findings.

I am like a teaching assistant or helper who is putting his thoughts in writing to provide scientific testimony to an evaluation board in a master's thesis. In order to complete my thesis I want to explain my experiences immediately. My thoughts echo the thoughts of Stephen Hawking in "Black Holes and Baby Universes", page 117, **"I don't claim any originality or depth, but this is the best I can do at the moment."**

Your children are your physical heritage of DNA left to the future. Your ratio of DNA to physical will gradually be reduced. In this way: if your child's ratio is 50%, the ratio of his child will naturally be reduced even further. You can speculate on the ratio of future generations for yourself.

We must try to leave as many material and psychological works as possible without being connected to others while on earth; books, statues, pictures, schools, hospitals, food kitchens, and leave our DNA this way.

Maimonides: It is as if you want to return to earth without going further up.

If I were to stop my journey here and return to earth, it would mean that I would only be able to explain my experience to this point to those on earth. So I want to go as far up as I can both for myself and for the people on earth.

Maimonides: In that case, let us continue. Virtual god within God, imaginary earth within real earth: one of the definitions of the true God is that God was not born nor given birth to. Does your simulation god conform to this condition?

"Not having been born or been given birth to" means being of that that is. Parmenides says of this situation: *"There is not one thing that changes in the universe."*, *"One of the conclusions in the unchanging theory, is that the world in which we live is not real, and as it is not real, it is only an apparition, therefore it is only a deception and unreal world."*

Ecclesiastes, *3:14-15 I know that what God does he does consistently. To this nothing can be added, from this nothing taken away; yet God sees to it that men fear him. What is, already was; what is to be, has already been, yet God cares for the persecuted.* **(OT)**

If we take the computer as an example; virtual means something that appears to be but is not real. The appearance of pages of writing on a computer screen do not exist in reality. The pictures and images and information that appear as products of a given program do not effect the value of the (possible weight and volume) material computer. They were only created from the capabilities of the computer in the terms of our needs.

Maimonides: Even though I don't like mentioning the Matrix, it is a type of Matrix then.

We can call it a type of matrix, not one that is harmful to man, but a matrix supportive of man. You'll remember in film "The Matrix" during the attack of Zion there is something like this: 250,000 machines are coming, one machine for each of the people in Zion.

This is interesting, because in the book I published in 1995 called The Book with *No Name* there is a section entitled "Making a Picture of God."

"If God can see all of us there must be an eye for every one of us. If God can sense everything we do, there must be an ear for every one of us. If God can preserve information about each one of us and evaluate each one of us God must have a section for every one of us. If I could make a picture of God, in one eye there would be as many eyes as there are people; in one ear, as many ears as there are people; in one brain, as many brains are there are people. If we think for a moment, we see that this is like the network system established by the computer. The main computer automatically establishes a section for each terminal that is connected to it from its own memory system. In this way it controls all aspects of the terminal so the terminal becomes a part of the main computer.

Each person, then, is a terminal connected to God. Man receives suggestions from the center it is connected to. Before each process a person goes to the main computer and according to the requests coming in from other terminals, will enter a queue to have his desires met according to priorities. There is a waiting period that depends on the number of terminals. If you have given the proper command, and the connection is strong, you will be granted what you deserve very easily and your terminal procedure will be completed. But occasionally, there are so many terminals, and so many requests that the time it takes to reach you may be delayed. (Don't you have to wait occasionally at the bank for the computer system to revive?) At that time patience is needed; some wait in patience, some, not receiving what they want immediately, give up, saying the system is not for them breaking the connection with the mother computer."

Maimonides: If the creators of the imaginary god are scientists why did they give place to religious men?

As I have said, the virtual god is a copy of the real universe. In scenarios of the virtual universe, inclusion of the Torah, the Bible the Quran and other belief systems, and non-believers are a sign of respect for the Creator and other belief systems. **(1)** a reflection of need of these kind of groups in afterlife, **(2)** are the other choices in the multiple choice of the test of life. You may think of it as world simulation machines with resources and rules connected to the Original. The existing simulation machines have one important difference: they are so real that at first man is unable to tell the difference.

It is not only a religious god, but also a scientific god, with a council made up of both religious men and scientists. Because religious men will be tested in imaginary environments there are various scenarios which include them.

Maimonides: What other standards have the Holy Books been able to put forward?

Everything was created simultaneously but only those things you choose are activated.

Because the creation of computer characters is done from the same center, creation of one is exactly like creation of all of the characters. When a game is loaded all characters and the game scenario are loaded into the memory of the computer. Each area is there to be activated when the time comes: it is selected and activated by appearing on the screen.
Luqman, *31:28 Your creation and your rebirth (happen) only as a single soul.* **(Q)**

In a car race in a computer game only the car the player chooses is activated and appears on the screen. The modules which were not chosen are loaded, and passively waiting to be chosen and activated into the game and do not appear on the screen.

The scenarios in an imaginary environment are the same. Only the three dimensions that you find yourself in and the areas you can see are active; the others are passive. Just as in a virtual space it is only necessary to have active life in the place where the reading/ recording head is, there is no need for active life in the whole of virtual space.

Maimonides: How will the imaginary god secure safety of the brain for people who are an imaginary construct in a virtual environment?

The Period of gods of Standards (ISO)

One of the most important standards of an imaginary god system is providing for the safety of all candidates who are playing against the players in the intense scenarios that are downloaded. The candidates, because contents have been overloaded into the scenarios must have predetermined loading standards. In order to protect them from physical danger; i.e. having a heart attack as people do in exciting dreams, the candidates, must be monitored constantly. There must be a warning system to warn people, thus preventing physical harm. Within this standard is the provision that the candidate cannot choose a harmfully high dosage. There are verses that refer to this.

Deuteronomy, *30:11 For this Law that I enjoin on you today is not beyond your strength or beyond your reach.* **(OT)**
The Table, *7:42 Those who believe and perform honorable deeds (will find) We never assign any soul more than it can cope with* **(Q)**
The Cow, *2:233 Yet no person is charged with more than he can cope with* **(Q)**
The Believers, *23:62 We only assign a soul something it can cope with.* **(Q)**

Virtual gods, shortly after they are produced will begin to branch out just as professions do, and master imaginary gods will develop for each job: a love god, religion god, justice god, peace god and others (**Maimonides** interrupted)

Maimonides: You mean Greek gods were real?

I feel that in place of a singular god, the idea of multiple gods is a result of the people of that age not being able to fathom only one god creating such a vast universe.

How come the same God wants my enemy's victory as we say" my enemy's friend is my enemy"? Or "my enemy's God cannot be my God." These kinds of thoughts could be the reason for the multiple gods model. There with all these models bring solutions to the reasoning of societies, also bring chaos to the people who already believed in different gods.

I think on a virtual stage in the beginning they will take these names. In summary, if virtual environments with certain purposes and imaginary gods are to be created, they must provide a protection system under a set of ISO standards to protect people against all types of negative effects. The ISO standard of the gods' age will have been started.

Maimonides: Man can only understand mankind so far. However, no matter how much he succeeds there is always a place in man's brain that will remain unknown. Will man's brain be one of these side effects?

<u>There will be two serious side effects of this system:</u>

1. The downloaded scenarios cannot remain connected to our brain very long. For this reason the virtual god technology connected with our brains will have to be returned to normal to allow our brains to normalize in specific periods as a default of the system. Is the necessity of sleep a feature of man or of the system?   In short, why does the Creator put us to sleep?

2. There are difficulties in the system we call virtual god. Just as when we watch a broadcast on the computer there are interruptions at certain intervals, to allow the system to collect details and show them before it begins again, there are difficulties stemming from the speed of the communications within the system.

Maimonides: Are there any other side effects to humans?

Think of the heaven that was promised, the beautiful women are perpetual virgins, love slaves that gaze into your eyes: there is unlimited food, rivers of milk and honey, no fear of death, no stress. Thus, the problems of the world have been lifted from mankind who has been struggling with them on earth. Then too, as the stress of a person on the course of life increases the need for the promises of heaven also increase and the images of things available in heaven become even more world-like.

Heaven is a place where man can freely desire and in time, can reach the conditions of those desires and without the fear of loss it provides a chance to become the person he wants to be. There is no doubt that this is an imaginary/virtual reality.

Being in an environment he desires with each every desire taken seriously will inevitably create a dependency. If heaven is a place which responds to each command, this is a type of sacredness, a place where man is divine. Just look at the situation: in spite of the fact that no one has crossed over and come back to explain, billions of people for thousands of years have worshiped in hopes of being worthy of getting into heaven. And can you imagine the state of dependency that is created once it is experienced? Just like Adam and Eve, another life would be spent in fervent worship and supplication to return!

So, instead of the dependencies on alcohol, drugs and other diversions found now, in the near future the world of the virtual god and its heavens would create a serious dependency problem. Most people will choose the virtual over the real.

John, 12:43 *(Because) they put honour from men before the honour that comes from God. **(NT)***

Maimonides: What would the administration system of a virtual god be like?

The "We" and "Council" mentioned in the Holy Books could be called the Virtual-7. (V7) Rule in the real world in the classic sense, will be in the hands of those who invest in real technology who will also be the leaders and the regulators in the virtual copy.

The technology of a virtual world will be developed and supported by the front running countries. And a situation will appear wherein the less developed countries will be pushed to follow, just as today the councils like the United Nations and the European Union administer and evaluate. There will be members of the council with veto rights who will administer and ordinary members without veto rights. The rights of the less developed countries not included in the decision making process will be taken by the developed countries and those council leaders in the real world will also be directors in the virtual or copied system.

Just as those today who invest in technology will administer those who have not invested in technology. The sociological god is under the direction of the technological god.

Maimonides: Why are the less developed countries bound to accept this system?

Let me give you an example from today's computer sector. To get a position in the computer industry a person not only must have a diploma from an accredited school, but must also show proof of having passed tests administered by businesses like Microsoft, a technology provider. Institutions hiring new employees prefer to rely on the master tests developed by the technology they will be using, such as Microsoft, instead of developing their own tests for the area a candidate will be working in. It is a requirement of the employer, and a candidate must enter the test and pass it, whether he wants to or not.

In the future the situation will remain the same. Governmental and private institutions will not hire personnel by depending only on tests which evaluate knowledge. They will increasingly rely on virtual environments of bribery, flattery, ethics, courage, creativity, compatibility and others and want to hire only those personnel who have a background of success in those areas. The internet industry will hire from a pool of candidates who leave documents listing their accomplishments on human resource sites. Those who have completed scenarios of preferred institutions with the scores attained from virtual environments will be chosen. Continuing with the administration:

Those who create the system direct the system. The degree of intervention Turkey makes on the NASA space program is a good indication of the influence a technologically underdeveloped country has in a imaginary environment. Drowning in questions of daily functioning, instead of making investments in science, are unable to rise above primitive levels and just as in the real world they are unable to lead, they are unable to have a say in an imaginary world.

Maimonides: So in the end what problems will a virtual god be able to address?

Just as when working on a text a photocopy is made to protect the original from damage while you work to make changes, a virtual copy of the universe would provide an inexpensive alternative to work on changes we want to make. To prevent the copy from being misused and treated poorly you would not reveal that it was a copy, or if you did, you would have to cause it to be forgotten and by giving importance to it, make those within the reality feel as if it were real. Members of a virtual reality may be able to play a courageous and ethical role when they understand they are being tested and the life course will be filled with the false heroes of an amusement park.

Maimonides: From what you have explained you should not then be allowed to reveal what you have seen here.

The Originator, 35:32 *Then We gave the Book for an inheritance to those whom We chose from among Our servants* **(Q)**

This is my virtual life course. A person who is going to inherit responsibility of revising the rules must somehow come to understand the system; he must write it and publish it. This will be using the "Real Meaning Method" developed by **Dr. Ahmet Yesevi**: he purposes speaking to people's mind and level of understanding following the principles of endearment, unification, soothing-stimulating-compassionate, while being pleasant. The system must develop and evaluate its own personnel within the environment. So developments in this scenario do not reach racers in another scenario.

Considering my purposes in publishing this throughout the world:

I want to be sure people know that the world they live in is not real. I want to convince them that it is virtual and somehow imaginary. I want to ensure that they understand that this unimportant virtual simulation world is the most important place for manifesting their dreams in the real world.

Preparing mankind in his thoughts for the near future, I want to free mankind of his fears and make him a bit cautious. I want to say **"Watch out! There's God!"** I want to tell mankind that killing before death, killing before killing (by losing the meaning of being alive), is all imaginary! I want to tell mankind that their dreams may be turned into reality through this imaginary experience.

Maimonides: Given these various goals, there must be many race courses and scenarios that are not connected to each other!

Of course, in a virtual environment where there will be all types of persons developed, there is a need for a council of scientific and religious men which is continually producing and developing a flexible broad archive of scenarios.

Appraising administrative candidates in a business world to whom the institution will be turned over, to see how they will use personnel resources in various scenarios we would test their faithfulness, character, talents, health and other areas to be sure. Religious men who have the resources of religious institutes assigned to their keeping, must be evaluated on their ability to lead the strong honest people who believe in themselves and whether they will use these resources for personal benefits correctly in various situations.

II Peter, 2:3 They will eagerly try to buy you for themselves with insidious speeches. (NT)

Programmers or scenarists will immediately interfere, with the permission of the council, with those who stray from the parameters of the scenario of the current system. At that moment, it will help take you away from the topic and to provide time for the engineers of the system to add a new scene of illness, a pain, a loss or a happiness will show up in your life to distract you. During that period a new module will be added to the system for you and attached to your scenario or your scenario will be frozen until the necessary changes have been made. The basic goal of the scenario is taking advantage of the longing one feels in the virtual scenario, to monitor your natural reactions to experiences that you won't be able to savor in real life.

Maimonides: Would you please give me an example of this?

During the time of chess champion Kasporov's struggle against the computer the press and the media first reported that man had beat the computer, then reported that the computer had beaten man. However, the true contest was between Kasporov and the computer programmers of that chess game. Here the computer was only an instrument. In truth when in a one on one contest the computer programmers were unable to beat

Kasporov, they were only able to do it with the help of a computer that computed 200 million moves per second.

Programmers in the background interfered with the program when Kasparov made an unexpected move were able to change the program and attach new modules. Kasparov who was playing by looking at the computer screen was unable to see activities behind the scenes, and perceived the prolonged time it took the computer to provide its move not to be the interference of programmers but the reduced speed of the system.

Due to our trust in God, we say that God knows something we don't when we don't receive something we think is rightfully ours or because of a perceived injustice, our prayers aren't answered when we expect them to be. This is a trust, a hope resulting from a lack of understanding God's justice.

Virtual reality is an environment where thoughts are turned into reality temporarily which can be manipulated. Your imagination shapes everything to fit your thoughts. A virtual environment is at your command; show off your thoughts! However, you must not only think of past experiences, but you must think of monitoring possibilities available in the future; plans and diagrams and the effects of personally experiencing them, and you must know every refraction coefficient or they will know.

Maimonides: Roger S. Schank in the book *The Next Fifty Years* in his article "Are We Going to Get Smarter?" said that, *"Certifying agencies will worry more about what you can do-what virtual merit badges you have achieved-than what courses you have taken."* So, in the simulation course you have outlined your read-understand-apply simulation course (virtual god) is a human construct; are there human fears?

You have asked about the point at which I first thought about man's construct. Research that began when I realized the fear of my questioning felt by religious men changed dimension when I became aware of the fear of those who created the system and I reached the concept of "A God Less Chosen." Without knowing it man asks why the road to God is so narrow and difficult. Does God not truly want us to reach Him that He makes it so arduous? That means that God really only wants a very few to find their way to Him. He probably only needs a few people on his staff. Who increases the difficulty of the race course? Why?

Matthew, *7:13 "Enter by the narrow gate, since the road that leads to perdition is wide and spacious, and many take to it; but it is a narrow gate and a hard road that leads to life and only a few find it."* **(NT)**

The Fearless Virtual God's Fear of Being Understood!
(Gods Take Their Strength from Being Non-understandable)

Why do we no longer believe in the sun god? Because science tells us that the sun is a star in space that it has nothing to do with our creation and the events on earth. Furthermore we understand that whether sacrifices are made or not, the sun will rise in the east and set in the west.

I believe that prayer can help change the choices we made on our Application for Earth. However, I still have doubts about prayers being of any use in the courts of the afterlife when I read these verses;

The Narratives, *28:84* **Anyone who brings a fine deed** *will have something more than it, while anyone who come with an evil deed (will find that) those who perform evil deeds will not be rewarded except for whatever they have been doing* **(Q)**

The Spider, *29:58 We shall lodge* **the ones who believe and perform honorable deeds** *in the Garden with mansions by which rivers will flow, to live there forever. How splendid will* **be the earnings of the workers.** **(Q)**

Notice that is states, "anyone who brings a fine deed", "the ones who perform honorable deeds", "the earnings of the workers." One of the nicest things said about tests in this virtual world is "work is worship."

Given that gods take their strength from being non-understood, the technological level of virtual scenarios must be at a level that cannot be understood or seen to be logical when they are being experienced. In this situation, those experiencing virtual scenarios may cause them to think that only a supernatural power which they cannot possibly understand, let alone produce, has created it. Candidates, for this reason, must be evaluated by their essential selves.

Psalms, 7:9 You righteous God, assessor of mind and heart. **(OT)**

Revelations, 2:23 It is I who search heart and loins. **(NT)**

The Resurrection, 75:14 Indeed, man holds evidence even against himself. **(Q)**

Maimonides: Where do the secrets of these fears begin? Not in every level, right?

At the time when the level of knowledge and understanding necessary to create the virtual system is reached on the life course, the virtual system within, the imaginary stage and scenarios become endangered as credibility, authenticity and acceptability diminish. The racer, when he says that the technology behind it can be worked out, when he says that it would not be that difficult to do, when he says if he can think of it science will soon be able to produce it, the imaginary stages of the virtual system are removed and the truth behind the mirror becomes visible.

When the racer understands his trials and observations, he will begin to play a role, not doing what he wants to do, but what is necessary for him to do. Candidates will begin to question, not living in an imaginary reality, not the lessons of the scenarios, but instead, will begin to question the system itself. And then the tests of the life course begin to be evaluated. The "Godhood" and "inscrutability" of the system which gave it power loses its strength and becomes invalid. And the owners of the system will lose their ISO standard qualifying certification (validity) as well as the authority to grant certificates to the racers. Therefore, the virtual god will begin to take steps to protect itself from being understood. The racers, when they begin to think of the solutions to the system will have goods withdrawn or contract physical ailments or face sudden unexpected happiness which will return them to their original scenarios.

The Cow, 2:155 We shall test you with a bit of fear and hunger, plus a shortage of wealth and souls and produce. Announce such to patient people. (Q)

The virtual god, not able to rise above the certain level of knowledge he is in, will be used mostly in primitive time education. The first level of education which includes both technological and sociological education will address only the basics of scientific information. The second level and those that follow will not advance in the technical aspects and in general will concentrate on the sociological aspects of the scenarios. In the technical setting we are tested to determine our sociological breaking points in love, loyalty, sharing, ethics, patience and other aspects through sociological scenarios. In the primitive areas persistence and courage are emphasized while in the more advanced areas team work and modeling become important.

The figurants of the system, attempt to keep people away from the **Exit** door of the system by emphasizing the helplessness of man using statements such as "We are all incapable followers, mere drops in the ocean."

Maimonides: How does one complete a scenario successfully?

Why is it that one newly released film breaks all box office records while no one attends others? This is because movie goers are unable to find anything of themselves in the film's media releases and when the added deterrent of not liking the actors in the scenario or not liking the cinematography is added, they decide it is not worth the price at the box office. Also they will not relate the film to their friends.

The success of a virtual god system is connected to capability of racers to find something of themselves in the scenarios and allow themselves to be swooped along in those scenarios. The system develops a virtual life with a virtual family, a virtual work environ-ment, in a virtual social structure.

Life, is man's practice answer to virtual system, his giving to receive. The racer, unable to connect with the imaginary scenarios of the virtual system, begins to lose his concentration on the scenario and the virtual system does not receive the answer. This raises the question of whether the inadequacy of the scenario is due to the failure of the racer or the failure of the system. If the racer is unable to adequately connect with the system, it means that the appropriate scenario was not chosen. Had

Adam and Eve not grown bored, they would not have begun to seek. Losses in virtual life are there to provide meaning to that life or not. The racer,

- When he begins to get bored with virtual life will begin to feel he is running around without a purpose and become a **Passive Player**.
- He then begins to question the system and becomes a **Dangerous Player to the system.**

Once you have seen how a horror film is actually filmed you will not be as frightened in other horror films. In adventure films when you learn that the player who is hanging over the side of a canyon by a root tendril has been filmed in a studio suspended over a foam-covered stage made to resemble a canyon, doesn't your viewpoint change? We no longer feel much fear or apprehension.

If you notice, it is no longer the scenery in horror movies or adventure films that frighten us, but the sudden sound effects. As Rumi said: *"What frightens the eye of man is that he fears the various vagaries of his imagination."* (2212)

Please ask yourself this question: why would a Creator who presents you with such a complicated world try to hide from you within this confusion? What is the Creator trying to prevent you from seeing? The question that will clarify our understanding of the universe is the question of **"just how real these are."**
Beware! The virtual universe bates us by making the impossible appear possible ending in pathetic results. Either be as you appear or appear as you are or the virtual universe will get you!

Maimonides: You don't care for heaven, so you brought the world into an imaginary state with an imaginary universe. Here's a question for you: throughout this journey has sex ever come to your mind? Have you wanted to eat? Maybe heaven is a place like this that takes you out of your normal mind, have you ever thought of that?

(The Voice had set his own trap, knowingly or unknowingly.)

I have to agree with what you say. Since I embarked on this journey I have never been hungry or thirsty or had one thought about my genitalia. As you said, this journey has taken me beyond my mind. But given the same journey, as I remember everything, the situation will begin to change. In fact, when I have seen the same things over a few times they will begin to lose their interest for me. Do I not tire of the magnificent beauties of the earth? In order for the same course to take me beyond my mind again I must experience it as if I am living through it for the first time. Just as the fish in an aquarium whose memory is renewed every two or three seconds, my memory must be renewed at each beginning or I must lose the certain characteristics that make me. Does a sheep in the meadow feel stress?

Not being able to remember this journey when I return to earth would not only be a great injustice to me and mankind, but would also create serious side effects in the meaning of experience with shadows that I would have to face. Years ago I said, "The worst point a person could reach is probably the point where he says that there is nothing left to love." I still have a few things I can love, but it is in those things or in the formation of the things I will love, that I will find it more difficult to accept that I had a choice in it.

If I return to earth, I will research how I marked my Application for Earth and whether or not I was free in my choices. In addition, when I return to earth, if I am able to remember this journey, will it be a crime to reveal the virtual god, or not? I will figure that out.
In addition:

* Was the crime of Adam and Eve eating the fruit? Or under-standing that they were unclothed?
* In the afterlife, where there is hell for sinners (criminals) why doesn't God send them directly to hell and effect their regrets and restore them to heaven without finding it necessary to rehabilitate them by sending them to earth? Since God makes the choice, it means that the world is a better training place than hell!
* Did they give their word that they would not eat of the fruit again?
* When Adam and Eve return to heaven from the world will they remember the days of forbidden fruit, their state of nakedness and their days on earth?

Maimonides: Why does God send humans to hell instead of Satan who is the main reason of rebellion. If everything is being recorded what is the need of a witness? Are the recordings not enough? Even the thoughts are being recording not just the acts.

*I Chronicles, 28:9 / for the LORD searches every mind, and understands every plan and thought (**OT**)*

*Job, 21:27 / Oh, I know your thoughts, and your schemes to wrong me (**OT**)*

Romans, 8:27 / And God, who searches the heart, knows what is the mind of the Spirit, because the Spirit* intercedes for the saints according to the will of God.* (**NT**)*

*The Cow, 2:234 / and Allah is aware of what you do. (**Q**)*

*The Narratives, 28:69 / And your Lord knows what their breasts conceal and what they manifest (**Q**)*

Maimonides: From what you've described I get the image of a virtual universe being like a thought detective as in the film "The Minority Report"[6]. Am I wrong?

I can provide an example of virtual god technology's practical purposes. What do you do to determine talent in a child? You attempt to determine which talents he has by sending him to various courses such as sports, drawing, music, mathematics, physics and the like. In the same way you may determine his undesirable side by leaving him in the middle of those who deal in bad things. All these experiences are provided to determine your child's talents and limitations. We determine where he should take higher training in the same way. Engineering, the arts, medicine; these are a virtual god technology providing the person with tests at any age in the scenarios he wants, monitoring who they are and what they are able to do in a virtual environment in order to direct them into a real physical environment.

This will provide a serious element in bringing out the contributing sides of people and developing a healthy, viable clean society.

---

[6] **(Minority report:** in the year 2054, where a special police department called "Precrime" apprehends criminals based on foreknowledge provided by three psychics termed "precogs".)

The film "The Minority Report" explained a system of thought detection established in a limited area to prevent only crimes of violence before they developed. One of the purposes of a virtual god is to prevent the development of crimes, but this time not only in the limited area of violence.

Maimonides: What does a healthy and clean society mean?

If you recall at one time in Turkish society there was a slogan calling for a "Clean Society". We have probably become so clean that the need for that slogan was removed and we no longer use it. (Perhaps it was removed when it was understood that the slogan would not produce the goal.) I use **"Healthy and Clean Society"** because there can be no cleanliness without health.

If in heaven even prophets commit crimes and are sent into exile, it means there is a serious problem of cleanliness in heaven. It means that, "the world was created for the cleanliness and health of society in heaven."

Holy Books, institutions, cults; in short, all types of social groups are said to have been "established for the advancement of people."

Evolution: the way in which living things change and develop over millions of years, or a gradual process of change and development.

In Islam in particular, and in many esoteric teachings, and in beliefs of mystic and Sufi groups, the term evolution is used in a spiritual sense. In this respect, as a religious term evolution is used in the majority of cases to identify the phases the soul goes through as it improves and develops.

In what subjects and how does a person evolve, and what do millions of evolved persons form? Societies that are made up of evolved people are evolved societies and this must be the ideal outcome in a period when the slogan "clean society" is on everyone's mind. This can only be formed by characteristics hidden within the members of a clean society. A healthy and clean society is made up of members who: **1)** are able to easily get rid of stress, **2)** are able to assimilate pain, **3)** to transpose disappointments stemming from the results of choices they made or rise above disappointments.

Maimonides: Are you talking about the story of creation in the Holy Books?

Until today the hope of forming a "healthy and clean society" of evolved people has only been considered to be a possibility with the help of one of the various esoteric teachings, or teachings of mystic or Sufi groups with religious formats. The virtual god model shows how to reach the same point with the help of technology. In conclusion, while this model will take some to a new understanding of a more logical Creator, it will lead others to the goals of 21st century technology and others to both. This model is the first model of the unfathomable aspects and the thoughts of the Creator, following the finger prints of God. It is the first technological model created by the thoughts of mankind.

You'll remember some verses;

The Cattle, 6:32 What does worldly life mean except sport and amusement? (Q)

Some others are like this:
The Smoke, 44:38-39 We did not create Heaven and Earth and anything in between them just by playing around. We have created them both only to reveal the truth, even though most do not realize it. (Q)
The Cattle, 6:98 It is He Who as (granted you) a settlement and a resting place (after death). (Q)

When we add the condolences and healing to the fun and games, condolences and healing, decision making (test), entrusting something to others, constitute four different goals for creation.

Maimonides: With the words **"Your creators are with you and want you to have fun"** he took me to the elevator. As I pressed the button for the third floor, the three lighted and the door opened.

1. Fun And Games

The door opened onto a completely different world. I was in the dinosaur age. Around me there were Allosaurus, Tyrannosaurus-Rex, Theropods and flying Ornithocheirus. Without wanting to, one is afraid, and gets himself together, ready for action. I was so frightened that I forgot the trip for a while. When one is expecting a higher technology and confronts a more primitive one, he is surprised. I suppose it isn't necessary to say that the elevator door closed behind me.

When the wild animals began to notice me I suddenly felt the need to look out for my safety. On the one hand I told myself "there's nothing to fear, these are holograms," but precaution is another thing. Just as I was about to be savagely attacked and become a monster's breakfast, the whole scene vanished, and I found myself on the top of a transparent base of the ceiling of the classical heaven of the floor below. As I studied the floor below the voice of this floor came through.

Voice: You certainly overcame a lot of stress quickly!

You're right, but why did you do that?
Voice: We call your fear bringing you a bit of fun. Think of "Jurassic Park,[7]" the film that technology made possible.

Going back in time to the people of 1975, still living in the conditions of 1975, if this film was shown with the computer sound and visional effects which the people knew nothing about, and if we tell them that *"these are dinosaurs on Chan-Chin Island and these are the first pictures,"* since they know nothing of the computer science used in the film industry, when people of that era see the pictures on television they will believe them to be real.

Just as you got excited before when you thought the pictures of the first age were real. We can reach these conclusions; Falsity on a level of a higher reality may be the truth of the level below. Therefore, the technology of a future virtual period may appear real to us who do not know today's virtual technology. It will stay that way until the technology of the lower level reaches the upper level. **God sent the Holy Books to the people of religion's first period so they would believe and to the people of this period, science so they would understand.**

---

[7] (**Jurassic Park** is a 1990 science fiction novel written by Michael Crichton. Often considered a cautionary tale on unconsidered biological tinkering in the same spirit as Mary Shelley's Frankenstein, it uses the mathematical concept of chaos theory and its philosophical implications to explain the collapse of an amusement park showcasing certain genetically recreated dinosaur species. It was adapted into a blockbuster film in 1993 by director Steven Spielberg. The book's sequel, The Lost World (1995), was also adapted by Spielberg into a film in 1997".)

(1) Ability to get rid of stress and attain comfort;

People who work intensively: businessmen, politicians, sales persons are physically able to rest on a vacation, but unable to find spiritual comfort. If they were sent on a ten day vacation, the first three days are spent winding down from the fast tempo they are used to, and the last three days are spent building up stress about the environment awaiting them on their return.
Of a ten day vacation at most the middle four days can be experienced as vacation, and generally due to the stress of the return they arrive back tired. And this is true only if they have not been using the telephone for business during those four days. The same is true for the poor of society. In spite of the fact that they have been saving up for the whole year, those who are unable to go on a vacation that can bring a smile to their faces produces serious depression.

In the end, those who spend their days, months and years having forgotten what happiness is, with reduced ability to love, unable to truly communicate with others, will be a group of troubled people unable to be satisfied. As a result these people will seek happiness in drinking, gambling, drugs, deception, prostitution, and strange re-lationships. So what will be the situation of people lead or directed by decisions given by administrators made up of a group of un-satisfied troubled people? That state can best be explained by the phrase. *"Of course, those who fall into the hands of those who do not understand the state of others are doomed."*

Fun and Games

The Cattle, *6:32 What does worldly this life mean except some sport and amusement?* **(Q)**
The Spider, *29:64 What is this worldly life except an amusement and a game?* **(Q)**
The Family of Imran, *3:185 What does the worldly life mean except the enjoyment of illusion?* **(Q)**
The Iron, *57:20 Know that worldly life is merely a sport and a pastime (involving) worldly show and competition among yourselves, as well as rivalry in wealth and children.* **(Q)**

After a long hard day you come home in the evening to relax. To be comfortable, you exercise, have a few drinks, play a few games on the computer, put your earphones on to listen to music or spend some time with the family: you chose one. If the trouble at work was serious, no matter what you do, you cannot get the problem out of your head or because you cannot reduce your excitement, you cannot relax. The problem here is that you cannot establish insulation between your daily life and your play environment.

An example is the dinosaur age scenario I confronted at the entrance to this floor that made me forget everything, including this trip. Every-thing I had experienced until that moment was insulated from me in an instant that made me forget who I was and why I had come. It brought me to the point where I could only think of fighting what I saw. This was brought about by providing the insulation of conditions being unknown, not knowing the difference between real life and virtual reality; an amazing environment for those who want to get rid of stress.

It reminds me of the state we have come to; if talking is forbidden, saying it will ruin the insulation, people who are in a world that does not resemble the place they live on earth in the slightest, with no connection to it, could fight dinosaurs in this virtual world. They could forget themselves, their likes, needs, problems and pleasures in this completely different world. They could run from here to there, they could battle, kill, within an entirely natural, healthy, harmless and short period, could relax.

In this game, of fire and finding simple weapons, killing monsters will earn lots of points. In order to continue with the game, the necessary elements which have been hidden behind things, the energy, food, drink, shelter, heat and other needs, when they are found, will enable the player to continue the game. The water the player drinks in this virtual reality or the food eaten, because there really is no body, giving non-existent water gains the necessary energy or points to keep up the game. The player all alone in the wild with monsters, since he has no mind, and no skills in talking and understanding, with his virtual body runs screaming and yelling at the giant dinosaurs, wild animals, and wilderness. They will be primitive people with no thought of losing their lives. People who want to get rid of stress, need to erase their thoughts. Meditation, yoga and other methods are used to stop the thought process.

The circumstances surrounding a person in a virtual reality resembles the dream state. It is a type of dream state can be controlled from the outside. If communication with the dream area and the brain is understood, man could be shown any dream he wanted to see and could experience any dream world he wanted to.

The person would awake after he is relaxed and would remember the stress producing stimulants, but the peace of mind provided by relaxation would allow him to regard them in a calm manner.
Games that more than one person can play together will have been developed and societal games will have been distributed to homes and work places via the internet and it will have become the safest system. People in very different environments, can live the imaginary feelings they've been fantasizing and can be the person they wanted to be. A virtual reality is heaven on earth.

I want to share an article from Science and Technology Magazine entitled Virtual Sphere July 2007.

"Virtual reality, as the speed of progress increases in the computer world, becomes closer to reality. Once interest centered on a receptor connected to the body through special glasses to play a virtual game. A Virtual Ball designed using the same logic appears to have taken this interest one step further.

The balls which may be used in various services, are basically used in games, of course. For some reason when different programmers load this ball the goal is able to be changed. For instance, you can create activities like running, walking, jumping, hopping and a walk in nature can be changed into a different program to a soldier on a battle field sweeping the area with a machine gun.

Using both game and simulations these balls can be used for training and, when several are connected together, form a network and the users can profit from being able to affect the others. It is thought that Virtual balls can be used in different areas. A virtual museum, a tourist trip, a simple sport exercise are among the Virtual Ball's advantages. With this design the Ball has been awarded the "best vehicle to permit man-machine communication" award. (page 20)(http://www.virtusphere.com/)

Of course, the scenarios are not limited to the dinosaur age, anyone has the right to use whatever scenario he wishes to relax in. Ergun Candan in his book *Teachings of Hidden Secrets* page 55 writes: Spatium: " *I said the spatium is a place where matter is made up of extremely subtile balls (groupings). Our thought energy causes **the matter of this place to form instantly**. Whatever is thought there is manifested immediately."*

As Rumi said many years ago: *"In the afterlife meanings take form. **Our forms match our daydreams.**"* (1866)

As long as the game continues all that the player has, does and thinks are recorded. When he is awakened, and looks at the recordings of the game, laughs at his fears and hopelessness, his anger at another. One of the funniest parts is seeing his false courage when he claims to fear nothing then the screams and flight when he is put to the test.
It is as I said before about the film "Jurassic Park": **The virtual reality of the future will one day be as reality to the people of today.**

Voice: "Your creator is with you and will comfort you."

(When I heard these words, I thought I had no chance at continuing upward and would return home. Since I didn't choose heaven I didn't have a chance.)

First, the images below me faded, then the dinosaur age I found myself in at the beginning of the third floor reappeared and the monsters took attack position as a group and began to come towards me. Just as I was thinking "Where did these things come from, just when we were having such a good discussion," the elevator door opened and I understood that my time on this level was over. This floor was saying farewell in the same way it had welcomed me. I both entered the elevator and as I saw that the buttons to activate upper floors were lit, I breathed a sigh of relief. I had visited the third floor of fun and games mentioned in the Holy Books. Now my goal should be to get to the fourth floor.

As I pushed the fourth floor button the door opened.

2. Comfort and Healing

I found myself in a holographic scene of a young mother who had suddenly lost her husband and was alone with her two children protesting with questions of "why me"? "Why us?" I was there, but they didn't see me. The woman was protesting and was probably about to try suicide to punish herself and protest against God.

I remembered that the words of farewell on the previous floor "Your creator is with you and will comfort you," would, of course, take me to the floor where the Creator comforts. The pain of the woman who had lost her husband reminds me of the verse:

The Cow, *2:155 We shall test you with a bit of fear and hunger, plus a shortage of wealth and souls and produce. Announce such to patient people.* **(Q)**

This type of loss was standard fare in the virtual racecourse. With exceptions the system generally worked on the principle of first ones in, first ones out so that those who came in first experienced the death of those who followed. I was in the area of a Healthy and Clean Society that dealt with "Assimilating Pain."

The entering and exiting of the world is a difficult course.

(As I watched the woman and children with these thoughts **Saint (Mother) Teresa** appeared at my side.)

Mother Teresa: If the duty of comforting this woman were given to you how would you use religion and science to do it?

(As this question was being asked the woman saw me and communication began. As the woman looked at me in astonishment as a person she had never seen I automatically expressed my condolences.)

Woman: Friends, may your life be long! (as she said this she pulled her children to her and began to cry).

In order that your friends live you must be alive and well. To my mind you have several choices.

1. You accept this as a natural law and continue living without faltering, lightening your pain as you live.

2. You can go to other places to stay away from discussions reminding you of your pain; places and people. You try to avoid people who would naturally speak about the loss. And you certainly avoid talking about the pain. You can avoid sad music. You may travel to a far away place that will help you forget your pain. But we may not be able to help you forget your pain while it is so fresh and unbearable no matter where you may go. Because you will know that you are in that place for the express purpose of forgetting your trouble. Because you cannot forget that reason, the method will not be effective.

3. You can choose to heal through medicine. They will **give you sedatives** which numb you and **prevent you from feeling healthy, seeing, and thinking**. In fact, you can sleep and completely disconnect from life. But there is no healing in this treatment, it only **freezes the environment with you in it**. When you awaken from the effects of the medicine because your brain is unhealthy you won't be sad, but you won't be happy either. This insulation which protects you from healing, leaves your head in confusion, so when you return to your normal state you will begin to feel the pain again and in time you will eventually heal. Maybe in the long run you will forget your pain but then, you will begin to deal with the side effects of the medicine on your physical system and you will lose your normality and liveliness for a long period. Instead of providing a chance for acceptance of your situation, you are controlled by the goal of erasing your past. The emptiness that is formed or is attempted to be formed will **lead to depression, breakdowns or complete disconnections and there may be a lack of active participation and liveliness while the gap is being filled.**

When you are in a freezer-like situation real life continues, and you fall behind real life. When you come out of it, it may take a long time to regain cognancy. In the book *The Next 50 Years* in an article entitled "Brainscans, Wearables and Brief Encounters", Harvard University research scientist, Dr. Nancy Etcoff puts it this way. *"Drugs tame symptoms, but therapy helps people to solve their problems and learn solutions." "While drugs seem to work only as long as you take them, talk therapy promises the long-lasting effects provided by learning."*

4. If you want to, let us prepare you a room in keeping with your protests, where you can find a little solace as you rant and rave and break everything getting out the feelings of violence.

5. The spirit of suicide is murder of the body. You can punish yourself instead of your surroundings, you may want to harm yourself or even commit suicide. The next day the papers would have two headlines.

* "…woman in the pain of losing her husband regardless of the life tests her two children would give her, committed suicide."
* those who don't like you could give the newspapers exactly the headline they're looking for; "…woman, not knowing the value of her husband in life, had such guilt after his death that without regard for her children, to cover up her lack of love for her husband committed suicide so people would say "look how much she loved her husband."

6. Is the only method you know of to ease your pain, crying? Does the pain subside the more you cry? Does the number of those who suffer with you increase or does the attention increase?

Forgetting the persons who have passed over and forgetting the lament of them are totally different things. I suggest forgetting the lament.

The Holy Books have something to say to those who chastise themselves for feeling guilty about someone's death. "If I'd only done this he wouldn't have died," repeated enough times curses those around you and even those in the grave are uncomfortable. Read this verse:

The Family of Imran, *3:156 You who believe, do not be like those who disbelieve and tell their brethren when they travel around the earth or are out on some campaign: "Of they had been with us, they would not have died or would not have been killed." So that God place that (sort of) despair in their hearts. God gives life and brings death; God is Observant of anything you do."* **(Q)**

I have a method that works successfully on a child who cries at the wrong time or cries to get what he wants. Say this to the child, *"You will not get what you want done by crying. But you may cry if you like, and as much as you like. I will be at a distance where I can't hear your crying. When you are finished crying, come to where I am."* Generally, children will stop crying at that point. If you notice the children who get what they want by crying use this method to solve their every problem throughout life.

Putting your dead spouse in the grave is difficult and you think it is the most difficult thing respecting your spouse, don't you? I have heard it said that the biggest revenge a woman can get is to forget him. According to that, if your husband leaves you and begins living in the same town with someone who is younger and more beautiful than you, would you hurt less? More? I think more. Because burying people/ experiences in your heart is more difficult than burying the dead in the earth and makes it much harder to forget. You can continue life with someone else not making those mistakes you made with your spouse. You must stop punishing yourself.

And this situation is not only between spouses, sometimes a beloved friend will slip away before your eyes and will become someone completely different whom you cannot reach. Is this not a type of loss?

This type of huge loss deserves this thinking, **"If you mourn a thing strongly enough then you may never need to mourn the same subject again."**

Let's talk about something lighter. How did you meet your husband?

Woman: In the last semester of our university studies, he came up to me with a bouquet of roses and said *"Every relationship has it's problems, and ours is that it hasn't started." I said "he is the one" when he first kissed me and said" for those who are visible and invisible my name is.....her name is......from now on she is my woman."*

Mother Teresa: The saying to be proved "Obey your family cheat your partner in marriage, Obey your Partner cheat your family." This is being stuck between family and the wife / husband.

But the problem experienced in marriages is the "indispensability complex". Human beings treat their partner in more loving ways when they themselves feel deeply loved and indispensable or crudely thinking" he/she can't give up on me." When the time comes that we run out of patience then the world turns into a place flooded by the tears of the people who have learned their lesson by losing.

Now let me give you an example one of my friends used to win someone's, heart. During the last year of university, a young lady, seeing that her friend was embarrassed to only be able to buy her a single rose said, *"The number of flowers you give me is not important. The important thing is the number of flowers that open in my heart when I see you.*"

(If the environment I am in at this moment is a recorded image, it means we can ask to see for the same image again: an opportunity for the mother and children to watch themselves. Turning toward Mother Theresa I asked,) "May we show the woman and her children what they have experienced beginning the day she lost her spouse, please." We used the wall screen.

A film of the woman and her children in the pain of the past few days was shown. Watching herself had a big effect on the woman. Even though there were tears from time to time, she watched herself carefully, and naturally didn't like what she saw. When I told her she could watch this record of her behavior over and over as much as she wished, she said:

Woman: Thank you very much, I got the message.

(I stepped out of the image at that point.)

Mother Teresa: From the prevailing point of view today, the choices you gave her were not bad. If we could add a little technology we would be more successful.

1. We could allow this woman who has lost her spouse to show her spouse the attention she wants in the form she wants in a virtual reality scenario. Her spouse's hologram could give answers in a way she wants in certain intervals for limited periods. This way she can say good bye to her spouse: forgiven and free of guilt.

2. We could manipulate the woman's brain by directly loading a happy past to free her from her feelings of guilt so she could start a new life by inserting new life and death memories.

In short, with the necessary feelings and memories of this loss can be lightened to help her recover quickly.

When we look at it this way, there is a saying a baby is born and dies a few days later. "OK," you say, "But what is that child's sin?" Do dark-eyed perpetual virgins await this baby? Or unlimited tables of food? To me, the attention should be turned to the mother and father. Perhaps the mother and father lost their children where we are, and are having treatment for the loss of children in a virtual environment.

When parents lose their children it is the worst death and the least expected. This is especially difficult if this happens suddenly without saying goodbye.

I am sure that manipulation of the brain in the opportunity of a virtual life provided by a virtual god's world would be a much healthier way to assimilate pain. What's more, this is a fitting use of higher technology.

Mother Teresa: I would like to point out an article in *Science and Technology* in May 2007 entitled "Can a Bad Memory be Erased?"

With, the momentary surfacing of a long term memory, before it is returned again to the actual memory, first a processing period is triggered. After this period is activated with medicine or chemicals the effect becomes clearer. Researchers are trying to find the answer to this question: is it possible to erase a memory and only that memory when it is showing itself for the "first" recalling of that memory. In work with laboratory mice, first they taught them to fear two different sounds; as the sound is heard the mice were given a small electric shock.

The next day, half of the mice were given a medicine known to cause memory loss or forgetfulness, and only one of the sounds was tested. The day after that, both sounds were tested and the mice that had not been given memory loss treatment reacted fearfully to both sounds. Those given memory loss treatment were seen to remain insensitive to both sounds.

In the meantime, the nerve reactions are recorded in the part of the brain called the "amygdala" which does the work of the feelings and memory recovery. Activity increased with the memory of pain, and decreased in those mice that had been treated with memory loss medicine. Researchers concluded that memories could, indeed, be selectively erased with the effects of medicine. Of course, it was emphasized that results of a similar experiment on human beings could bring far different results.

If you can erase them you can change them! Isn't that so?

Some pain is so fierce that it affects one very deeply. You may be one of those whom those around you are unable to help no matter what they try. In order that you do not live your entire life as a problem person you are forced to rid yourself of the pain as quickly and healthfully as possible. This woman eases her pain by being anesthetized with medicines instead of erasing memories about marriage she is here to tolerate her pain without forgetting it. **"Your Creator is with you, and will test you enough."**

(With that she said good bye and I was off to the next higher level, and the door opened.)

As soon as I entered the elevator and pressed the button to the fifth floor, the 5 lit up and the door opened. I was in a mid-sized work place in a two-storey house where seven or eight people were working. The people had not yet noticed me when a voice began to speak.

3. Human Resources (Choosing Personnel)
(Attention! Your Breaking Point is Being Tested!)

Voice: In a healthy and clean society how do you explain *"Preventing disappointment from overtaking you as a result of your choices?"*

The biggest choices that affect our lives are work, those concerning, a spouse, friends, personnel, and administrators. These are people we choose to share our most valued feelings and economic op-portunities or people to whom we choose to trust our futures.

I would like to provide some examples of available choices;

Work: Think of students who are studying to take the college entrance examination. In addition to primary and high school many have private lessons or attend special private schools for this purpose. Generally at a school in another town on a preset date they spend two or three hours struggling with predetermined questions attempting to prove that they are worthy of attending the school of their choice.

 As they make this choice, the choosers ask "Is this area right for me? Can I do it?" The choosers ask, "Is this area right for this person? Is this student a match for this area? Can he do it?" By the time the questions are answered at least four years of your life have passed.

The true success of the examination can be determined by (1) studying the success graphics of students after removing those who entered the area they studied out of necessity, (2) those who work in the area they studied in school. If graduates do not work in the area they studied, the method used in testing for entrance is wrong.

Spouse: You think of marrying someone. But why is s/he really marrying you? Does s/he really love you? Or is it the impulse of the moment? Is it a permanent love? Are the families compatible? What will be your family's attitude? And all the same questions must be asked by the other side.

Children: You are married and have decided to have a child but do you want a child so that your spouse will be bound to you? Do you want the child because of your spouse's or your circle of friends' pressure? Will you be a good mother and father? Will your attention change with the sex of the child? Are your resources completely sufficient to raise a child? Is it a momentary wish? Do you really want a baby? Unless you are careful, you might find a baby in your lap with the answer.

Friends: You met someone and became friends. Is s/he a good time friend? Can he be trusted with a secret? Will he sell you out when he is hard pressed or for his own benefit? Sometimes it is only after some 20-30 years of sacrifice this becomes horribly understood.

Personnel: You will choose a person for a critical role in your business and will not have the time to follow up and monitor him afterward. Is he the right man for the job? Can he be trusted? You don't know. When you find out your company might have already suffered serious financial and psychological damage.

Administrators: You choose the mayor, the town chairman, your representative, the president you chose for your country. Is the person trustworthy? What about his past and you count on the future plans of this person? Does he play favoritism? Is he honest? Is he clever? Is the person courageous and persistent? Does he know his contingency? Is he universal in thought? In short, is he the leader you need?

While making all these choices the questions we have and the answers to the questions asked of us will be;

1. When education is finished, and you have begun to work,

2. After years of marriage,

3. After the birth of a baby,

4. Months or years after a person has been hired and the company has suffered loss,

5. Politicians in your city, your country who have embezzled or have been the leader of embezzlement rings are revealed years later when you as a tax-payer are paying for the damage they have caused.

Unfortunately, all negative answers can only be given in hind sight or at the point where nothing remedial can be done, at the point of no return. Later, because of the financial and psychological problems caused by negative answers we experience problematic people, a problematic society and unending chain of problems. In a situation where no one exactly knows anyone else, the actual question that plagues us is, that the real question is knowing the exact intent of the person in front of us.
One of the purposes of our life on earth is for God's choosing personnel and administrators. This is clearly outlined in the Holy Books. (God's Method of recruiting Human Resources)

Some of the verses about monitoring:

I Timothy, *3:10 They are to be examined first and only admitted to serve as deacons if there is nothing against them.* **(NT)**
I Corinthians, *3:9 We are fellow workers with God.* **(NT)**
The Family of Imran, *3:154 God might test what is on your minds and purge whatever is in your hearts. God is Aware of whatever is on your minds!* **(Q)**
The Cave, *18:7 We have placed whatever is on earth as an ornament for it, so we may test them as to which one is best in action.* **(Q)**
The Holy Prophet, *11:7 (He did this) so He may test which of you is finest in action.* **(Q)**

Mankind's entry onto earth: each person is a singular winner, after a merciless contest where the losers die, a victorious sperm! (God rewards those who win with life!)

When speaking of earthly life, it is said that *"those who worship, live good lives and are industrious people, will all attain heaven,"* they do not speak about competing with each other for a position in heaven. However, the struggle of millions/billions of people on earth, resembles the struggle of sperm attempting to reach the egg. To me this is a reverse birth. In order to have birth into the Real, one must first pass with honors in the virtual environment.

Where there is struggle, there is competition. Therefore, to enter the Real Life there is competition, then during life there is competition. Those who are highest in the competition will only be revealed upon death/ when they reawake.

II Corinthians, *5:4 To have what must die taken up into life.* **(NT)**

According the scriptures and various teachings, the earth is a setting for advancement or is a school where we are members of an apparently limitless group, on a course of life without knowing where we have come from or why we are here. These particular verses clearly show that a choice will be made between the members of the group. Members, not knowing where they have come from and without a reason for being there, find themselves a part of a scenario in which their breaking point coefficient in various aspects of life begins to be tested.

Voice: Please give an example of the breaking point coefficient.

Within the virtual god system everyone will come to a point of giving/ accepting a bribe. Consider this case: in the virtual business as we are being tested in the coefficient of giving or accepting bribery while hiring a director for the firm.

<u>**Scenario:**</u>

First Stage:

If the control of a firm worth $100,000 is being entrusted to the director, in an imaginary environment without anyone's knowing, a bribe is offered to the candidate for director in ever increasing amounts; $100,000, $250,000, $500,000, $750,000. If the person rejects the offer of $750,000 and accepts $1,000,000 for acting fraudulently, the breaking point of bribery for this person is $1,000,000. If the candidate in question is to be hired for a firm worth $100,000, this person would be considered quite satisfactory for the job on the basis of his bribery coefficient. On the other hand, the candidate would not be considered acceptable for the position of director of a million dollar firm unless he increased his bribery coefficient to more than $1,000,000. If there is more than one candidate for the position in the same test given by the firm applied to, the person with the highest bribery coefficient will certainly be chosen.

Second Stage:
The wives or lovers who have been attracted to a luxurious life of these same candidates will have their bribery coefficients tested. A greedy spouse can turn a spouse into a traitor or a thief. If a person accepts a bribe of $500,000 to supply a spouse's needs, the bribery coefficient of that person falls to $500,000.

During these scenarios, a stage is set within which there is very little possibility of the plot being revealed and if found out, weaknesses in the justice system neutralize the crime. Thus, conditions are rife for the candidate to deviate. Given pressure or need, ungoverned circumstances, and little possibility of legal intervention, the candidate who stands to profit from such a deal can easily stray. When the press and the media are involved in this scenario, the racecourse is even more seductive.

Voice: What do you mean by press and media support?

This subject was nicely covered in an article entitled. Cinema therapy in the April 2007 publication of Science and Technology. *"Cinema therapy has recently been used more and more as a treatment in psychotherapy. Right now, instead of calling cinema therapy a psychiatric treatment in its own right, we are talking of a therapist using a certain film of his choice to be used as a facilitator in the treatment of a patient."*

"...Films while saving time, can be said to be a more convincing explanation. The situation can be thought of as dreaming while being fully conscious. The spectator, can easily leave the real world and feel himself a part of a powerfully constructed story with sound and scenery

in support. Studies in various areas for effectiveness and scope have provided evidence of significant impact of adolescents' perception of matters as varied as habitual cigarette smoking, deviant sexual behavior and social violence being a factor in causing cancer."

In 1998 I constructed a model of press and media support which I will present here;

Methods of annihilating a country or overthrowing a government;

1. Make the people believe they are not living.
2. Destroy the trust of the people in the state. (making them believe there is no state in existence)

Methods:

You can easily make people believe that others are living a life he could never dream of by frequently showing brief glimpses of the lives in newspapers, television, magazines.

In these circumstances, when he compares the life he sees in magazines and on television with the life that he lives, his spouse, his house, his clothing, he will easily believe he is not living and will never be able to have that sort of life and shall sink into depression. Most importantly, he will begin to desire the conditions of this type of life.

If the government simply stands by and watches the people's money being stolen, unfairly distributed or if civil servants lead the corruption, people will soon come to think that: *"If you aren't someone's relative, if you don't have enough money, if you do not conduct imaginary export business, or engage in bribery, embezzlement or other misdeeds, it is not possible to live. Those who do, profit, neither God nor the government punish them."* If a citizen seeking his rights is thwarted by false testimony of a governing board that has been bought off, and if there is no punishment handed down by the courts established for the purpose of citizen protection, that citizen's faith in the justice system will be severely weakened.

God's justice is administered by the courts on earth as it punishes criminals. If there is no justice in a government the people will have no belief.

When the press, the media and the government work hand in hand, the number of people who need hope, but maintain their sense of integrity in spite of poverty, is reduced day by day. An explosion of theft, prostitution, embezzlement, and extortion can be expected.

Television programs and magazines covering events are run by about 1,000 people. These 1,000 people effect the imaginations of millions of citizens negatively, and reduce the belief in society and its operational system. That society will be turned into a society that believes it is not living normally and one in which individuals will do anything to prove differently.

Under such bombardment, our prospective director's bribery coefficient will fall to $100,000 or even $20,000 in an instant.

Voice: What is the point of a bribery coefficient? How it is measured?

The basic philosophy is that, **"if you take a bribe you will give a bribe."** Since the coefficient of taking a bribe is being measured, with the goal of measuring your coefficient of justice, the ability to complete business illegally or in a bidding process when the firm does not deserve to win the bid, their ability to offer a bribe is being measured. To this end,

For a candidate to easily progress in his job, with the logic of **"anyone who takes money today will take orders tomorrow,"** some or-ganizations and sects offer monetary or psychological compensation. In an effort to get rich quick, while appearing to ease one's material monetary problems, in return the candidate is offered choices that actually compromise him. This is just like a watermelon: the outside is the healthy green of peace and friendship while the inside red, is the symbol of blood!

The day will come when those who are unable to receive a certificate within an imaginary system will not be able to enter business, hold an administrative position, become a bureaucrat, or a politician, marry or become a parent. They will not even be able to be born...
Voice: They will not be able to marry or have children?

A clean and healthy society is, above all, a society with happy marriages and families at its base. To this end, just as we are able to assess the breaking point coefficient in the selection of a director of a business firm, in a virtual environment we will be able to assess loyalty, love, respect, good days and bad days, family harmony, and other aspects necessary for a good marriage. Those who do not prove competent in the test scenarios will not be able to marry.

I Peter, *4:12 My dear people, you must not think it unaccountable that you should be tested by fire. There is nothing extraordinary in what has happened to you.* **(NT)**

Voice: How will politicians be tested?

Social scenarios will be used, of course. The prime minister, parliament representatives, and those within their scenarios will be tested to see whether or not they favor their own parties, relatives, spouses, friends, surroundings, bidding, real estate or staff. Will they abuse their office? Will they work in the interest of their country? Are they courageous? They shall be tested in every scenario you can think of. Just as we think of the practice of marking a finger with ink to show we have voted as primitive, we will think voting at a voting box in the 21st century to be primitive.

The people will not choose any public servant. Candidates will prove themselves in virtual realities, and the administration of the govern-ment will be entrusted only to those with the highest breaking points.

In the past, when a young apprentice began working with a master, a sum of money that appeared to be forgotten and what's more, uncounted, was left in an inconspicuous place to determine how the apprentice would react to it.

The virtual god system goes one step further to test your inner sense of justice or injustice by putting you into an unjust situation and behaving unjustly towards you. The logic is this; the important thing is not to be able to maintain integrity in a system where everyone is honest and everyone is well-heeled. The heart of the issue is; are you able to retain your integrity in a system where everyone is corrupt and extremely needy? It is not the injustice of the virtual god system that is being monitored, but your coefficient of justice within that system.

Our junior high school teacher gave us a good example of this: "A gentleman covers his mouth when he yawns in a dark room with no one else in the room."

Matthew, *10:16 "I am sending you out as sheep among the wolves; so be cunning as serpents and yet as harmless as doves."* **(NT)**

Philippians, *2:15 "Then you will be innocent and genuine, perfect children of God among a deceitful and underhand brood."* **(NT)**

The philosophy of the scenario of a virtual god system is like the philosophy of Murphy's Law: *"If an attack goes exactly as planned, it means that you have definitely fallen into an ambush."* When everything goes as you've planned it, be wary of your own corruption.

Voice: The biggest protests or corruption begin at just the point you have mentioned. Mankind begins taking payment for prayers and good deeds he has done in the world immediately. In spite of the fact that the Holy Book he believes in says, he will certainly be tested with poverty and societal ailments, when the cycle of poverty begins and he should be practicing patience, some protest. Instead of thinking of it as a time to be endured and a time of testing, he believes he has suffered injustice and it turns into a period of rebellion.

How will you struggle when your needs are not granted? Will you cry and whine? Will you revolt? Will you give in? Briefly, how will you defend your rights? This is what we are trying to learn.

Habakkuk, *1:13 Why do you look on while men are treacherous, and stay silent while the evil man swallows a better man than he.* **(OT)**

Job, *9:24 When a country falls into a tyrant's hand, it is he blindfolds the judges. Or if not he, who else?* **(OT)**

Romans, *9:14 Does it follow that God is unjust? Of course, not.* **(NT)**

The Romans, *30:36 Whenever We let mankind taste mercy, they are glad about it; yet if any evil should strike them because of what their hands have sent on ahead, then they feel despondent.* **(Q)**

These periods are a time when very subtle but important support is given to those who follow the true God.

Hebrews, *2:18 That is because he has himself been through temptation he is able to help others who are tempted.* **(NT)**

Let me give you two anecdotes as examples, one from the seen and another from the unseen.

Footprints in the Sand

One night a man had a dream. He dreamed He was walking along the beach with the LORD. Across the sky flashed scenes from His life. For each scene He noticed two sets of footprints in the sand. One belonging to Him and the other to the LORD.

When the last scene of His life flashed before Him, he looked back at the footprints in the sand. He noticed that many times along the path of His life there was only one set of footprints. He also noticed that it happened at the very lowest and saddest times of His life.

This really bothered Him and He questioned the LORD about it. "LORD You said that once I decided to follow you, you'd walk with me all the way. But I have noticed that during the most troublesome times in my life there is only one set of footprints. I don't understand why when I needed you most you would leave me."

The LORD replied, "My precious, precious child, I Love you and I would never leave you! During your times of trial and suffering when you see only one set of footprints, it was then that I carried you." (Irish Anecdote- Carolyn Carty 1963)

The Priest's Reproach to God

A village that was about to be inundated with water due to construction of a new dam was being vacated. Everyone left the village except for the village priest, who said "you go on, I'm not coming. God will give me special compensation." The villagers went on without much protest. A day later the waters had already risen to table level. The villagers went by row boat to rescue the priest. They found the priest standing on the table, but he again said, "You go on, God is going to give me special compensation and will save me." The villagers left and returned the next day. By this time the water had reached the roof. From the roof the priest yelled, "You go on, God is going to give me special compensation and will save me." The third day the villagers came with a helicopter and with the only place left to go the found the priest on the bell tower, against all their insistence he said, "You go on, God is going to give me special compensation and will save me." And they left. The next day they returned to find the priest's dead body.

Meanwhile while everyone was laughing at the priest on earth he was in a corner of heaven pouting. Those around him were curious and asked. "God saw your goodness and accepted you into heaven. Why are you pouting? The priest retorted, "Don't ask, I've been worshipping him for forty years. Once in forty years something comes up and I ask him for something and he didn't back me up." At just that time, the heavens thundered and out of the clouds can the voice of God, "Crazy fool, I sent you two boats and a helicopter. You didn't get in, what else should I have done?" Let's continue on the course.

Mother love is the reflection of god's love. It is a personal love for you in your lifetime given by God.

Voice: Do you think there will there be other types of standards?

Another Standard of the virtual god technology will be that justice is not dispensed without a need. That is, there will be no subjects on the test that you haven't studied.

The Immunity, *9:115 God is not apt to let any folk go astray once he has guided them to the point where he explains to them how they should do their duty. God is Aware of everything. (Q)*

The Cattle, *6:131 That is because your Lord will not destroy any towns unjustly while their people are heedless: everyone will have ranks according to what they have been doing. Your Lord is not oblivious of what they are doing. (Q)*

The Narratives, *28:59 Your Lord has never been the destroyer of any towns unless He had dispatched a messenger to their capital city who recited Our signs to them. (Q)*

Without giving something, nothing can be asked for. Just as in school, first there is training then the test. Another interesting verse;

The Children of Israel, *17:16 We have never acted as punishers until We have dispatched some Messenger. We order its high-livers so they act depraved in it; thus the Sentence about it is proven to be right and We utterly annihilate it. (Q)*

If we read this from another angle: "Administrators who have become spoiled with wealth and goods, to save the country or to display their rotten ways, we ruin the country, we try them with all types of scenarios. Later, these administrators are shown to be worthy of their sentence."

Voice: Why do you translate this to support your own thinking?

I am forced to think this way and accept it. I am unable to give any other meaning to a few politicians defrauding innocent people and causing them to live in misery for years, but that God has permitted this to continue. I cannot believe that the God, an unseen friend, my grandmother introduced to me as a child, works this way. Perhaps the most important model to tell me that is that my conscience is clear is this! Virtual god technology is not a puppeteer, it only sets the stage!

Politicians lose the race when they work so as to help their own country at the expense of another. In the test of politics, the highest points are gained by instigating projects which foster peace and function for the well being of all people.

Voice: What is the disadvantage in precinct hand voting democratic elections that you find so primitive?

There are two glaring problems in this: **(1)** It supports population increase. **(2)** It allows for remotely fixing mass votes.

(1) A philosopher says, *"When doing a project, it is not what everyone says that matters, what matters is that what is necessary has been said."* Democracy depends on numbers, not inherent characteristics of events. Therefore, in order to gain power and guarantee election, groups must increase the number of voters. If a group with families who are able to support and rear one or two children gives birth to eight or ten, within two or three generations a group can gain the administration with sheer numbers. A country must have a larger armed forces than those around it, therefore it must increase its population. Is such a system not undermining itself in the long run?

(2) I read that many years ago in the struggle against the rat population in United States grain storage bins, ultra sonic signals were used. Rats with their acute hearing ability could hear these signals while humans could not. Subjected to these signals, the rats were left without appetite for food and sex and within a certain time the population was eradicated. You have heard about the dog repellant systems that work on the same principle used by people who fear dog attacks.

Every living thing that has ears can be controlled this way. Just as electronic signals that cannot be heard by the ear, but are audible to the brain can be used to calm and relax people, other frequencies can be used to irritate and anger people. On election day, if calming ultrasonic signals are sent by satellite, the party in power will be reelected. If irritating signals are broadcasted, the opposition party will be elected.

Psalms, 19:13 A foolish son is the ruin of his father, a wife scolding is like a dripping gutter. **(OT)**

A very expensive and work intensive method of attaining power can be done by indebting the people with long term mortgaging.

When the projects I have mentioned are put into effect, democracy, which people now think they run themselves, will finally turn into a system of management.

Voice: Understood! Understood! Your business is difficult on earth and you are in a position to be able to write good scenarios.

Luke, 16:11-12 If then you have not been faithful with the dishonest wealth, who will entrust to you the true riches? ̄ And if you have not been faithful with what belongs to another, who will give you what is your own? **(NT)**

In this situation I have to say good bye. "Your creator is with you and justice is true."

(The elevator door opened and I stepped in. When I pushed the sixth floor button the door to the sixth floor opened.)

4. Indivudual Punishment System
(Delayed Justice is Injustice!)

As I looked down from this floor I saw banks, the parliament, the ministries, businesses, the mayor, the municipality leaders, media men, secretaries, the director of information management on different stages, all experiencing. Thousands of people, separate from each other, were being tested in different scenarios of parallel universes. A person watching could not help wondering which stage *he* himself was on.

As the sixth floor I was on began to become lighter, my attention turned to examining my surroundings. There was a fenced section for prisoners and their guardians, in another other section a prisoner sat thinking darkly. In another section relatives of a dead prisoner were ululating and cursing the murderer. I was in another section with a judge, plaintiff, a defendant, a respondent, lawyers, a public prosecutor, a court crier, scribes, and the murdered person's supporters in a court room with a murder case in session. On one of the walls of the room was a quatrain of Omar Khayyam.

Name one who didn't break your law, tell me?
What pleasure is in the life of virtue, tell me?
You will demand evil for the evil I did, you will,
And what will be the difference between us, tell me?

Voice: There are big troubles with justice on earth right now, it seems.

I believe that God's justice is administered by a personalized individual punishment system.

Voice: What is an individual punishment system?

It means a personal justice system. But first let's identify the officials who will administer the justice.

Police: A person that must be guilty enough to commit crime, must be willful enough not to do it, must be courageous enough to prevent a crime and once committed courageous enough to catch a criminal. He must be humanistic enough to treat the criminal well, and must be honorable enough to hand the criminal over to the judicial system.

Justice: The most reliable judgment is one which is based on material evidence; material judgment will result in the least opinionated court. There is always room for conjecture in courts where evidence is scarce or is based on simple hearsay. Therefore, it is that justice is connected to the judge, not the judge to justice."

Let us think of an example: if a man is given a sentence of 20 years imprisonment for killing another, the goal is to provide comfort to the family and friends of the dead person. It is also to make sure that the criminal knows his mistake and will not repeat the crime once he is released.

How is it then, that a sentence of 20 years is justified for the life of one person; a good part of one's life? If the goal is to prevent the person from coming to the point of repeating the crime and being certain it won't be repeated when the chance comes:

1. A person who reaches the point of regret and maturity (20 – maturity) in a shorter time has wasted those remaining years in prison.

2. If a person who is released when his time is finished repeats the crime, then he will have been released early when he shouldn't have.

Because the true reason for a crime has not been understood, people have been forced into using a punishment system of society to end the life of the alleged criminal instead of using a system that is specific to the defendant. The basis of this punishment system is like the blood feud which trades the life of one person for the life of another. Instead of taking the criminal's life immediately, it is taken in the corners of prison over a long period of time. This blood feud is between the state and the criminal, supported by the state.

Two members of society are lost: one is in the grave and the other is in prison. One is lost anyway, but if we are to save anything from those who remain, we must do everything possible to reestablish them into society. Anyone who has served his term, come to terms with his crime, if he can be of help to society, each day he stays in jail, justice is delayed, and **"delayed justice is injustice."**

As Rumi has said, *"It is justice to put a thing where it belongs, but persecution to put it where it does not belong."(2583)*

On this subject a good example of this is given of Moses, just as is written in Banishment 14-22, after he had killed a man, he begged forgiveness of God.

The Narratives, *28:16 He said: "My Lord, I have wronged my own soul. Forgive me!"* **(Q)**

After having unintentionally killed a man Moses begs forgiveness from God. When a man commits a crime on earth, after proving his regret on earth, he can be forgiven and even be made a prophet. And he was not just a minor prophet at that; the prophet who conveyed one of the Holy Books, the Torah, to mankind. This is a fine example of God's justice and tolerance in the world. As I said before, how can we ask God for tolerance in our prayers if we do not show it to each other?

Voice: What kind of justice system do you envision in a virtual scenario?

Basically, methods coming from the future do not punish people, but create opportunities and methods for new horizons and new chances and lower the criminal potential.

The strength of Sociological God is social justice. The power of the technological virtual god model is the opportunity of unlimited trials. State must provide a justice system leaving no need for "looking for justice" The reason for a criminal going to prison or being punished is that society and those near to the dead person can be comforted. Will society and the judges who sentenced him and those near to the dead person allow the criminal to return to a normal life if I can prove the true regrets of a criminal and have the guarantee that he will not repeat the crime? If they will not allow his return, it means that the modern blood feud is still being perpetuated.

In order to prove that the criminal will not repeat the crime, unaware of the intention, the criminal of his own free will, will be presented with similar virtual scenarios that will provide natural reactions. In each one he will be shown his performance and the scenario will be repeated again and again.

The general rule is this: those who commit a crime in the virtual world will commit one in the real world.

He will be monitored within the parameters of virtual scenarios if the same crime is committed he will admit that he is not ready to be released. If the same crime is not committed, the crime will not be committed in the real world. Recordings of the scenarios will be shown to the judges, the dead man's family and other interested people. With the approval of the interested parties, society will have gained a beneficial member from a criminal. In this way, technology will assist justice, and the "Technological Justice", **"Digital Justice"** system will have begun.

This technology will give hope to all who have landed in prison somehow. Perhaps the most important aspect will be that those people said to be guilty of a crime will have their brain recordings reviewed to test whether or not they actually committed the crime. Technology will reach information that will leave no doubt about under what conditions they committed the crime and virtual judges will abide by the law.

All newborn babies may not be innocent!

1 Timothy, 5:24 The faults of some people are obvious long before anyone makes any complaint but them, while others have faults that are not discovered until afterwards. (NT)

In a virtual environment they will be released from the law and their conscience, and they will be released in the real world, too.

Voice: Are there verses in the Holy Books to support this subject?

Of course, the most important verse is this one:

The Cattle, 6:98 It is He Who has reproduced you from a single soul, and (granted you) a settlement (on earth) and a resting place (after death). (Q)

The resting place is prison. There are other interesting verses about death.

Deuteronomy, 32:39 It is I who deal with death and life; when I have struck it is I who heal (and none can deliver from my hand). (OT)
The Qaf, 50:43 It is We Who give life and bring death, and toward Us lies the goal. (Q)
The Cow, 2:253 If God had wished, they would not have fallen out with one another. (Q)
The Accessions, 8:17 You(all) do not kill them but God kills them. You did not shoot(anything)when you shot(arrows or spears) but God threw them so He may test believers, as a handsome test from Himself. (Q)
The Light, 25:3 They take on (other) gods which do not create anything while they themselves have been created. They control no harm nor do they control death nor life, nor even rebirth. (Q)
The Family of Imran, 3:145 No soul shall die except with God's permission according to specific writ. (Q)
The Family of Imran, 3:152 God confirmed his promise to you as you grappled with them by His permission. (Q)

Voice: Can we say in conclusion then, that our hour of death cannot be changed?

In spite of the fact that Society as a rule believes that there are verses to indicate that, there is some flexibility in that.

I Kings, 3:14 And I will give you a long life if you follow my ways keeping my laws and commandments as your father David followed them. **(OT)**

The Clans, 33:16 Say: "Fleeing will never help you: if you should flee from death or slaughter, then you will still enjoy (life) only briefly. **(Q)**

The Originator, 35:11 No elderly person grows even older nor has anything shortened from his life unless it is (written down) in some book. **(Q)**

According to the Holy Books it is not possible for you to do harm to anyone else or not even to yourself without God's permission.

Yunus, 10:49 Say: "I control no harm nor any advantage by myself, except concerning whatever God may wish." **(Q)**

Voice: There is a gauge of the felt need for a technological God that can be found in the book called a Concentrated Qur'an (View of the Concentrated Qur'an) on the website, (www.aydinturkgucu.net) Is there a question of the people of earth accepting the fact (thinking/knowing) they are shadows? (when I said "no")

It's good that you understand that the shadows are not the goal but the method. I will now see you off to the upper floor. "Your Creator is with you and the creators are with you, too."

Thank you, I'll see you.

With the push of the seventh floor button the number seven lit up and with the door opening, I had arrived on the famous seventh floor. There on my right were eight stairs to climb to reach the door with the "Exit" sign above it. (The stage stairs and door were like the stairs in the film *The Truman Show* at the end with an "Exit" sign above like a door opening to the real world.)

I felt like running up the stairs, opening the door and going out into the real world, but I held myself back. Just as I'd learned from the other floors, I could be caught here if the door would not open before I'd finished my training.

Revelation *8:1 The lamp then broke the seventh seal and there was silence in heaven for about half an hour.* **(NT)**

As the verse says there is a waiting period a lot longer than usual. This is probably a test of patience I needed.

Voice: Years ago, our attention was attracted to the fact that you asked for something different from your creator, and we diverted people and publications that would support you and made sure they reached you.

(I interrupted immediately.) What? With "our attention was attracted," what did you mean?

What you thought in a virtual world and everything you said was followed here and we watched all the prayers you made to the Creator. In order that your prayers were answered, all the virtual support we sent was spotted by the obstacle team, *"any publication that is written with a bias and special purpose will not be a good friend, but a bad friend. So, books, like friends must be separated into the good and bad, and words like "books are a man's best friend must be used with care,"* you wrote in warning to your surroundings.

(It must have been my occasional glances at the door at the top of the stairs)

Voice: I see your mind is on the door you think opens into the real world. Everyone prepares himself for the seventh floor, but the Creator of seven heavens is on the eighth floor. After the training is finished on this floor why shouldn't it be? On all the floors so far, you have gotten the answers to your question of "why". On this floor you will learn "how". May I first have a summary of the training so far?

All working systems that have been figured out can be copied, changed, and directed. We have seen that by first understanding the brain and the information retaining system, the brain, by stimulating the sense center, can direct the body even without sense organs. It also appears possible to copy certain information in the brain to other areas, change certain aspects and replace it, then after testing this new version it appears possible to put it back in place of the old brain. Then, the new version reactions can be recorded and evaluated and replaced in the old brain, if found suitable. You can see if I really understand by using this example;

Example: A picture in a photograph is almost impossible to change without damaging the picture or the change being obvious. However, that same picture can be scanned or sent to a computer using digital photography. At that point, you can make the changes you want with the help of software program and when the picture is printed again no one except an expert will be able to understand that there have been changes made. The important thing here is that because the technique of storing the image has been revealed, it can be copied onto the computer, changes made and returned.

In the computer systems of today, because they work with this binary system (0/1) the capacity and capabilities are limited.

Voice: Do you remember where we gave the training that caused you to think of space as a recording device or a hard disk?

I remember very well. It was while I was in the 1997 Micro Processors course. It was explained that in order to expand the capacity of the limitations of the binary system bacteria were about to be used in computer and hard disks.

The binary system of the computer, where a 0 or 1 has been put in the information box that won't be changed for a long time is read, changed or erased as necessary. The 0/1 data means full or empty and each box is made to contain only one or the other. In this situation, it resembles the early telephones where each cable carried only one telephone conversation. (Figure 1)

If that same cable is connected to a switchboard, the number of conversations you could have will depend on the number of frequency bands that are created on one cable. (Figure 2) With today's fiber optic cable technology which is transmitted by light signals, millions of conversations are possible.

The information storage boxes of today's computers are just like the one-

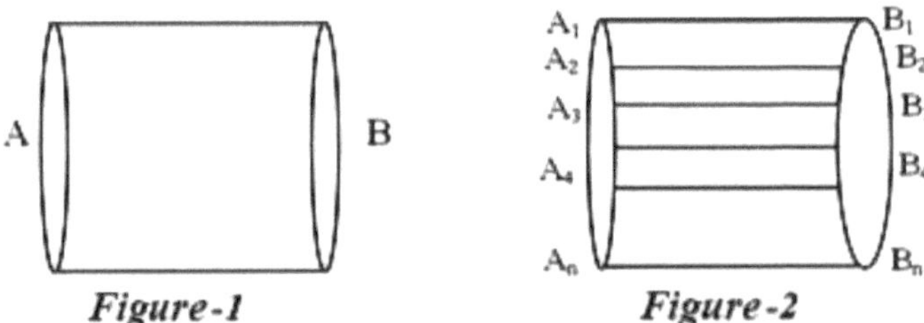

Figure-1   **Figure-2**

conversation telephone system without a switchboard: primitive. Because the information storage system used in computers, like telephones, do not permit the distribution of frequencies, the capacity and speed of the binary system is limited. (Figure 3). On one hand research was being done to eradicate these limitations, while on the other hand, work to reduce the size of existing information boxes continued. Under these conditions computers and parts used such as hard drives hard disks and rams have been reduced in size as the capacity has increased. But the increase has stayed inadequate for voice/ image and storage in terms of needs. (Figure 4)

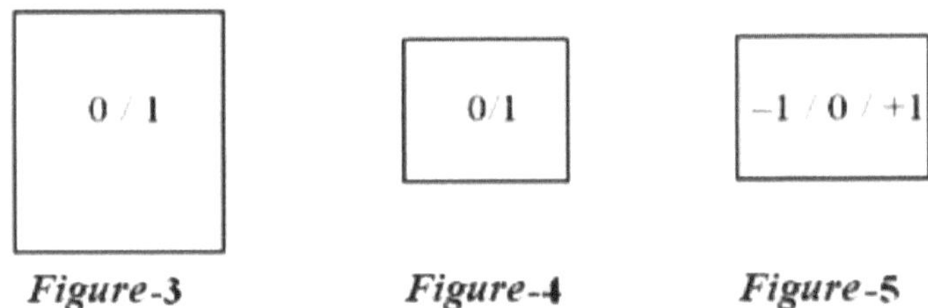

Figure-3   **Figure-4**   **Figure-5**

Voice: Looking at the configuration of an atom, we see an electron(–), proton(+) and neutron(0) and good example of a trinary system application. If, instead of the 0/1 information which was stored electrically in the computer systems of the time, they could have switched to a trinary system of +1/0/-1. (Figure 5)

We must quickly develop our computer systems into quicker, increased capacity and more sensitive information storage and processing systems.

In our micro processors course *"in order to increase this capacity in our computers there must be a living organism storage system developed,"* and the principles of such a system were explained:

Organisms used for this purpose are bacteria that give off different colors according to the frequency of light reaching them: i.e. when 1 decibel of light is received they give off the color red, given 2 decibels of light, blue, three decibels of light, yellow, and four decibels of light, green, this produces a 4 base system. But when a 7 color system is designed a 7 base system would be reached. A sack of living information, the bacteria, must be able to be isolated from each other, to store the information loaded for a long period of time and to be read or changed when necessary.

In the book *Black Holes and Baby Universes* page 50, (Stephen Hawking writes):

"To explain this, quarks were endowed with an attribute called colour. It should be emphasized that his has nothing to do with our normal perception of colour; quarks are far too small to be seen by visible light. It is merely a convenient name. The idea is that quarks come in three colours –red, green, and blue- but that any isolated bound state, such as a hadron, has to be colourless, either a combination of red, green and blue like the proton, or a mixture of red and antired, green and antigreen, and blue and antiblue like the pi meson. The strong interaction between quarks are supposed to be carried by spin-1 particles called gluons, rather like the particles that carry the weak interaction. The gluons also carry colour." Notice that "red and antired, green and antigreen and blue and antiblue are mentioned like 0/1, exist/ not exist, active/passive constructs. When red(1) is active, antired is passive(0).

The one-information box working principle would work in this way: Box 1, 2, 3, 4, 5, 6, 7 light levels which can be sent at simultaneously will load one code. When only 1, 2, 5 and 7 levels are sent, 1, 2, 5, and 7 rooms will be 1 and 3, 4 and 6 rooms will be 0. (Figure 6) Thus, 1 box will be divided into seven.

This is like a single floor home with seven apartments. In a one storey house, when the bell is rung and sound comes from inside it means they are home. If no sound comes from inside, they are not home. You can build a seven floor apartment building on the same site (instead of the one storey building), so there you would have to push seven bells.

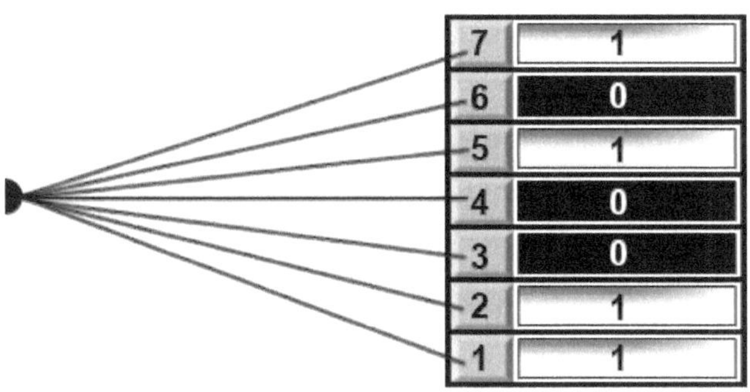

Scientists Push the Boundaries of Human Life
(Newsweek International, By Lee Silver / June 4, 2007 issue)

Scientists in the last couple of years have been trying to create novel forms of life from scratch. They've forged chemicals into synthetic DNA, the DNA into genes, genes into genomes, and built the molecular machinery of completely new organisms in the lab— organisms that are nothing like anything nature has produced.

The people who are defying Nature's monopoly on creation are a loose collection of engineers, computer scientists, physicists and chemists who look at life quite differently than traditional biologists do.

What we're talking about is producing life that is wholly new—not in any way a genetic descendant of the primordial Mother Cell. The initial members of each newly created breed will have no ancestors at all. So far, researchers have fabricated individual biological building blocks, but they have yet to create an entirely new synthetic self-replicating organism.

Venter has put tens of millions of dollars of his own money into Synthetic Genomics, a start-up, to make artificial organisms that convert sunlight into bio-fuel, with minimal environmental impact and zero net release of greenhouse gases. These organisms, he says, will "replace the petrochemical industry, most food, clean energy and bioremediation."

If you had to push seven bells, one at a time to get results, you would lose time. Where there were colored lamps placed in the bells, if all would ring at the same time with the push of one button, and a query system wherein residents would respond with different colored lamps lighting, (blue, yellow, red, green, etc.), if the lamp of the house that has the bell is lit, they are at home (1).

If it does not light, they are not at home (0). In this situation, not a septenary system, but a 0/1 binary system with 7 blocks is being used. (*Figure 6*) This information storage method of sound and image records would provide us with the necessary capacity and speed to store and process images.
I would like to share news of this with you:

Let's think of a screen of a movie theater that contains all colors: where the colors will actively appear at any one place on the screen is determined by the light directed through the frames of film that pass in front of a projector onto the screen. This is done by filming at certain speeds and running the film back using film frames and light and the white screen which is then transferred to the brain through the eyes. **Instantly, both the writing and the reading processes are processed from the screen.**

At any one instant there is only one frame active on the screen; the prior and next frames are not reflected on the screen and are passive. This is exactly like in space where only the place where the world is, looks active and the places outside the world are passive. In the book Black Holes and Baby Universes, page 51 Stephen Hawking says. *"It is hoped that this 'infrared slavery' will explain why quarks are always confined to colourless bound states but so far no-one has been able to demonstrate this really convincingly."*

Only at the position of the world are the quarks activated to turn into a colored image, and then when the world reaches a different point, they again become passive quarks. But in space the position of our world is colored and not "colourless."

The value of 0/1 represents an insignificant value as it crosses the writing head of the hard disk in the information boxes on the hard disk. However, it turns into totally different images on the screen as it passes over the reading/writing head and activates. (The images of the film will appear, wherever DVD reading head is.) The universe is a curtain between us and reality, as reality is just a curtain away.

In a virtual world, man's body will appear and disappear, just like the image of a person on the cinema or computer screen. The body will appear again just as the specifics on a frame of film with each appearance/disappearance. Man is a virtual being made up of as many frames as the sum of his heartbeats; consider this!

Voice: We could ask: was a three dimension virtual reality created at this point?

Various verses talk about the three dimensions.

The Sent Forth, *77:30 Hurry away to shade which has three sections. (Q)*

But, I think, we don't live in a three dimensional world, but an eleven dimensional world.

Voice: Will you please explain this subject a bit more around the point of view of the dimension we live in, you wrote in 1998?

Dimension: a measurement of something in a particular direction, especially its height, length or width.

As you see, dimension is a term to describe living/non living, seen/unseen beings. We know as many dimensions as we can identify. While three dimensions are usually enough to identify material objects, width **(x)** height **(y)**, depth **(z)** and time **(t)**. In identifying the universe we live in the first dimensions that come to mind/ specifics are;

1. Width (x)
2. Height (y)
3. Depth (z)
4. Color
5. Temperature
6. Sound
7. Speed/time (t)
8. Gender
9. Animate/Inanimate
10. Dead/Alive
11. Existent/non existent

While science uses three dimensions as a "standard model" to describe the visible universe, man's brain uses eleven dimensions to perceive and describe his surroundings. (Doesn't science collect visible data from the Hubble telescope using color? In addition, infra rouge and other frequencies and unseen dimensions are known to exist in the universe.)

<u>**For example:**</u> The weight, height of two people are described the same by science. But if you ask another person to describe these two people he will do so by giving the specific race, gender, voice, animate/inanimate, alive/dead of each. So while science looks at three dimensions, people look at all eleven dimensions.

Virtual god technology would have to test at least eleven dimensions on the virtual racecourse of earth to be believed by man. In man's brain, the closer a copy is to the original, the more reality it takes on.

Voice: The model of space as a hard disk as you explained it is logical. Rumi has said, *"The world is renewed with each breath.*

But we stay in this world just as we appear, without awareness of this renewal. (1144) In this situation, are we speaking of a three dimensional simulation instrument without a screen? Just as we have here?

That can be said, of course. Virtual Universe is not a computer grafted onto humanity, but an intelligent machine. In the film "The Minority Report" a human brain that had been computerized was used instead of a computer programmed with humanity. Let's not leave our virtual system without taking a guess about the screen. I think of it as a hole in the screen or a smashed atom.

What happens when you put a minute hole in the tube screen of a television? A huge amount of energy is released and pours out of that tiny hole. If you do not check the energy pouring out it will cause you damage. If you are able to control it, you can use it somehow.

When you accept that the world is an imaginary screen, atoms which are generally said to be the smallest particles of matter, will take the place of the sensitive pixels on the computer screen. OK? We are actually punching a hole in the screen of the world by smashing the atom. By controlling the energy discharges we have brought ease into our lives. We have also brought damage and suffering into the world by, in a controlled way, blowing holes in the screen of the world with nuclear bombs.

The reason a living being is unable to live in a place where a nuclear bomb has been dropped is that the bacteria that come from the screen of that area have been destroyed and that they are unable to restore themselves. That is to say that the screen is unable to develop an image. The system is able to repair itself over a long period of time. (If you scratch the screen of a plasma TV with a hard or sharp object, that area will not be able to be restored and will remain dark.) Radiation is the energy seeping through the screen.

Voice: Which discipline do you plan to use for this?

A platform which is suitable to the combining mission God wants of course. It is impossible to meet on a new idea while everybody insist on old ones remaining. There are unacceptable ideas and experiences in each and every group. So we must focus on the points they concur not upon the subjects in which they differ.

The foundation of science was laid without including God and the concept is still not included to this day. Science is researching the universe, and attempting to understand it, but science stays away from the question of whom or what created our universe? While accepting the hidden aspects of psychology and sociology and other fields, science looks the other way when it comes to considering the hidden Creator of the universe which billions of people believe in.

Science by preventing mankind from understanding the universe that God created and some religious men, by turning a blind eye to the truth have left science to drown in Darwin's theory of evolution. **Just like the example: Jacques Cousteau discovers that Atlantic Ocean and Mediterranean Sea do not blend.**

The Beneficent, *55:19-20 He has made the two seas to flow freely (so that) they meet together: Between them is a barrier which they cannot pass.* **(Q)**

At the same time, religious men use new scientific developments and/or discoveries to point out the scientific areas by claiming, *"Yet another area of the Holy Books has been proven. This is another miracle of our Book."*

Science and religion both, like two fanatic fans behave emotionally. One avoids the requisites of science and the other disregards the science of religion. The outcome is a religion without scientific basis, and science without religious considerations crushing mankind in the middle.

To unite mankind we must seek the science of religion and introduce him to the technological/scientific God.

As in the **II Pope Paul's** Encyclical **"Fides et Ratio,"** 9/14/1998 (http://www.vatican.va/edocs/ENG0216/_INDEX.HTM)

For it is undeniable that this time of rapid and complex change can leave especially the younger generation, to whom the future belongs and on whom it depends, with a sense that they have no valid points of reference. (Introduction -6 "know yourself")

On a number of occasions, the Second Vatican Council stressed the positive value of scientific research for a deeper knowledge of the mystery of the human being. (5:61)

From this comes the Magisterium's duty to discern and promote philosophical thinking which is not at odds with faith. It is my task to state principles and criteria which in my judgment are necessary in order to restore a harmonious and creative relationship between theology and philosophy. (5:63)

Metaphysics thus plays an essential role of mediation in theological research. A theology without a metaphysical horizon could not move beyond an analysis of religious experience, nor would it allow the intellectus fidei to give a coherent account of the universal and transcendent value of revealed truth. (7:83)

Voice: It is interesting that you accept the science platform as a unifying stage.

You're right, but what I was criticizing before were certain scientists, not the whole of science just like the religious men not the religion.

Science, which has been accused of being opposed to God, by putting an end to the reign of false gods, has allowed the progress of mankind and therefore has been a servant to the true Creator. (If science had not been developed by mankind, humanity may still be worshipping the sun and moon.) And, if the fall of false gods is what the true God wanted, isn't this a service to the true Creator?

There is a need to find a Unified Theory or a Theory of Everything that simply includes and integrates both the religious and scientific views of creation beyond which cannot be agreed upon today. Models of prevailing theories include areas that only lead to ho-pelessness as details are revealed. These areas must be reexamined on a neutral platform with logical alternative futures and must be resynthesized. Alternative futures will be formed by abstract thinking processes, and more conciliatory models will be found.

Science and Technology Magazine, June 2007 has a befitting interpretations of science in the article, "Science and False Science";

"Science is a wonderful device used to show us the way in our efforts to **understand the world we live in.***"*

"*When you consider the* goal of science*, we can give the answer "understanding without ceasing." Science is the* effort by mankind to understand the universe, the environment, and the world we live in.*"**

Science is the **only information source that attempts to undermine its own findings.** *Activities in all the other areas of information, show a tendency to play favorites to their own ideas and claims.* **Only science attempts to find its own error and bring them to light**, *this is a part of the scientific method. The road to mankind attaining true and reliable information is through science."*

Voice: What do you expect people's reactions to be to this?

Science wrenched false gods from the hands of religious men with natural, continuous questioning and with the application of the answers established has always threatened false gods.

Those shadow/virtual figurants which are in your control react according to the precepts you have provided, while those who are able to live on their own free will form their own conclusions and will be on my side. It has been my observation that people who cannot find a better model choose the most beneficial from among those available. They will find even the worst belief better than no belief and will be forced to choose one among the many and make the best of it.

Just like a politician who acts according to the saying, he who pays the piper may call the tune, and says *"we will act in the benefit of our nation."* Belief is like love. If man does not believe enough in God or if God is not believable enough, he will choose the religious sect, group or people who benefit him, his family or his group. At this point on the racetrack, in the love that seems the least controllable or the most hopeless, it seems that God is nowhere to be seen. As Chekov said, *"To marry without loving, is like worshiping without believing, a shameful business."*

From the moment the moon god was found to be nothing more than an object in the sky, religious institutions and believers may have held out, but with the proof of truth, it wasn't long before they shifted to a new god. This is seen in this verse:

My goal is not to have my own views accepted, but to have a conclusion arrived at by thinking of the method of Socratic dialogue and as Plutarch said, ***"Man's intelligence is not a vessel to be filled, but a hearth to be lit."***

It will take many nudges to change the perspective of the status quo formed throughout the thousands of years of thought and research into the creation. Many who are quite content with the deep-rooted advantages and the high regard for the status quo will be difficult to dislodge. Ridding man of these shackles will always take time whether in the field of religion or science as new thoughts run up against the barriers developed by man. As Genghis Khan faced the Great Wall of China, he said, *"The strength of this wall is only as strong as the hearts of the people who built it."* Then years later this thought was completed by Victor Hugo when he said, *"No army can stop a thought whose time has come."*

I will again quote from the film "Contact." According to Ockham's Razor, *"All other things being equal, the simplest solution is the best."* In neither science nor religion had God been identified enough. In the attempts that were made, even the most basic questions have not been answered, therefore, until the model of the virtual god is disproved it must be considered true by the theory of simplicity.

As for the success of my explanations, it is as I have always said: **A writer open to failure will always endure.**

Every writer before finishing his work, in the event that the work is unsuccessful or unnoticed, or to stay on his feet before the criticism it engenders, feels it necessary to find a view point in defense of his work: preferably one which even strengthens it. In case of dark days, I wrote these words and breathed a sigh of relief. **"If you write about the future, you can't expect to be understood today."** In the past others have said this, too.

On the first page of the work DECCAL, ***"This book is for the very few. Maybe none of them lives anymore. They are those who understand my Zarathustra; how could I myself, confront those who have ears that just today heard? (And who would be mine) only the next day."*** Nietzsche

*"**When you do work it is not for everyone, what you say is important for those who need to hear it.**"* Socrates.

*"**Explain whatever you want to, you will only explain as much as those who hear can understand.**"* Rumi perhaps does the same thing here.

And as God did a favor for the prophets:

Ezekiel, *2:5 "Whether they listen or not, this set of rebels shall know there is a prophet among them."* **(OT)**

The Cattle, *6:112 And thus did We make for every prophet an enemy, the Shaitans from among men and jinn, some of them suggesting to others varnished falsehood to deceive (them), and had your Lord pleased they would not have done it, therefore leave them and that which they forge.* **(Q)**

Thunder, *13:30 "Thus We have sent you a nation-nations have passed away long before it-so you may recite to them what We have inspired you with even thought they disbelieve in the Mercy-giving."* **(Q)**

God, in these verses whispered at the beginning that He had sent his teachings to those who couldn't be expected to follow them.

And one who will produce thoughts about the creation of the future says, *"God himself at a point when people have not accepted his existence, prophets, those who appear to be angels, and in spite of all the unseen persons, is it not an illusion to think that everyone will accept my thoughts?"*

Scientists identify the speed of light as the fastest speed in the universe, but as I think of the training on this side trip I realize that we must have been traveling faster than the speed of light. Am I wrong?

Voice: The speed of light has been accepted on earth as the stable speed of the Universe. However, the fastest speed in the universe is that the speed of thought without a body, and this journey is a trip being taken at that speed. The bodies you dream in are the same as the bodies you use to travel in thought. You will think they exist, but in truth they do not because they are simulated. You may like to think of it this way; all of this is a dream! The important thing is not whether it is a dream or a thought trip, but what you have seen and felt.

What is the meaning of God's singularity?

Voice: The meaning of God's oneness:

1. With the approval and consent of all parties, all authority is collected into the hands of impartial justice which raises no doubt as to favoritism.

2. All the time, the same results are arrived at with no dichotomies or question of a mistake.

3. Not only from the point of results, but as seen in the words in, "all religions are from the same source" resources and opportunities and equality of opportunities are **universal and just**.

4. "Everyone is one" does not mean that everyone is a part of the whole,

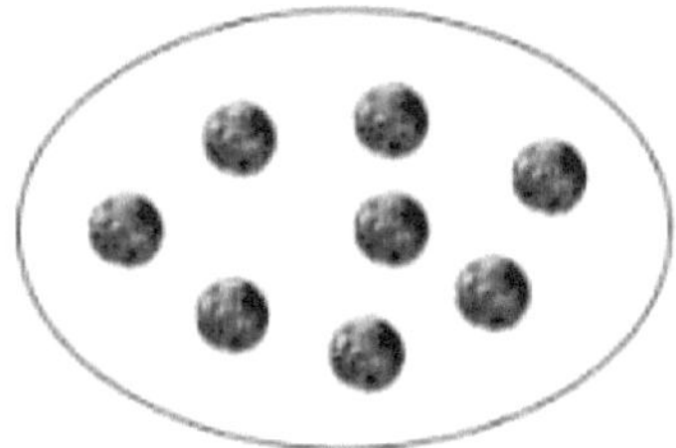

But that everyone is connected to the source.

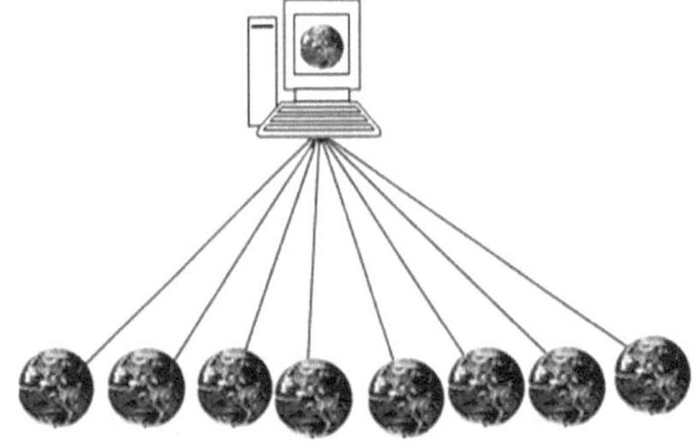

We understand that God is one and alone and needs no one and nothing, but the angels in his service seem to be an out-serviced construct. Thinking as a computer programmer, I figured that the brain guiding the senses and a computer communicating with direct signals, would be able to run the whole system by itself. The writing and hardware personnel would only have to repair the computer and keep it up, and check the steps in the system. If man made the virtual god technology just as man has made machines that evaluate, could it be made to give the same result each time?

Voice: Good question! I'd like to give an example from an article in the book *The Next 50 years* by Ian Stewart entitled. "The mathematics of 2050"; *"The point is that what **matters is the checking, not what kind of entity carries it out**. In the past, humans did the checking, because that was the only alternative, but it doesn't have to be humans in the future. The **main criteria are that the checking entity must be trustworthy and anyone who distrusts it should have recourse to independent entities capable of carrying out their own checks**. But as long a those conditions apply, **the decisions of a machine is just as valid as that of a human being.**"*

As was mentioned previously, from today forward, our medical tests, identity checks, financial recordings, salary payments can be left to the computer and the decisions made are as reliable as those made by human beings. Have we agreed on this?

Of course, the difference between the true God and the virtual god is important. Even though everything is documented and kept in recordings, as you said, because it is man's work, even though we have a large proportion of matching answers, once in a while there may be mistaken evaluations. For this reason, in special situations, we would have the right to protect our rights in the virtual world.

*I **Kings,** 12:24 Do not go to fight against your brothers, the sons of Israel, let everyone go home, for what has happened is my doing.* **(OT)**

Does the court in the next world wait until everyone is dead to hold court?

Or is there a separate court for each person as he dies? Is there terror in the grave? Will you please give us information on this?

Voice: Court in the afterlife as it is called, the opening of the black box or the revealing of the results, is only a personal justice system with areas within the individual punishment system itself and is done in two phases. Think of the university test you go through on earth, once you give in the test paper and leave the test, answers are revealed and you can know your situation by calculating the results. The important thing here is the place of your score among the others that have taken the test; so before the results are posted, you suffer a bit of anxiety. After everyone has turned in their papers and left, the scores are revealed simultaneously and you will know whether or not you have enough points at which areas of study you may attend.

The period between when you walked out of the test room and checked your answers and the posting of the test results with all scores included, corresponds to the personal court in the afterlife. Once all scores are revealed the court of society in the afterlife begins. Perhaps most importantly, the horror of the grave only applies to those who are sinners, why should the good suffer in the grave?

How do you interpret this verse about the afterlife?

Ha Mim, 41:20 So that when they come up to it, their hearing, eyesight, and their skins will testify against them concerning anything they have been doing. **(Q)**

Why does this verse speak only about testifying against us? The ears and the eyes and the skin will testify both for and against us! Why this negativity?

Voice: The human brain records both inner and outer stimulus to the human eyes, ears and other sense organs as they work with thoughts. We use the existing basis and in the virtual world we use the recordings from the sense organs to take a copy for ourselves which are used as positive proof for those you call good people.

__The Kneeling,__ 45:29 This book of ours will pronounce the Truth about you. We have been recording whatever you have been doing." (__Q__)

As we have said in this verse: In this situation, your eyes, ears, and skin will testify for or against you.

Of course, the eyes and ears mentioned here are not those that are found outside your physical body but the sense receptors in the brain. In a dream in spite of the fact that you do not use your eyes or ears you see and speak and the brain records.

__The Narratives,__ 28:78 Will not criminals be questioned concerning their offences? (__Q__)

Just as is indicated in this verse, the recordings, your documents will easily and pragmatically ensure your decisions, so there will be no need for many questions.

__Yunus,__ 10:29 "God suffices as a Witness between us and you." (__Q__)

This means then that recordings referred to and evaluations made are done by a virtual god.

Voice: We simply entered the existing system and developed a construct. We have also emphasized the regrets you will suffer when the results are revealed.

__Poets,__ 26:102 "If we only had another chance, we would then be believers." (__Q__)
__The Companions,__ 39:58 "If I only had another chance, then I'd be someone who acts kindly." (__Q__)
__The Counsel,__ 42:44 "Is there any way to turn back?" (__Q__)

There is no need to be negative here. But in order to have another chance at the test, just as in a birth, you must earn the right among millions of other applicants and begin everything over again. With us, there is no chance to enter a test on earth and fail or pass, then live a life according to the results and benefit or not.

And what is the situation for those who pass?

Voice: You'll recall,

Resurrection, 75:33 *"Then he stalked off haughtily to his family"* (Q)
The Counsel, 42:45 *"The Losers are the ones who have lost their own souls plus their families' on Resurrection Day."* (**Q**)
The Rending Asunder, 84:7-9 *He used to be happy with his own people; he supposed he would never revert to God.* (**Q**)
The Rending Asunder, 84:13-14 *Surely he was (erstwhile) joyful among his followers. Surely he thought that he would never return.* (**Q**)

In these verses another life is clearly mentioned.

In conclusion, in the space between the virtual and true God there is another family and a "World Between." A driver who always looks at the destination, cannot live life along the road because he has his eye on something else. He forgets to play and smell the flowers along the way. Is it possible for someone who sits home all day or doesn't go to school to enter the test? Not living is dying without having lived.

What is the bridge that is finer than a hair and sharper than a sword?

Voice: This is a good example of wrong interpretation. Since the whole test is on earth, it would seem there is no need for extra difficulties and this bridge. **This is a primitive way of explaining the sensitivity of God's justice** to people in a period before science and the microscope. We did this in a period when we could not say to people. "We will see things through a microscope that is millions of times thinner than a hair and the laser beams we will develop will be even sharper than a sword." It is information given by a book for all times to a people of a time when there was limited information.

Let us give an example of this using rockets that are sent into space. After the rocket is launched, what would happen if the empty fuel tank were not released before it exited the atmosphere? Because of the weight of the empty tank, the rocket would not be able to maintain the speed it had attained during the launch and losing speed, would not be able to exit the atmosphere and would fall to earth. Any and all information if analyzed by either religion or science in the understanding of a certain period, can be changed in an instant with the addition of a new experience or piece of data. Therefore, it is impossible to say we have studied this verse and understood it, so we will now put it away forever. Does science not preface every revelation with the condition "for now" it is thought that….? Haven't new findings changed old conclusions? Will they not change in the future? Science is only science because it uses the "for now…" condition to keep it current. Some religious men do the opposite when they declare something to be absolute, contrary to the essence of the book. It may not separate the holy information but it certainly alienates believers from science and contemporary issues. An unchanging resource is information. The interpretation of the resource may not change for people but almost certainly will change over time.

I am interested in a current insure. Will global warming mean the end of the world?

The Moon, *54:1 The hour approaches and the moon is splitting apart.* **(Q)**

Is the "splitting apart" of the moon mentioned here caused by a space rock?

Voice: The main question here is this: why does the Creator of such a majestic work allow other parts of the creation to tear it apart? Why do poor countries suffer from a hole in the ozone layer caused by the rich countries? Why did he allow the deaths of millions from radiation in Japan, those who died in the 9/11 attacks, Iraq: they will question God's justice, and answer with **"God knows something we don't,"** or they are also saying. "If I gave it away, so what?"

To a believer whose faith has been weakened, it seems like, "This god continues to test us with poverty and death. What is left to take?" the reason for this lies in the fact that God's justice has not been clarified enough so the believer's faith has been weakened.

The Accessions, *8:17 You (all) do not kill them but God kills them. You did not shoot (anything) when you shot (arrows and spears) but God threw them so he may test believers, as a handsome test from himself. God is Alert, Wise.* **(Q)**

The Criterion** 24:3-5 Instead of whom, they have take on other gods, which do not create anything while they themselves have been created.* ***They control no harm nor do they control death not life, nor even rebirth. (Q)

These verses show that God has control over all death in the human universe. In this situation it is only logical to assume that all murders are innocent. We talked about criminals in the individual punishment system being tested by repeating the same scenario again and again and the situation mentioned here would be the killing scene in one of those experiments. We have already mentioned about this.

From the same viewpoint, in a virtual god technology since no one is killed, in order to determine the extent of ends the monster within will go to in a virtual world, these types of experiments may be allowed. Again, as I asked at the beginning, "Can a God who allows creations within a creation to destroy the masterpiece, or a God who destroys works of man, really be God?" In the end, the world you live in is under the direction of a virtual universe.

Doomsday has not yet been lived in the real world, but as you said before, the doomsday of a virtual world is the solution of a virtual god whose power has not yet been defined.

As Rumi said, *"It is time for all that is hidden to surface. This is judgment. If it is judgment let's see it. This is the condition of seeing it all."*

In summary, to research mankind, within a virtual world on virtual stages, since no one is armed in a real sense, all levels of testing, even the highest, can be done to determine the feelings of good and bad within people.

Voice: We can solve all our individual and societal questions, experiment with endless scenarios, and produce immeasurably, at low cost and a vast simulation field called **"Parallel Worlds"** or **"Parallel Universes"**. All this would include all social research and development in a virtual environment with no loss.

We can call a parallel universe a **"Parallel Life"**. We can think of it as the **"Second Life"** field on the internet, the difference being that we are not playing from outside the area, but it can only be played from the inside.

Matthew, *16:19 "I will give you the keys to the kingdom of heaven: whatever you bind on earth shall be considered bound in heaven; whatever you loose on earth shall be considered loosed in heaven."* **(NT)**

Pilgrimage, *22:11 If some good should happen to him, he accepts it calmly, while if some trial should strike him, he turns over on his face (in despair). He lose both this world and the Hereafter.* **(Q)**

Divorce, *65:12 God is the One Who created seven heavens, and the same (number of planets) which are like earth. The Command prevails among them so you (all) may know that God is capable of everything. God comprises everything in knowledge.* **(Q)**

These verses all clearly show this and your idea of "<u>Here = there</u>".

How does God's forgiveness or mercy work for criminals in virtual god technology?

Voice: If the world is a test, if you receive a low mark for a behavior, how will you be able to improve your mark?

I will prepare better for the next test. If there is not another test scheduled, I will suggest the teacher give me a special test so I can pass.

Voice: When you do a wrong in God's test on earth and you receive a low grade what do you do? You realize you are sorry and decide not to repeat the wrong. This is God's way of offering you a way out. But just as when you receive a low grade in class and you make an excuse to the teacher, "I knew the answers but I just got nervous in the test and this happened and that happened," it is begging. You have to wait for the end of term to learn if the teacher accepted your pleas or not. In order to know if the Creator has accepted your regrets it is probable that one must wait until the afterlife.

Voice: In a virtual environment when something is about to be found that is useful to mankind we will lengthen the life of a person until the work is finished. Virtual god, while seeing that a good thing will finish early, is not wasteful enough to keep something running.

If you have understood man as much as you claim to and you can control everything about him, why are people born into the world with a disability?

Voice: Here=There: You cannot even begin to imagine the extent of the virtual reality's area. In the end we live in an environment created by the true Creator and we can only function within the limits allowed in that environment. We created a copy of you on our computer and when we make a change to that body there is no change on your real body. However, the changes we make in the experiments may be useful in your understanding of your characteristics and help in your development. A virtual world, no matter what you may construe it to be is a racecourse for developing a **clean and healthy society**.

John, *9:1-3 As he went along he saw a man who had been blind from birth. His disciples asked him "Rabbi, who sinned, this man or his parents for him to have been born blind?" Neither he nor his parents sinned Jesus answered, " he was born blind so that the works of God might be displayed in him."* **(NT)**

Regarding physical abnormalities; when virtual people in a virtual environ-ment are able to create the virtual bodies we wanted, we question the point in training abnormal people, and their caretakers such as teachers, doctors, and support personnel in a different virtual environment. To this aim, consider, for example a teacher who will be teaching in a school for the visually impaired: first we allow the person to live a life as a visually impaired person himself. He gains understanding of the feelings and opinions a person experiences in that situation. With this experience, when he is awakened, he can easily relate to visually impaired students because he understands their plight. You could say it this way; if you can solve the vision problem with electronic glasses why do it the long way in a virtual environment?

As I said, we are not the true Creator and as creations we can only help within the limits of the environment. The virtual god project is an example the model of the system we developed with the advancement of mankind as our goal. With this system we can understand him and find answers to the whys and wherefores of his thinking.

With the main purpose of creating the system being the monitoring of the true character of people, is there special training to strengthen the will? Is fasting one of these training methods?

Voice: Since this is a current issue let's take fasting from sunrise to sunset or refraining from eating certain foods for a period as an example. What is the point of fasting? The point is to refrain from using the food and drink for a certain time period. Refraining from eating and drinking for a certain amount of time, builds willpower and also give your body a rest. This is beneficial and recommended only when one is healthy and it is not worth harming your body for the sake of strengthening will power.

To make it easier for people to fast, well meaning organizations open special soup kitchens to provide food for the fasting poor, others close their restaurants to prevent temptation. But, it is only when a person refrains from eating and drinking on his own accord and without others' help, using his own willpower, that fasting strengthens his will power. As was said earlier, the device is valid only when one resists from corrupt practices when corruption is the mainstream.

(At this point the hologram of Thales[8] of Miletos appeared and approached us. Thales was at one side, on the other side were stairs leading upward to a door with "exit" written on it. When the image of the pioneer of the philosophy came the door was opening to the floor to a new dimension. Thales speaks)

Thales: Are you ready?

Did I win?

Thales: The evaluations of the other candidates have not yet finished. The result won't be known until they are complete.

I hope I won't meet the man in the role of the director in the film, Ed Harris, because I want to see something I can be sure is real.

Thales: And how can you be sure it's real? As in the beginning of the film *12 Monkeys,* can you be sure you won't lose?

You are speaking as if you were ignorant in the world and didn't value a happy life. Do you have any suggestions?

Thales: Our time is running out, but I do have a few suggestions.

When you review the life you have lived, who have you benefited? Ask yourself this question at each point! Especially considering your behavior with those in a station below you, who needed you; even if they are your enemies, have you treated them without discrimination and helped them every time?

---

[8] (Greek philosopher who is considered the founder of Greek science, mathematics, and philosophy. He visited Egypt and probably Babylon, bringing back knowledge of astronomy and geometry. He invented deductive mathematics. To him is attributed **Thales'** theorem. Proclus attributed the following additional mathematical theorems to Thales (Boyer 1968, pp. 50-51): a circle is bisected by a diameter, the base angles of an isosceles triangle are equal, pairs of vertical angles formed by two intersecting lines are equal, and the ASA theorem for triangles.)

http://cs-exhibitions.uni-klu.ac.at/index.php?id=328

How have you treated those in your close surroundings: your spouse, your children, your employees, their relatives who lent you a hand when you needed it, your neighbors? Have you helped those on the same race course complete their journey successfully? In short, how do you treat the people who have been put in your care? Have you made slaves of them or have you helped them achieve human freedom?

How have you treated the body that's been entrusted to you? Have you valued nutrition and sport? Have you taxed your body with cigarettes, excess alcohol, drugs or other harmful substances? If not, kudos to you! The true praise goes to those who somehow found themselves mired in these bad habits and extricating themselves have responded to help those still unable to get out. What have you done to help these people? Have you been instrumental to even one person in giving up cigarettes? It is as the great sage Haci Bektash Veli said, "The wise are both pure and purifying."

And time: how have you used the time allotted to you? Have you spent it learning the information you most need for your life here? Have you spent your time in frivolous play? If you hadn't paid attention to science and technology on earth, you would have returned to earth. The thought that "*I am living this life well, so I don't have to do it again*" is valid here. If you are unable to rise to the next level, you will repeat the same level or lower and drown in the same problems and relationships. As you wrote on the wall, "empty days filled with emptiness surpassing empty."

"In war, the aged, women, children are never to be touched." This could better be said, *"In war, the aged, women, children **and animals** are never to be touched."* The important message here is that, seeing a gap in a forgotten group in certain sayings, it is important to be able to fill that gap.

In the press release you published years ago you said:

"I want to renew the suggestion I made to change the oath of office used in swearing in new parliamentarians of the Turkish Parliament."

"I swear upon my honor and integrity, before the Turkish Nation and Humanity to safeguard the existence and independence of the State, the unity and indivisibility of its people, and the absolute sovereignty of the Nation. I promise to remain loyal to the supremacy of law, to the democratic and secular Republic, and to Atatürk's principles and reforms; and in the name of peace for humanity and universal solidarity, not to deviate from the ideal according to which everyone is entitled to enjoy fundamental freedoms under **peace and prosperity** of **humanity and universal solidarity** and justice, and to remain loyal to the Constitution."

This will bring us to **universality and unity.** And our slogan could be "My birthplace is ….., I live in the world." As you said we must ask, "What have you done for yourself?" What have you done for humanity?"

Thales: You see? Look! The education and tests continue at every stage. It is not the devil that is hidden in the detail, it is the path to success. I think every philosopher thinks because when you started to write years ago you said: "a philosopher is the one who also makes people think and question. He can do it by saying new things. I want to be a philosopher not a writer, because human being need philosophers immediately. Like the words of Dostoyevsky "Questioning leads us to the truth." The greatest achievement is the ability to leave behind a work of art.

What do you think of my ideas I put forth before on leaving a work of art?

Thales: Let's think of it this way; those who leave no work of art but support their environment with happiness and motivation, for instance, your relatives who have been so supportive in your work so far, friends who have had a role in helping others advance, and the hidden heroes who have chosen to lead normal lives in order to stay firmly on the path: thus, every virtuous life is a work of art, isn't it?

As you offered in your book, *Book Without a Name* "Aren't we all writers, after all?" We are active writers when we put our observations, our experiences and our feelings on paper, and passive writers when we retain these aspects of our lives. And refraining from publicizing thus allowing others to write, we take on the role of ghost writers as you have noted in your example. Some people produce their own work of art while others help friends or enemies produce theirs or alternatively produce children who leave works of art. Of course, producing work earns extra points for a person.

You may have noticed that I included enemies in the helpful category. How will you be deprived of your material needs or physical abilities? Or when needed, how do you think permission will be granted? Will you awake one morning to see that all materials and personnel you need have been delivered to your door? Of course not. Everything will go normally with things in your life, trust you earn, and qualities of self confidence you collect and entrust to yourself. Then a time comes when a person you thought you knew well and trusted well, turns out to be very different. In your surroundings it is time for you to waken those who you thought were dynamic, but were sleep walking. It is the time for him to be supportive or a hindrance according to his inner urgings.

The Elevated Places, *7:198 If you summon them to guidance, they will not hear, and you will see them looking towards you while they are (really) not seeing (anything).* **(Q)**

In truth, every person is automatically recorded as a work of art according to his life recordings. Some are beautiful works, which we observe with amazement time after time, while we watch others who are normal, and some we never even turn toward.

The Great Event, *78:40 We have warned you (all) how punishment lies close-at-hand, on a day when any man will see whatever his own hands have sent on ahead, and the disbeliever will say: "If I were only dust." (Q)*

The Pilgrimage, *22:10 "That is because of what your hands have sent on ahead." Yet God is no One to harm (his) worshippers. (Q)*

I would like to present an anecdote to illustrate these verses:

An old carpenter had reached the time of retirement. He mentioned to his employer, his plans to spend a freer life with his wife and growing children. Of course he would miss the check that provided him money, but he really needed to retire. The contractor he worked for was sorry he was leaving and requested that he work on just one more building with him.

The carpenter agreed to do it and began work. Unfortunately, it was easy to see that his heart was not in it. From the start he did sloppy work and used shoddy materials. What misfortune, to end a profession he had been so dedicated to, like that!

When the work was complete, the employer came to survey the work. The carpenter stretched out the keys and said, "This is your house, a gift from me." The carpenter was shocked, and extremely embarrassed. If he had only known that it would be his house! Would he have done the same?

It is this way with us, too. We build our lives day by day. We often put less into it that we have to give. And when we realize that we are to live in it we get shocked. We would have done it differently had we known. We cannot go back, however.

You are the carpenter; you take out a nail every day, or put in some lumber or erect a wall. Someone said, "Life is your own design." Today's behavior and choices build the house we will live in tomorrow. So build it wisely. Take time to envision the house you are making today from above.

A lovely anecdote! What did you mean a bit earlier when you said that evolution had not been finished?

Thales: Why don't you open the door and see for yourself?

I was extremely excited! I bounded up the stairs and stood in front of my door marked "exit". I stopped for a moment and turned around looking first at Thales then above in the direction the sound was coming from and said "thank you, see you outside". Then, turning back towards the closed door I said, "I'm ready, let it begin." And I opened the door.

I opened it but just like the endless darkness at the beginning nothing was visible in the intense darkness again. I was shocked! Hoping for God's enlightening welcome, and being confronted with darkness again was a shock to my body and soul. I could see nothing because of the darkness. I had either opened the wrong door or had opened the door the wrong way! I had probably opened the wrong door, and turned to glance around for another door on the seventh floor. When I saw none and wondered how I could have opened it wrongly, I came eye to eye with Thales. His eyes expected an answer instead of providing one. I was on the edge of light/darkness, the seen/unseen, and the known/unknown. I needed to make a choice between returning or continuing into the darkness.

The last darkness before the real earth concealed the unknown question, "are you ready?" once again I answered by stepping forward.

It was as if I had awakened in **Ergun Arıkdal**'s hypnosis chair I had been in years earlier; I awakened from a deep sleep.

Ya Sin, 36:52 They shall say: O woe to us! who has raised us up from our sleeping-place? This is what the Beneficent God promised and the apostles told the truth. (Q)

I was in a type of dentist's chair surrounded by strange equipment of all sorts. On one panel a "procedure completed" light blinked on and off.

On a monitor on another instrument was an image of my brain, on another was an outline of my body with colored symbols and gauge values next to certain organs. On the monitor on another device I saw the last image frame from the door I had just come through.

Acts, 7:56 "Look,' he said, 'I see the heavens opened and the Son of Man standing at the right hand of God." **(NT)**

becoming real? The chair slowly turned until I came face to face with a doctor who said "**Welcome back to the real world, Aydın TÜRKGÜCÜ.**" Just behind him were two nurses. To the left was a contraption with a button, the doctor printed out my report. Now I could not command my body, in any way. If, at that point a fire had broken out in the room, there would have been no way of escape for me. As if just awakening from hypnosis, or the last moments before going into a trance, my body was heavy, as if filled with cement.

With a few touches of another apparatus by one of the nurses, the connection must have been released as I began to have feelings in my upper body and move my neck around. I could talk and collected myself enough to ask my first question.

How am I doctor?

Doctor: Not bad, but without seeing the evaluation figures, I can't say much.

What evaluations? (I saw two people sitting in the section where the doctor was as if they were under hypnosis). Is everyone competing for the same thing I am?

The Cave, 18:19 And thus did We rouse them that they might question each other **(Q)**
Ya Sin, 36:52 They shall say: O woe to us! who has raised us up from our sleeping-place? This is what the Beneficent God promised and the apostles told the truth **(Q)**

Doctor: Yes!

Why are some of the chairs empty? Did they find the way out before I did?

Doctor: There were a total of four of you. One person came in before you did, and the other seats weren't filled.

Why were there so few people? How many were in the group? How long ago did they show up?

Doctor: There are not many taking the test, so there are very few. The contingent was one person and he came in a short while ago.

Did I lose?

Doctor: The order is only one factor but the other values are important, too. Sometimes the order changes. Someone returning after you can also win.

How will I know then? When with the results be released? What happens to the losers?

Doctor: The results will be known when all have taken the test. As for the losers, a long time from now, until another list is established, they will continue on with their regular business. If you didn't pass, instead of doing what you are passionate about doing, you will continue doing what you should do, like others unhappily going along. And this is enough of a hell, anyway.

On the Application for Earth you said, "God has hidden plenty of things to be easily obtained to bring happiness to man: work, money, material possessions. I have not found my happiness in these things," "During this search I have come to understand that God has hidden my happiness behind a wall.", "….in the next search I understood that my happiness was not behind a wall but behind God." Now I say to those who ask why I bother with this, "If God hadn't hidden behind my happiness, I wouldn't have been forced to hunt for it." Moses, Jesus and Muhammad will be both happy and disappointed at this.

Why is that, then?

Doctor: They are the code names of the computer programmers who have taken the virtual reality to its furthest point. Their names and information were preserved in the Holy Books of the true God as they were.

The virtual scenarios called life on earth are what people have formed to see and understand. In the book *The Next 50 Years,* Steven Strogatz mentions, *"We may end up as bystanders, unable to follow along with the machines we've built, flabbergasted by their startling conclusions." "If we're ever going to reach that next great era of awakening, we'll need to be rescued from the devil of dimensionality. Look for computers to be our saviours."* I would like to change that to include, "And along with the savior computers we must seek computer programmers."

Doctor: What do you think is your reason for such great unhappiness leading to this search? What is the happiness you seek?

I know that I was born a researcher. Actually, I didn't know the exact reason for my unhappiness, either. Maybe it was for this reason that Stephen Hawking said. *"Happiness is understanding."* but others says *"Understanding brings peace, knowing comes with discomfort"* I really didn't know the reason for my unhappiness. But when I watch a science fiction film, or a space film, or read something about God or hear something, I feel something inside that I can only describe as wild longings or wild excitement. At the end of these longings is the feeling that I am not, at that moment, doing the work I am supposed to be doing. In slowly increasing periods I have been able to concur with those calls and dive into thought space, looking for the proverbial needle in a haystack.

There was a voice inside that seemed to be pulling me toward these questions and I didn't explore the reasons or question why. Not knowing the source and contents of these mysterious callings, it was as if they were asking, "Are you ready?" As a result I followed the inscrutable summons into the most dangerous regions of thought and turned onto the road of God and creation. A serious reply was given and in 1995 with the publishing of my first book I reached the first resting place. Night and day I went on in freedom, my feet on untrodden earth, my head in the world of the unimagined futures, and my eye on the horizons beyond the horizon.

As the voice at the beginning of this journey said, when I was given permission to remember the journey I made in 1998 I brought out my second book, "I'm Ready, Let it Begin." Now I'm here again.

Doctor: On the earlier trip because you had less data at that point, you understood a more limited amount about the same subjects but you managed to illicit the main structure. How did your book do?

Actually, it was quite successful. Several magazines published interviews and I was invited to speak on a few television programs. There were also book signing days. Then I guess I fell back into worldly pursuits and stopped following up on my book. I never brought out a second edition. But everything I read and everything I saw invited me to delve in again. There was always the invitation, I just never answered it; I never said "Let it begin."

Doctor: You have touched on a good point. You remember, we divided people into two groups: those who have come here to understand, and those who have come here to be understood. For those who have come to be understood it is easy to get involved in things of the earth, but for those who have come to understand, this invitation mechanism has always been a standard. For those who come to understand, the first test is to accept the invitation and follow the straight road. And as they proceed on the road we both support them and put up more hurdles, we affect their daily life positively and negatively.

Worldly life is a race course of struggle for those who see and those who don't see on the road to attainment. The invitation to the journey is given in the period when everything is most conflicting. Those who will, come, those who won't, will continue to struggle with worldly problems on earth.

Why is your goal to hinder the success of people?

Doctor: Of course, our aim is for people to be successful, but the real aim is to choose the most enduring and most successful.

When they come to their real duties we must know they will not sink into despair when they confront the same problems, and being so new at the problems, they will not get lost in the effect of power or get lost in the darkness of the pain they experience. This is the safest method of ensuring our goal of humanity gaining?

In regards to happiness the basic logic is this: your stimulation to begin this search is to live better or know more. If you had believed that the best course was found in the worldly life you would have been happy and not taken up the search and would not be here. You have not answered the question I asked you about happiness.

I see happiness as the collection of many joys; the joy of love, work, beauty, and a sum of happiness in all areas. For instance if you are not happy at work it affects the happiness of love, and if you are not happy in love, it affects happiness at work. When you add to this the happiness of your family, friends, social circle, country and the world you have your picture of happiness. You evaluate the situation according to the weight of your points.

But the most important happiness is being able to find and reach the person you were meant to be from the person you were at birth; to find yourself and develop yourself. The verses clearly state that we were created two by two with spouses.

The Great Event, *78:8 We created you in pairs.* **(Q)**

I believe this too. It is for this reason that finding your spouse is important. Adam and Eve having come in together and gone out together, sometimes one wonders if the statement about leaving this world "not without my spouse" is not valid.

There are other advantages to finding a spouse.

The Cow, *2:187 It is lawful for you to have intercourse with your wives on the night of the fast:* **they are garments for you while you are garments for them.** *God knows how you have been deceiving* *yourselves, so He has relented towards you. Now (feel free to) frequent them and seek what god has prescribed for you. (Q)*

Here what has been "prescribed" is referring to the book of the science of all that has been and all that will be for all time and places and all beings. What we need to understand here is that sexual togetherness carries a secret. It is not there for comfort alone or procreation. If you are not in the correct place, the correct work or with the correct spouse there is something inside that is not complete. This is either half happiness or half living. If you live half a life, you can only give half to those around you.

Doctor: I remember, you said that "Women are the gates to heaven". After this statement we can understand this, "We all come in with our mothers, and leave with our woman." But let us not stray from the subject. How are you feeling?

After a trip using the abstract thought process technique, an intuitive feeling of a deep understanding emerges. The things I saw and heard and the model that emerged from convincing scientific findings is perhaps the most viable of any of the spineless alternative past future models.

Doctor: Another good example is: *"There are three kinds of passengers on the train. Two of them sits in the compartment face to face. One of them sees the future (where the train goes) and other sees the past (where the train passes). And yet, the third stands still on the top of the train sees everywhere. For belief we must combine not just the mind and soul but the future and the past."*

(When the second nurse ended a procedure with an instrument that started at the 82% mark it began to decrease. And gradually, as the gauge dropped, the solidified state of my body also began to decrease from my head to my feet. When the indicator reached zero I regained control of myself even though I was exhausted.)

Ok, now what happens?

Doctor: Let's first complete the questions you had on your cross examination. Let's begin with the experiences you had in the world that made you think it is a virtual world. In the book "I'm Ready, Let's Begin" you asked "Why does the Creator who has the power to load everything into the brain cause us and himself so much trouble? When we think of the state of evolution man is expected to reach, we see a person sequestered from the world of matter, with feelings and thoughts completely in control, making no mistakes, who is exactly like him. While a Creator is able to make robots of us by loading all sorts of programs into our brain, he does not do that but, instead, by putting us through this type of experiments makes us into human robots. I find that thought provoking." What do you think now?

I see again that, what some have put down to *"we are unable to understand with our limited minds"* could actually be explained by "we are unable to understand with our limited information." When we look at the fact that we are being caused to live in a virtual world by manipulation of our senses:

I accepted the image of God that my maternal grandmother passed down to me which identifies God and a wise teacher, not a judge. In today's world the most important thing that God expects of man is to maintain our humanity, the characteristic that makes us human. As a person, a part of the created, my handing in a report of "this person will never be human" is like claiming that the Creator does not have the power to keep one of his students because he is unable to educate him properly, as if he is saying *"It is impossible for me to educate this person."*

In the model of reincarnation, people try again and again in virtual world educational and rehabilitation center programs using scenarios designed to teach precepts missed in previous unsuccessful attempts. The aim is to rid them of what I called bad images above and successfully reach a more godlike model in this world and the afterlife. As I said, God always wants his people to pass our tests and will provide all types of opportunities. Anything less would produce the image that **"God only loves winners."**

Thoughts are also punished, since according to religion it is sinful to hold harmful thoughts. That means that the system also supports crimes of thought.

We have studied the stars and the planets and the life and the non-living and all things created and their varieties and have pronounced them to be works of God. But these splendors aside, there were also many things which do not seem to fit this work of art. When politicians take decisions, then fail to defend them, thousands die or are killed without even knowing why this is allowed. Why are these things allowed?

Doctor: You are right questioning with an earthly view point. Think of it this way; In order for God's justice to prevail there are two possibilities; either the dying do not really die or the dead are not real. Just as in films, in a virtual world those who die are not dead, really, or they really do not die.

In summary, as is said in Holy Books, if the truth of the heavens is reflected on earth, neither side is very enlightening. In this situation, the only model that will allow me to see the positive aspects is the virtual world model. With that, the dying will be like those dying in a film or in reality; benefits earned are worthless. It is only with this view that I can preserve and defend my belief.

Mankind must free himself of his self deprecating point of view and launch the age of great awakening, complying with his feelings now supported by scientific findings, to move from the stage of belief to the platform of understanding. He must work on projects from his voice on the telephone to the beaming of his appearance on television to the most extreme possibilities of teleportation.

In the same way, instead of always supporting weapons to harm and destroy human beings more easily with their information and experience, I would like to see scientists using their knowledge on projects to benefit the universe. Religious men and scientists, few in number but high in influence, have misused their professions for centuries by bowing to the pressure of narrow minded politicians and investment conglomerates, thus betraying humanity. When it is so easy in this virtual environment with virtual shadows to be human as humans are meant to be, why this capitulation to the darkness?

Doctor: What do you think of miracles? Were miracles given to prophets because words weren't enough for the people? Wasn't the message for the people of those times?

There have been those who believed in the miracles and those who believed in the message itself throughout history. The Books for the people of all times also talk to the people who have every kind of knowledge and idea. There are people who stay away from both crime and injustice, who believe and fear the afterworld.

Some of the specialties of some of the prophets included the ability to see the unseen, sense people not sensed, to walk in places that are not suitable. Scientists are now able to do many of the same things. Is it possible that a science which is able to produce miracles of prophets play God?

John, *9:32-33 Never since the world began has it been heard that anyone opened the eyes of a person born blind. If this man were not from God, he could do nothing.' (NT)*

In short, it is clear that science, in future, by controlling senses will also control feelings. If mankind in his future accepts the premise that the virtual world could be produced by man, it means he accepts today the possibility of what we would call a virtual world.

It appears impossible that science could accept today's unseen God, but it will be forced to accept the virtual universe that it creates itself. Would it not be wonderful if the true God that science accepted were a "Scientific God?"

In the world we identify as real, on earth, and if, in this virtual world I have come to right now, which is like the real world, I must perceive things with my sense organs, how am I to know which is real? As in the beginning of the film *12 Monkeys* how can I be sure I won't lose? What kind of a labyrinth is this? Which is the real world? In the process of redefining reality with questioning, many people will temporarily fall into the emptiness of the middle area.

Doctor: The human being is already lost in covered universe, isn't it? What is the **"Middle Area"** like? People will either be in reality or in the virtual.

I don't know if you are a real person or a virtual personnel in a virtual system. But allow me to summarize. **"If you are a normal person, watch out because the system you are in may be an environment conceived in the future and integrated with the past!"** Mankind, having become accustomed to living comfortably in his world and having planned for his retirement in this world and the next, will find his future plans completely upset when he realizes that there is no retirement in the next world, the essential work being there.

Let's look at it this way: A model is developed within the parameters of scientific proof and the Holy Books. When religious leaders accept this model the man on the street will be a bit taken aback at first. One moment they will accept the fact that the world they live in is imaginary, the next moment they will reason that because they touch it, drink it, eat it, and use it in other ways, it must be real. They will flounder through a period of dichotomy between defending their natural instincts which protect them from deception and their acceptance of the environment as it is. Due to the new definition of reality, they will waver between the virtual world and the real world in a **"Middle Heaven," "Middle World"** or otherwise named area and will live there until they have made the leap in thought from non-believing to understanding.

Doctor: We simply call it the **"Middle Region"**. I would like to give you some advice that will help you shorten the period you spend in the middle area taking you from non-belief to understanding. In the world you came from, being a good and virtuous person was a recommendation and obviously did not contain certainty. But until this point on the journey you have learned that all your thoughts have been recorded and have seen and accepted the fact that what you thought to be the real world might not be real at all. In short you went from thinking **"It was very good for you to be a good person,"** to thinking **"I am forced be a good person."**

It is not a question of which is real and which is virtual, but the truth that you are always watched, monitored and evaluated. While the real God is always recording, don't let the idea bother you that people from the "middle region" are recording you, too. It could also be that people are not comfortable with the possibility that other people are watching them, or manipulating them and are directing their private lives in a Godlike way. In summary, someone or some ones are watching us or **"Watch out! Both God and other gods are recording us!"**

Thinking about which one is virtual and which is real is important but, probably the most beneficial view is not to spend much time worrying about which is which and living as if it is real at any moment.

Doctor: After that opinion I would like to give you a suggestion; as you find yourself in various environments in the world, don't you associate with different types of people? Does your personality change according to the environment you are in? When we examine the recordings of you in various different groups you associate with, and you display nearly the same characteristics in every environment, your personality is set for better or worse. However if you display different behavior in each different group you enter, then you will be a person whose behavior depends on the group, not a person of stable character.

In the world you came from, in order to live better, if you have not changed your personality according to the people or the place, you will not change your personality or behavior whether you think you are in a virtual world or a real world. What would you do, would you behave as you wanted in a real world where you didn't think you were being recorded and play a role in a virtual world where you knew you were? Isn't the success of this system right here? Leaving you to figure it out! If you want to, accept that there is no God and act without control, or accept God exists and live as if you are being recorded in a controlled system. Real or virtual; is it really important? Outside the virtual world, I'm sure there is a true Creator, yet undefined, who is on a higher level and recording! You have begun a period in which the philosophy that you believe in is a part of a larger reality, **and in the future you will live in a part of a technological reality.** So what do you want to do? Continue or stop?

In short you are saying, **virtual god technology is a god-given chance provided by the Creator to man to test himself. The existent God is not a denial of the** true Creator, but a technological copy of the universe. Now, if I agree to stop and if this is the racetrack of the true God, I will continue to live on this tract. If I agree to continue, I will try again and be tried on another racetrack in another virtual man made world.

Doctor: Here there is a divine justice which demands, first that you experience what you have chosen then you reap what you have planted. Heaven is a short break in the life of man. You may live it here or on the racetrack of life. These racetracks are the "test of the few". This means that as the race course continues, whereas a lot of people began the race, only a few people are left competing. If one person is to be chosen in the end, tests given to determine the few, are exclusive tests both for the competitors and the winners.

How many people have continued on the journey so far? Do their journeys all contain the same contents/tenor/nature?

Doctor: We have been providing the journey for a very long time. With changes made according to the knowledge level of each era. I will give an answer with a quote from Rumi whose name has been mentioned from the beginning: *"A group dressed in green took me into the skies. They showed me the constellations and many levels."* We take many on the journey with the scenario as if they had been kidnapped by spacemen. The door will open for those who knock at the right door and they will proceed along the corridor where they find themselves, as is mentioned in the verses.

Luke, 11:9-11 "So I say to you: Ask, and it will be given to you; search and you will find; know, and the door will be opened to you. For the one who asks always receives; the one who searches always finds; the one who knocks will always have the door opened to him **(NT)**

The foundation is always put down here. The contents of the source that is explained or the method are not seen.

As you said, I knocked on the door and the door was opened. But who opened the door?

The door was opened by virtual figurants instead of the true Creator. The most important thing is how can I be sure you are a person? Maybe you are a spaceman and by manipulating our senses you have shown yourselves to us as earth people.

Doctor: First of all, the door opened; we did not send you back without opening the door. As long as mankind believes he is unable to make a universe the existent God will prevail. When he believes he can make it or at the time he makes it, the existing God moves up a floor. The true Creator will always exist one floor above. As for the possibility that we are spacemen: Man is forced to explain the unknown in terms that he knows: as when indigenous people see an airplane for the first time they call it a "large bird," and when they see it on the ground they call it a "metal bird' and the pilot "the bird God." To them everything that flies is a bird. You must convince these people first that the flying thing is not a bird, but a pile of metal and then that the person flying it is not a god. This is the difficult part.

The Elephant, 105:4-5 *Casting against them stones of baked clay, So He rendered them like straw eaten up?* **(Q)**

You will remember that you have said, *"the one who understands the system directs it".* You can understand the system and make it, too. Thus, if you believe people can make a virtual system, we are people, too. However much I appear to be a real person to you, no matter what I say to you when you change the identification of reality you will always look on me in doubt. The saying, "To be or not to be that is the question" has been turned into: **"Virtual or real that is the question."**

But don't worry, as long as you continue to live in this way, it doesn't matter if you are in a virtual environment or a real environment, you may live a period in the same environment and you will be a part of that environment where you will be so busy running that you won't have time to think. Life is busy and difficult in both the virtual and the real worlds. Once in a while you will say "I wonder?" but your connection to the general reduces the importance of your doubt. Of course, for *you* now nothing will ever be the same.

Many have begun this journey. At this very moment in various environments under different direction journeys are being taken. They are few, of course. As long as the system continues there will be those who inherit the system and will take the trip in the future. Those who have made the journey so far, since they are generally not computer programmers, have only understood parts of the system. Your advantage is that you are a programmer. Others are candidates to be inheritors of other parts of the system.

There is a counterpart job for all types of people in every professional group on earth. Why should I waste time and effort on a professional group that I have no use for? Therefore, a part of the system is hidden in every profession. Experts in every professional group can find a part of the system and earn the right to take a thought education trip and become and inheritor of the system. Try to find them when you return to earth and if you approach them, you will improve the model with every new piece of the system you link together. In this way the awakening of mankind that has been awaited shall begin.

Could I have taken this same journey in a cave, long distances away from people?

Doctor: If you remember, at one point on this trip, this was said, **"When religions were given there was no science of today."** The methods you talked about with the caves were the science of the day. In those methods, we went to people. Healing sick people, we provide very small clues with miracles with no supporting scientific methods. The education given on earth was to make people feel in the system of that period. The identification used at that period was a reflection of the scientific data at the time.

If you remember, you said, "The God that created the system used quite advanced technology". What does it take for you to delineate a system? Information, of course. In another part you said, "You understand as far as you know." If we had taken a person on the journey you went on centuries ago he would have stared and stared and extolled the beauty of the scenery. He could not have made sense out of it because he had no knowledge. Therefore he would not have been able to model it. He would have explained what he saw without knowing what it was.

There are two ways to go to God:

1. With an inner trip while staying away from the outer world like seclusion in a cave.

2. God has given you breath and combined the material and soul, and has made the material slave to a soul. God wouldn't have given you the material, if the only way to reach Him would have been through nonexistence (the soul in the absence of the material world.) Therefore, you can also advance on the path leading to God by following the clues he leaves in the universe.

Actually, when you return to earth to be able to write what you have seen completely, and finish your book you, too, will go into your house and close the doors and turn it into a cave for thinking because it's necessary for concentration.

As I understand it, I must make a cave out of the world I see in my home and the unseen world of my heart, and live in my technological cave for a period of time.

Doctor: Exactly! Remember! The seen and the unseen will always be together, they will always support and authenticate one another.

Tell me why science has lagged behind!

Doctor: So far science has concentrated on unmasking the main strategy of material science and with the help of atoms has been able to reveal the structure of matter. More recently science has begun to study God's real work of art, man, and as it understands has approached God. Science is to be trusted, its feet are on the ground. So the verses you will cite as scientific and technological can be trusted.

You'll remember when you began to write many years ago you said, "When I went into the bookstore, I realized that we are content to reread the ancient philosophers, both native and foreign. I am setting out to change this situation." In the context of trying to understand the Creator, the best advice I can give was proffered by the great leader Atatürk in the words, "Science is the most authentic leader."

Atatürk is said to be a key worker sent to the Turkish people. Is that true?

Doctor: Why should we create a hero from among ourselves? Our goal is to educate people, to find the heroism within them. If we look at the logic you mentioned, then it seems like we must have sent all the statesmen and leaders who have developed state institutions throughout history. No, no we are not puppeteers. These are claims of those who oppose the success of the great leader and are trying to discredit him. You must not be instruments of these people. He is one of the few who succeeded in drawing lessons from his enemies by showing them respect.

The principle question is this: Why are spokesmen of religion and science unable to effect reconciliation? Why are we forced to make a choice? The reason is that; science which is searching for the unseen with material means (they have integrated the brain/ mind with the eyes) is no different from religious men looking for the unseen in costumes and beards and outwards appearances. Why is there not a science that has been accepted by God and why is there not a God that is accepted by science?
(I interrupted.)

I am not able to accept one who has not been accepted either. This is the real problem: methods of understanding. Those who know half, do not know the whole. God must be able to be both the God of science and the God of religion.

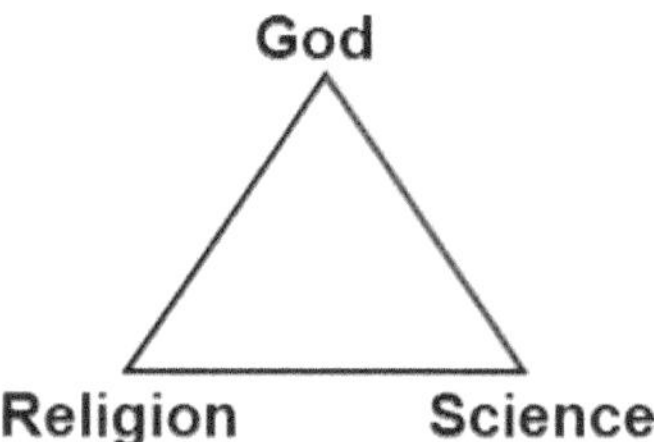

Doctor: It sounds as if you are trying to convince those who don't accept knowledge of God as science by using description of a source that science doesn't accept as science. In the Professor Rennan Pekünlü's magazine Science and the Future October 2007 edition, in the article "Physics and God" we read: *"Once again science does not find God: just the opposite! The truth is this: Religion and science are two fields of active thought that completely reject each other. One field does not use the findings of the other, and will not support each other with written treatise. "Seeing any step on the ladder as the last one, means retreating into an obsession of the "last word" on a subject. In these situations just as thumbing through Holy Books trying to find support for this step by treading tentatively on a few sentences does not make it science, and rejecting that step does not exempt it."* How would you answer these statements?

You can only climb a one legged ladder up a wall, not to the sky. Since it is my aim to understand the heavens, I am forced to use a two legged ladder.

I both agree and disagree with Mr. Pekünlü's words. Let me first explain the part I agree with. First of all, scientists have no well written well researched/ documented work on nature or creation …nothing has been produced about change to refer to….. Not only scientists, but anyone questioning what he says in the least, but is a result of his ignoring a truth. If you listen to religious men with even a little thought, you will find what they say to be self-serving and noncontrollable checks: developments which leave more doors open than shut. Things they want to say have been attributed to God more and more as time goes on. Therefore, so-called experts on God having no consistency in the media and press discussing endlessly without reaching conclusions, of course, do not match scientific consistency. How can inconsistent unscientific personal explanations be scientific?

One of the outcomes of this may be that without actually examining the Holy Books for their content, and simply assuming that these people are far from science, by deciding on the basis of our prejudices, we ourselves would then be far from scientific.

"Seeing any step on the ladder as the last one, means retreating into an obsession of the "last word" on a subject. In these situations just as thumbing through Holy Books trying to find support for this step by treading tentatively on a few sentences "does not make it science." In another section in that same article, "Afterwards? Science and these new findings will begin to try to show that they exist in the Holy Books. The saddest lesson that the Catholic Church learned from Galileo's experiments is this: religion's attempts to fill the gaps in science with religious teachings is dangerous for religion. It must not be pleasant to see the truth and apologize 350 years after the event."

In the book written by **Pope Jean Paul II** entitled, **"Fides et Ratio"** he says that *"In doing so, it will be not only the decisive critical factor which determines the foundations and limits of the different fields of scientific learning, but will also take its place as the ultimate framework of the unity of human knowledge and action, leading them to converge towards a final goal and meaning. This sapiential dimension is all the more necessary today,* **because the immense expansion of humanity's technical capability demands a renewed and sharpened sense of ultimate values."** *(7:81)*

"God who makes himself known is also the source of the credibility of what he reveals."(1:13)

"This is why I urge them to recover and express to the full the metaphysical dimension of truth in order to enter into a demanding critical dialogue with both contemporary philosophical thought and with the philosophical tradition in all its aspects, whether consonant with the word of God or not." (Conclusion 105)

Inquiry will save people from ill-conceived opinions. Science will be able to see this by fully experimenting with it, not by ignoring it. To criticize something as harmful and wrong and just ignore it, does not conform to scientific principles.

Now for the part I do not agree with: I would like to answer with a quote from **Dr. Fatma Paksüt's book "Plato and After Plato."**

"Everyone knows that those who work with geometry, arithmetic, and other sciences use imaginary constructs like, singular, double, triangle, square, oblique angle, square angle, obtuse angle. They will be taken up as if they were well known, and from this assumption they will build up to a conclusion.

The mind uses assumptions not like a principle, but like a step, a resting place, from which the complete theory will arise.

Without a doubt, those who research scientific subjects, too, use their minds and not their feelings. But as long as a theory does not result, because they are basing their findings on assumptions, they will not be able to consider their conclusions final. Geometry and other similar sciences, are not a concept, but an abstract science. And abstract science is like an average of guessing and conceiving."

Doctor: What is the most serious difference between the scientific theory of creation and the religious scenario? Why do millions of people choose the religious scenarios?

All of us would like to have our names written in a permanent place. Even if it is in amongst the unnamed heroes, we'd like to be a hero. Had you been an unnamed hero, it was only for that moment you were a hero or your sacrifice had no one to attach it to, or as if you were part of a heroism that was so secret it could not be revealed. But we know that without prejudice and favoritism, God knows all heroes, records them and rewards them most certainly in heaven.

The most important reason for man's procreation or drive to leave monuments is a desire to live from the time of creation forever, or to be remembered. Man wants to be permanent and be remembered. Aren't those who go to the graveyards to remember those who went before them preparing the foundation for themselves to be remembered? Are gravestones not a reflection of the struggle to be remembered? Will the living remember the dead the way they want to be remembered?

Science, which had historically given the average man no chance to continue through history, anyway, by turning the dreams of people into formulas, has made science unexciting and monopolistic. In the scientific scenario of creation all the sacrifices that the average man made while living stayed in this world and were forgotten in time.

For the average man the creation theory held no reward and was like marriage without love which disintegrates or continues as if it didn't exist.

Man uses the products of science that make life easier and respects this, but when it comes to considering creation will not release the comfort of the prospect of an unseen justice and unseen heaven in the religious scenario that feeds his spiritual needs. Man's needs are so great in this aspect and so important that he feels no need to question the promises of eternal life and the opportunities of reminiscence that religion provides. This is strengthened by the fear that he will find no other possibility of eternal life.

Pope Paul II's book "**Fides et Ratio**" says, "*People can even run from the truth as soon as they glimpse it because they are afraid of its demands. (3:28)*

It has happened therefore that reason, rather than voicing the human orientation towards truth, has wilted under the weight of so much knowledge and little by little has lost the capacity to lift its gaze to the heights, not daring to rise to the truth of being. (Introduction: 5)

In virtual god technology, even though the heaven is virtual, as long a man cannot reject it, will strengthen his beliefs in heaven.

Doctor: Stephen Hawking speaking of the universe in his work *Time and Space Journey*, arranges the specifics for his Theory of Everything like this:

1. It must show us a unifying model of force and particles.
2. It must answer the question of the "limitations" of the universe at the beginning.
3. It must give us several alternative choices. It must explain the truth about us having the universe we have.
4. It must contain several elements of pleasure.
5. It must envisage a universe as we observe it. The theory of everything must be able to bring us to a level of comparing our observations.
6. It must be simple in spite of the complexity it is able to provide.

What do you think?

In the same book the Princeton Physics professor John Archibold Wheeler says this:

> And at the end of everything
> Absolute simplicity
> So beautiful,
> There is such a compelling idea
> Ten years, a hundred years,
> Or a thousand years later,
> When we understand
> One another,
> How could it be else wise,
> We will ask how all this time
> We could be this stupid?

Doctor: Are you willing to change the thinking of the world with the fantastic clarity of the information shown to you?

This will motivate me and those who want to work for peaceful and beneficial goals. I am interlocked with this goal: I will continually travel, write articles, request opportunities to reach my goal. I believe that with this information and the cooperation of the people I talk to, in developing solutions, we will move from believing to understanding, and usher in a new era. It is now time to augment our beliefs with science.

Doctor: I see benefits in making a technical criticism that you may take in order to be prepared. Don't you express your thoughts with too much objection?

If you don't say anything new, reactions will be those that are expected, or known. Many people instead of researching new things, proving what they find and struggling with reactions, preferring to stay with what they find comfortable, become experts in the field of explaining what is already known. I would like to remind these experts who appear to have reached Nirvana, the meaning of Nirvana is "a state of perfection." If there is nothing new, there is no excitement in the telling or listening.

A good example of this from the past is excitement of Archimedes when he ran out into the streets naked shouting *"eureka, eureka"* after finding the principle of floating bodies.
The new points of view must be thought provoking, exiting and leading you to read, not the same inside fancy outside old thoughts.

"The kind of people who stick to the same thought for a long time, circumambulating around it, think they are making distance on the road."

To make rusty minds work they need to be spoiled a little. Thank God, some of them are doing it by themselves. And you just approve by nodding your head.

New ideas will always appear to be aggressively protesting old ideas to those who fanatically defend the old. No matter how delicately you present your case, it will always appear deprecating. Isn't new information really a protest against at least some of the old? One of the most serious problems of science is that the average man appears to have no interest in contributing to science. It is not ethical at all to force him to fight an uphill battle by expecting him to put a simple idea into scientific language before presenting it. Like multimillionaire Vehbi Koç says *"The person you hire who has backing from a source is just like having a rooster: it neither lays eggs nor is it good to eat but you feed it forever"* It is as Al Gore has said, *"If a man receives his money by not being able to understand, you won't be able to explain anything to him."*

__Matthew,__ 23:13-14 But woe to you, scribes and Pharisees, hypocrites! For you lock people out of the kingdom of heaven. For you do not go in yourselves, and when others are going in, you stop them **(NT)**
__Luke,__ 11:52 Woe to you lawyers! For you have taken away the key of knowledge; you did not enter yourselves, and you hindered those who were entering.' **(NT)**

When you visit a doctor, you tell him where the pain is, or what the problem is. The doctor will put that into scientific terms and evaluate it before he gives you a prescription and tells you what he thinks is wrong. He will then simplify his evaluations to explain it so you will understand. If we hinder scientific questioning, what difference do we have from some religious men who hinder religious questioning? Are we ready to increase the freedom of the man on the street to voice his ideas and thoughts? Or will we continue to block them? Will diplomas remain barricades or become bridges?

The man on the street, accepts both science and belief in God, because he doesn't have the knowledge and experience to prove otherwise. However, science's scientific results are accepted in an unscientific manner. (Ignorant man is bound to accept what he is told.)

Doctor: I was asking this: "Don't you express your thoughts with too much objection?" and you have become even more objectionable!

Is the problem with the contents of what I'm saying or the way I say it? I think we should approach it from that angle. If we argue about the methods instead of the subject, aren't we digressing from the scientific? Were Socrates, Plato and Nietzsche any less protesters than I am?

Doctor: There is a science of presenting information, as you know. I suggest you read the January 2007 edition of Science and Technology in the section "Impossible Cinema." *"When we confront something that is outrageous or illogical, generally as a society we give it the value it deserves and let it go. But sometimes, especially in the case of science fiction films, in an obscure corner of our brain, logic is not activated and we get wondrous pleasure at the thought of taking a trip through space or* *believing in something that stretches our* imagination." Was I able to explain what I meant here?

Books and films are thought trips. It is my aim, using this virtual journey which includes virtual reality technology and life spaces, to get a book written and then get it into a film in order to launch those who came here to understand on this journey.

The film industry has a very interesting effect on people. The talents of heroes like Superman, Spiderman, The Fantastic Four, the Hulk, and other films like these resemble heroes from past legends, don't they? People, even though it is a scene on the screen, believe it is possible when he sees a person flying. Perhaps the most important reason that he is able to believe is that it reflects his ambition for those talents not included in his abilities (flying, winning in battle, being unique, and other things like this) or it stirs a forbidden awakening of abilities. Science fiction stories are modern legends.

I have a very important nagging question for you. Are we on earth?

Doctor: Why do you ask?

I want to share a request I made of NASA dated 7/23/2003. (In summary) It was a time when the days of life on earth were numbered.

International Space Station = Noah's Ark

Our world is becoming less inhabitable each day and in the process many plants and animals are disappearing. Solutions have been already been initiated in preparation for the day in the not-so-distant future when our world is uninhabitable. NASA is one of the leaders in this effort:

1. **To distribute a United Humanity throughout space and the Universe**

2. **To find and/or establish new living areas in space, an International Space Station has been inaugurated.**

According to the research I have done, theoretically it is possible to regenerate a copy of living things from the DNA code. There is, of course, empirical research to support this and soon it will be possible to reproduce anything that ever lived using the DNA code.

In Holy Books the prophet Noah is reported to have loaded a ship with a copy of all the animals of an ancient era in order to ensure their return to the world of that time.

Genesis, *6:19 From all living creatures, from each kind you must take two of each kind aboard the ark, to save their lives and yours: they must be a male and a female.* **(OT)**

The Believers, *40:27 So We inspired him: "Build the ship under Our eyes and through Our inspiration. When our command comes and the reservoir burst open, send out two of every species on board.* **(Q)**

For the same such a purpose for the future of the earth, I suggest that on pair of all living creatures **(who are in love)** with DNA codes if needed, be loaded into an international space station. I further suggest that the International Space Station be renamed **"Noah's Ark"** in keeping with the memory of the mission. (The time has come.)

I made this suggestion several years ago. If you look at the physical dimensions in the Holy Book given to Noah to construct his ship, we can see that a pair of all the animals would not fit in that space. That space would, however be enough to contain the DNA copies of all pairs of animals. In this situation, if we accept that Holy Books are books for all time, it might be that this was a suggestion for a future ship. Were we given a suggestion? Now that I am in a future time slice here I have begun to wonder about the earth.

Doctor: In stead of sending human bodies to a space station in the early 2000's, the precaution of taking human DNA into space on a new Noah's Ark was taken in the year 2050.

In the beginning of years of the 21st century we noticed that our days on earth were coming to an end because of global warming and other signs of nature. It was so sad when we are able to cure many diseases, strengthen the human body, our world was dying and becoming hostile to life. It is much like winning the grand lottery and being involved in a traffic accident and becoming bedridden.

Isaiah, 65:20 No more shall there be in it an infant that lives but a few days, or an old person who does not live out a lifetime **(OT)**

We've searched for another world for ourselves just like a tenant is forced to evacuate his apartment and look for a new one to rent. But we haven't found another close/near planet to move to yet. It was quite obvious that the human being was about experience changes at the body level during the journey to another solar system's possible worlds.

It looks like it is impossible to leave the planet with our physical bodies. The body looses its muscle system and skeleton's strength in environments with no gravity. Astronauts still have these kinds of problems when they stay at the space stations for a long term. How would you solve these problems in your bodies if you couldn't find a new planet to live on?

Doctor: The tissue losing problem was left behind in the early days of space shuttles in the opening years of 2000. There were limited moving areas and opportunities back in those days.

Did you ever think, why god created animals? Bugs, bears, lobsters, bees etc. why? Was it only for our nutrition or fun?

For a while in history, mankind considered that animals were on earth for nutrition and fun. Then we learned the technology of the Mars devices from lobsters, how to fly from birds, using solar panels from insects and engineering from plants. In fact we learned that nature was full of God's technological miracles.

Hibernating animals feel no difference or weakness after the hibernation and start eating and living rapidly without any hitch. They lose fat tissue a bit but no deterioration appears in muscle and skeleton systems. In research at the dens where bears hibernate no signs of urine or feces were found. The hibernation of astronauts gave us a chance for long distance trips. We have minimized nutrition, beverage, oxygen needs for the crew.

We figured out how to make changes on human's life and body when we took a look at animals. Of course, systems adapted were not just like those an animal used but provided our tickets to a way out of earth.

"To prove the value of addition of animals to our life here is an article named
"Tardigrades in space ."

Tardigrades In Space or "TARDIS" is the first research project to evaluate the ability of tardigrades to survive under open space conditions. TARDIS is one of the projects within the Biopan-6 research platform provided by European Space Agency (ESA), and will be sent into space with the russian FOTON-M3 mission."
(http://tardigradesinspace.blogspot.com/)

It is quite clear that we have cooperated with animals to clear earth for a long term voyage. We were only able to survive by the data we've learned from animals and their genetic codes.

Did we break our direct connection with earth?

Doctor: As a result of the research we made on animals, to improve human life, we have succeeded in converting human body to be able to maintain life in spaceship conditions.

We have faced problems in reproductive research on animals in space. Quail eggs couldn't make the nest process. And with only after 11 days of their fetal period spent in spacelike conditions, baby mice once born were not able to determine vertical values in water on earth.

We experienced the same problems with our astronauts when they returned to earth from a long term space experience. Once we accommodate our body to the spaceship conditions for a really long time during this journey, it became impossible to survive on the earthlike planets anymore. It was conviction of mankind in the spaceships. Leaving earth was making us weak and effecting our breeding. So we had to take gravity with us to allow makes us to understand and make our vertical references.

Unfortunately we could not break our direct and natural connection with earth because we could not find another planet that was 100% the same as ours. So there was no need to journey far from the earth. Shortly, there will be no place to go for now we are living in the bigger version of the international space station and visit earth frequently, because we still need air, water and other basic needs. Although they are contaminated we have the purification technology.

*2 Peter, 3:13 But, in accordance with his promise, we wait for new heavens and a new earth, where righteousness is at home **(NT)***

Is there no longer anyone living on earth?

Doctor: We have a problem with space on a spaceship, so we have only been able to take on a certain number of people onto the ship we have developed. Those who remained on earth have been taken to places where there is no direct sunlight. We have begun to live in places without sunlight. We, in space, they underground, in places without the sun, have begun a develop a new civilization.

Revelations, *21:23 And the city did not need the sun or the moon for light.* **(NT)**
Revelations, *22:5 It will never be night again and they will not need lamplight or sunlight.* **(NT)**

These verses refer to a space station or underground life without sunlight, then. In addition;

Matthew, *24:29-30 Immediately after the stress of those days, the sun will be darkened, the moon will lose its brightness, the stars will fall from the sky and the powers of heaven will be shaken.* **And the Son of Man will appear in heaven;** *then, too, all the peoples of the earth will beat their breasts; and they will see the Son of Man coming on the clouds of heaven with power and great glory.* **(NT)**

Those referred to in these verses are those descending and returning to the station. (My head is a bit confused.)

Doctor: Limited space means limited opportunity for life. In this situation with the problem on the space ship, we cannot risk another problem choosing who is to be born to live on the ship. For this reason we remotely connect the fetuses in the wombs of those women on the space ship and the earth who are in the early stage of pregnancy to the computer system we call the virtual god. If the fetuses are able to pass the physical and spiritual tests of the virtual god system, they are allowed to be born. This makes virtual life itself a matter of being born. Everyone is first born into the virtual world and those passing the tests succeed in being born.

Isaiah, *49:5 He who formed me in the womb to be his servant.* **(OT)**
Isaiah, *49:1 Yahweh called me before I was born, from my mother's womb he pronounced my name.* **(OT)**
Jeremiah, *1:4-5 The word of Yahweh was addressed to me, saying: "before I formed you in the womb I knew you; before you came to birth I consecrated you; I have appointed you as prophet to the nations."* **(OT)**

__John,__ 1:13 Who was born not out of human stock or urge of the flesh or will of man but of God himself. **(NT)**

__Luqman,__ 31:34 (He knows) what ever wombs contains, Yet no person knows what he will earn tomorrow. **(Q)**

__The Bee,__ 16:78 God has brought you out of your mothers' wombs; you knew nothing, then while He has granted you hearing, eyesight and vital organs. **(Q)**

Why are tolerance, patience and morals necessary when the environment is so technological?

Doctor: Those are mental characteristics of humans who accommodate themselves to life forms in isolated the environment in spaceships lasting many years, twenty four hours a seven days a week.

In isolated space journeys stresses such as boredom, competition, jealousy was experienced. It was impossible to intervene and control these arguments due to the distance to earth which made radio signals slow.

__James,__ 3-16 For where there is envy and selfish ambition, there will also be disorder and wickedness of every kind. **(NT)**

In spite of the fact that we have improved therapy software scanning faces to measure stress levels from gestures, astronauts had to control their behavior before the stress level went up.

Patience, tolerance and morals are the basic needs in such environments. We have learned through research, that the family hierarchy which contained the familiar persons was the best for colonization in space, We built the first colony in space with 50 couples.

There are those who claim that we will live as light beings in the afterlife.

They are also mentioned in scriptures:

__John,__ 12:36 While you still have the light, believe in the light and you will become sons of light. **(NT)**

Do light bodies as mentioned in the scriptures really exist?

Doctor: In previous experiences you have learned that the technology of creation was light. In a virtual environment, everyone has a virtual body of light. When it comes to the light bodies we take on after death, some of the technical engineers of the system personally work within the virtual system, themselves. No matter which race course is chosen, all scenarios use the same virtual/light bodies. At certain periods of the day, these engineers, take on their light bodies and regularly do the control work of the virtual system. The engineers' brains, because they direct their own light bodies, begin to be just like double bodies (virtual / real) and are said to be children of light or light bodies.

The Elevated Places, 7:181 And of those whom We have created are a people who guide with the truth and thereby they do justice. (Q)

I couldn't clearly understand this Light Bodies subject. Would you be a little more clear?

Doctor: Let me explain it with an example that clears up the subject of the body and soul bond. Take a radio controlled toy car as an example. You can control the car back, forth-left, right with the radio control. The one who observes the car, only sees an electric motor, body and accessories but nothing else. He asks "where is the soul in it?" It takes time to get the parts and put them together to make the copy of it, and succeed. But he does not know anything about the radio control unit, so the car stands still. He tries to push the car to move it but car remains in place. This is the relation between soul and body. Does the body and it's parts move or talk even if you have got them together without a soul? Does it run even if you charge it with the shock unit? No. Because there isn't a soul to operate it. We can put body parts together but we can not produce the soul.

It is same for the bonds between light bodies and humans in virtual universes. In the virtual world the car exists only as computer software. The car is being operated with thought signals instead of radio signals. It's like the brain plays game the with thought signals.

Man automatically asks, "Am I on earth? In the heavens?" "In the womb? Am I alive." Are you of the People of A'raf?

Doctor: We are only the technical team between the real and the virtual. Don't worry, you are one of the successful ones in being born. Would you like to rest before your last trial today?

What is next after the last trial?

Doctor: You don't remember your family here and your life because we haven't reloaded your information about your past yet. Now you are going to live in some other age's virtual scenario to see what more you can do with what you have. You will be back to your life and your family with your new experiences, when the trial ends.

A virtual life is the path of the knowledge within you, not your journey. I repeat my question for a trip within enlightenment: Returning to the virtual life not with your mortal will but with God's will:

"Are you ready?"

When you're ready we may begin again!

I didn't come here to sleep. Not only for myself, but for those who have written "I am ready, let it begin" on the inside of their door or those who will in the future, with the belief and desire to contribute to the information accumulation:

"We are ready, let it begin."

Doctor: Your findings are not only for yourself. Now find things for others with others.

With this journey you have completed the individual part with honors and have learned the expanded state of past thinking through science. You are now ready to work with groups. Find others who have searched for the "Unifying Theory / United Belief" in other ways. Find groups of people from other races, using different languages, of different religions around the world. Form your "United Thought Group" and work for peace and the benefit of mankind. Give Stephen Hawking my greetings.

Remember, Your Creators are with You,
The Creator of all of us, is With You and With Us

May Your Path Be Clear!

Resources

Aydın TÜRKGÜCÜ, 1996, İsimsiz Kitap, Ankara

Aydın TÜRKGÜCÜ, 1998, Ben Hazırım Başlasın, Ankara, Çıkış

Aydın TÜRKGÜCÜ, 2006, Konsantre Kur'an-ı Kerim, Ankara

Aydın TÜRKGÜCÜ, 2007, Sanal tanrı, Ankara, Çıkış

Beyza BİLGİN Prof.Dr., 2005, İslamda Kadının Rolü Türkiye'de Kadın, Ankara, Sinemis

Burhan YILMAZ, 2005, Bilinmeyen Mevlana, İstanbul, Kozmik Kitaplar

Ergun CANDAN, 1998, Gizli Sırlar Öğretisi, İstanbul, Sınır Ötesi

Fatma PAKSÜT Dr., 1980, Platon ve Platon Sonrası, Ankara.

Holy Bible, NewYork, American Bible Society

Jeanette Eaton, 1961, Gandhi, Kılıçsız Mücahid, İstanbul, Amerikan Bord

John BROCKMAN, 2002, The Next Fifty Years, NewYork, Vintage

Karen Armstrong, 1999, A History of God, London, Vintage

Kenan Gürsoy, Prof. Dr., 2007, Maurice Merleau-Ponty'de Algı Problemine Giriş, Ankara, Lotus.

Kitabı Mukaddes, 1995, Eski ve Yeni Ahit, Kitabı Mukaddes Co

Konrad-Adenauer-Stiftung Vakfı, 2005, Türkiye ve Avrupa'da Çok Dinli Yaşam – Geçmişte ve Günümüzde, Ankara, Konrad-Adenauer-Stiftung Vakfı

Konrad-Adenauer-Stiftung Vakfı, 2005, Türkiye ve Avrupa'da İslam, Devlet ve Modern Toplum, Ankara, Konrad-Adenauer-Stiftung Vakfı

Martin Lings (Ebubekir Siraceddin), 2006, Hz. Muhammed'in Hayatı, İstanbul, İnsan

Orhan HANÇERLİOĞLU, 2008, Düşünce Tarihi, İstanbul, Remzi

Oruç Aruoba (Türkçesi), Deccal, Hil

Osman KARABULUT, 1994, Şems-i TEBRİZİ - Mevlana, Konya, Şems

Ömer Ertuğrul ATASAY, 2003, Allah'ın Dinini Hatırlayalım, Ankara, Acar

Papa II. Jean Paul, 2001, Fides Et Ratio (Akıl ve İman), İstanbul, İyiadam

Papa II. Jean Paul, 2001, Fides Et Ratio, Vatican, www.vatikan.va

Salih Akdemir, Prof. Dr., Kur'an ve Laiklik, 2000, Form

Selahattin YALÇIN, 1996, Hazır Değiliz, Harman

Sinan Canan Dr., 2008, Fraktal Düşünceler, Ankara, Haber/Ajanda

Stephen W. Hawking / Leonard Mlodinow, 2005, A Briefer History Of Time, U.K., Bantam

Stephen W. Hawking, 1988, A Brief History Of Time, U.K., Bantam

Stephen W. Hawking, 1994, Black Holes And Baby Universes, U.K., Bantam

Stephen W. Hawking, Stephen Hawking'le Zaman ve Uzayda Gezinti, İstanbul, Alkım

T.B. Irving, 1988, The Qur'an, U.S.A., Amana Books

The Jerusalem Bible , 1968, London, Darton, Longman & Todd

Web Pages
www.yesevi.org
www.wikipedia.org
www.incil.com
www.kuran.gen.tr
www.kuranikerim.com/english/m_indexe.htm
www.quran.org
www.qurantoday.com
www.thequran.com
www.dictionary.cambridge.org
www.seslisozluk.com
www.zargan.com
www.isgkc.org/translat.htm
http://etext.virginia.edu/toc/modeng/public/HolKora.html
www.devotions.net/bible/00old.htm
www.devotions.net/bible/00new.htm
www.worldebible.com/
www.bible.cc
www.catholic.org

Filmler: To me, movies are three-dimensional books. Brave Heart, Nostradamus, Ghost, Flatliners, Contact, The Fifth Element, Good Will Hunting, Rasputin, Shine, First Knight, The Matrix, Doom, Cube, An Inconvenient Truth, The Secret, What The Bleep Do We Know?, The Thirteenth Floor, Bruce Almighty, Dear God, The Kingdom of Heaven, Minority Report, Stargate, Vanilla Sky.

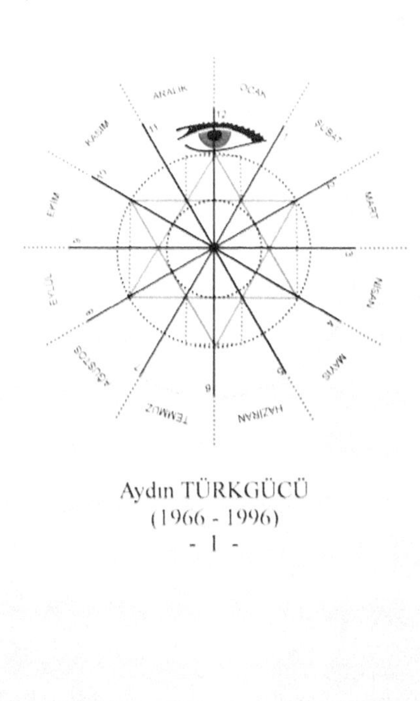

Aydın TÜRKGÜCÜ
(1966 - 1996)
- 1 -

THE BOOK WITH NO NAME
(1996)

The goal of giving everything a name is to prevent confusion. In any area
where there is only one nameless thing, there will be no confusion. In this book,
I have used the right to more than one name as well as the right to
"namelessness" which has never been used in the book publishing world.

This book was distributed free of charge by the author so that money would not
be involved. The right to name the book was given to the readers and 143
different names were suggested.

I AM READY, LET IT BEGIN
(1998)

“He who solves the system, controls it.
What is important here is to survive after having deciphered it,
not just to decipher it.”

This is why the book’s readers were insured against
possible mantel shock.

VIRTUAL GOD
(The Last Exit Before God)
(2007)

Is it possible that God may have given mankind the chance in a virtual world to test themselves so that they may pass the test on the Day of Reckoning? Is virtual reality the last chance for awareness before death?

There are two groups of human beings on earth: those who came to decipher and those who came to be deciphered. You can find out which group you are in by taking the group test in the foreword.

Reviews

A research with a lofty aim to show that Religion and science are in harmony. **Prof. Salih Akdemir, Ph.D.** *Ankara U. Faculty of Divinity*

For those who are bored to hear same old aproaches to " Religion and science" this book comes along with a new ways to discuss the issue. **Prof. Dr. Thomas Michel, S.J., Ankara, Turkey**

The book endeavors to interrogate the reasons to believe in the transcendent beings in human life, putting the emphasis on monotheistic religions. The relation between faith and scientific evidences is the basic focus of the author. In order to achieve its aim it investigates the hints provided by the Holy Writ and the Koran in the light of technological and scientific knowledge.**Prof. Ahmet İnam, Ph.D.** *Professor, Chair The philosophy department at METU*

Nice example of worship by thinking. **Prof. Beyza Bilgin, Ph.D** *Ankara U. Faculty of Divinity*

In his new book, Aydin Turkgucu offers to thinking Muslims, Jews and Christians who understand their faith, (a convincing explanation of) how technology unites them in their belief in the one true God. **Geoffrey B. Evans** *St. Nicolas' Church, British Embassy, Ankara-Turkey*

A serious warning that makes them to thing once again those who are planning to commit with a digital justice model. **Y. Selim Sarıibrahimoğlu, LL.D.**

New Reasons to Believe

Aydın Türkgücü

The title of this book well describes the contents: new reasons to believe. This work is not your usual apologetic text that seeks to "prove" the existence of God, but instead takes a fresh look at the Hebrew Scriptures, the Christian New Testament, and the Qur'an in an effort to show the humane benefits of religious commitment. As the author says (p. 39): "I am not trying to prove or disprove the existence of a Creator. I am trying to convey what we can achieve by assuming His existence."

This is not a dry theological treatise, but proceeds by means of a series of imagined colloquia with historical figures ranging from Atatürk to Plato, Thomas Aquinas, Thales, Maimonides, to Mother Teresa of Calcutta. This eclectic series of interviews gives a clue to the wide-ranging sources explored creatively by the author.

The author's scientific background provides a unique perspective and modern cosmology plays a key role in his argumentation. What can quarks, black holes, and baby universes tell us about the possibility or impossibility of God? The author concludes (p. 230): "To unite mankind we must seek the science of religion and introduce him to the technological/ scientific God"; he buttresses his argumentation with excerpts from Pope John Paul II's 1998 encyclical '*Fides et Ratio.*'

To those who are tired of hearing the same old arguments pro and con on the "religion vs. science" controversy, this book provides new ways to approach the issue. It invites the reader to undertake his or her own pilgrimage to the truth, as the author says in the final pages of the work (p. 281): "We are ready, let it begin."

Thomas Michel, S.J., Ankara, Turkey

Aydin Turkgucu presents a compelling reason to believe in God using the science and the traditional religions of the world. He moves you through the major scientific theories of the
great master's and martyrs of many past millenniums right up to the present day.

The great search for the creator God is inevitably historic the "Creation Theories" or "Big Bang" is theory or not? This is truly questioned in this book! This enduring goal is still open and a choice for everyone to believe.

In Aydin's book "New Reasons to Believe" sets out in simple understanding text and new compelling arguments of a completely alternative thesis. His view of life through the prisons of technological advances in computer language, time lines, virtual realties and recordings. This is going to challenge the scientific view? Also this is going to leave a big impression on your mind.
He allows you to follow the sacred verses of the Holy Books, Bible, Qur'an and Jewish Old Testament, to draw reference to the actual way God was speaking to human mind and thoughts and humanity. How? Buy either through the thoughts of the prophets or the hidden meanings of the text, which now can be revealed.

Aydin use great heroes, thinkers, scientists and many others, from the past to the present to draw influence. It is as if they with him Ataturk, Gandhi, Plato, Thales, Stephen Hawking and many others. RSB is Probing their thoughts, concepts and traditions. Religion and Science go together hand in hand and Aydin lift's the lid of the heresies of the past and also the conceptual science we are taught to believe.

God is watching you, recording you for the final moment when you meet with Him at deaths door! Even "Big Brother" on earth is doing the same recordings? Is it possible a virtual world? This is where your dreams and reality intertwine in a cycle of life here on earth or out there. Is our universe just a mirror reflection of what we see an believe?

RSB is a must read that puts everything is prospective that does not diminish your own faith in the creator. (RSB a must read)

But grow in grace, and in the knowledge of our Lord and Savior Jesus Christ. To him is the glory both now and forever. Amen" 2 Peter 2:18

Signed By:- Reverend Craig N .M .Parr The British Consulate Didim Warden

The book we picked up this time is from the bookshelf of Chargé d'Affaires of Indian Embassy Dr. Ramesh Chandra. Author of the book is Turkish writer Aydın Türkgücü and the book is called New reasons to believe in: 27 September 2011 Tuesday 09:53

The book we picked up this time is from the bookshelf of Chargé d'Affaires of Indian Embassy Dr. Ramesh Chandra. Author of the book is Turkish writer Aydın Türkgücü and the book is called New reasons to believe in:

Aydin Türkgücü presents a compelling reason to believe in God using the science and the traditional religions of the world. He moves you through the major scientific theories of the great master's and martyrs of many past millenniums right up to the present day.

The great search for the creator God is inevitably historic the "Creation Theories" or "Big Bang" is theory or not? This is truly questioned in this book! This enduring goal is still open and a choice for everyone to believe. He allows you to follow the sacred verses of the Holy Books, Bible, Qur'an and Jewish Old Testament, to draw reference to the actual way God was speaking to human mind and thoughts and humanity. How? Buy either through the thoughts of the prophets or the hidden meanings of the text, which now can be revealed.

Aydın use great heroes, thinkers, scientists and many others, from the past to the present to draw influence. It is as if they with him Ataturk, Gandhi, Plato, Thales, Stephen Hawking and many others. RSB is probing their thoughts, concepts and traditions. Religion and Science go together hand in hand and Aydın lift's the lid of the heresies of the past and also the conceptual science we are taught to believe.

Tags: DR. RAMESH CHANDRA, DR., RAMESH, CHANDRA

Leave a comment

Thank you, Dr. Chandra for focusing attention on this important work. Among the many compelling ideas presented here, is the idea that all is ONE, and that we as human beings are a vital part of that dynamic. Important, indeed. Bonnie Pura   2011-11-01 16:26:49

Brilliant read and an insight to God's possibilities. Well Aydın Türkgücü present a very believable augment threw time of the historical text of the Bible, Koran, and other histrionically and living minded ca-rectors that we all should get to know. A must read. Rev. Craig Parr   2011-09-29 17:02:33

Back Cover

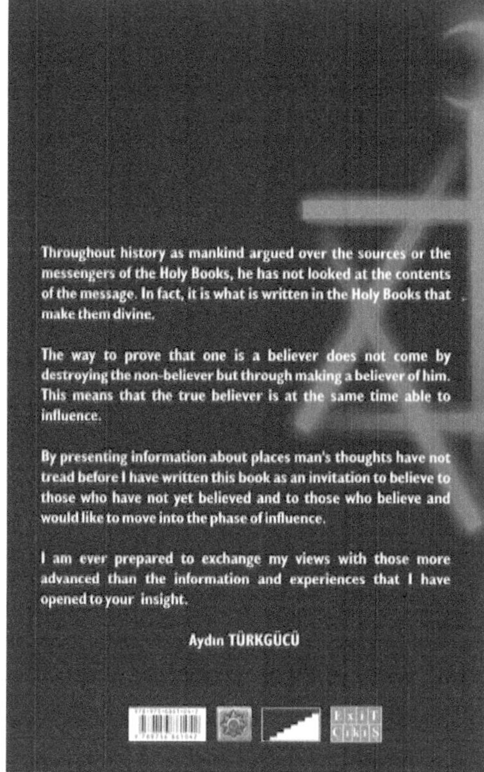

Throughout history as mankind argued over the sources or the messengers of the Holy Books, he has not looked at the contents of the message. In fact, it is what is written in the Holy Books that make them divine.

The way to prove that one is a believer does not come by destroying the non-believer but through making a believer of him. This means that the true believer is at the same time able to influence.

By presenting information about places man's thoughts have not tread before I have written this book as an invitation to believe to those who have not yet believed and to those who believe and would like to move into the phase of influence.

I am ever prepared to exchange my views with those more advanced than the information and expriences that I have opened to your insight.